# Modern MIDI

# MODERN MIDI

## Sequencing and Performing Using Traditional and Mobile Tools

Sam McGuire

**Focal Press**
Taylor & Francis Group

NEW YORK AND LONDON

First published 2014
by Focal Press
70 Blanchard Road, Suite 402, Burlington, MA 01803

And in the UK
by Focal Press
2 Park Square, Milton Park, Abingdon, Oxon OX14 4RN

*Focal Press is an imprint of the Taylor & Francis Group, an informa business*

**Library of Congress Cataloging-in-Publication Data**
McGuire, Sam.
 Modern MIDI : sequencing and performing using traditional and mobile tools / Sam McGuire.
  pages cm
 1. MIDI (Standard)   2. Sequencer (Musical instrument)—Instruction and study.
3. Software sequencers. I. Title.
 MT723.M35 2014
 784.190285'46—dc23     2013028057

ISBN: 978-0-415-83927-3 (pbk)
ISBN: 978-0-203-77331-4 (ebk)

Typeset in Palatino
by Apex CoVantage, LLC

Printed and bound in the United States of America by Sheridan Books, Inc. (a Sheridan Group Company).

# CONTENTS

Dedication                                              xiv
Acknowledgments                                          xv

1   *Introduction to MIDI*                                1
    1. MIDI Is Everywhere                                 2
    2. MIDI Is Incapable of Making
       Sound by Itself                                    3
    3. It Is Possible to Successfully
       Use MIDI without Knowing
       Anything about It                                  6
    4. Famous People Use MIDI                             8
    5. MIDI Isn't Just for Music                          8
    6. MIDI's Magic Number Is 128                        11
    7. The Key to Using MIDI Is Being a
       Skilled Musician                                  12
    8. MIDI Is a Huge Time Saver/Waster                  13
    9. The Differences between Digital Audio
       and MIDI Are Fewer and Fewer                      14
    10. MIDI Has Changed Very Little in the
        Past 30 Years                                    15
    MIDI Data                                            15
    Types of MIDI Messages                               17
    Channel Mode Messages (Subset of Control
    Change Messages)                                     19
    System Messages                                      22
    System Common Messages                               22
    System Real-Time Messages                            23
    System Exclusive Messages                            24
    MIDI Controllers and Subprotocols                    24

CS-10 Controller Assignments                          25
Understanding Parts per Quarter Note                  26
Binary Numbers                                        27
Reading Binary                                        29
MIDI Files                                            30
General MIDI                                          32
GS and XG                                             35
GM 2                                                  36
Running Status                                        36
Summary                                               37

2   *MIDI Hardware*                                   38
Five-pin DIN MIDI Cables                              38
USB                                                   42
FireWire                                              43
Ethernet                                              44
PCI Cards                                             45
Wireless (WiFi)                                       45
Hardware Devices                                      46
Local MIDI Settings                                   59
Global Settings                                       59
Local Control                                         61
Hardware Configurations                               63
Summary                                               70

3   *Mobile MIDI*                                     72
iPad Apps                                             73
iPad Instruments                                      73
Making Connections                                    75
Connecting Wirelessly                                 76
Audio MIDI Setup                                      76
Example App/AC-7 Core                                 77
Third Party Software                                  81
MIDI on Android                                       82
MIDI/OSC Control                                      84
Musical Instrument Apps                               89
Loop/Sequencer/Sample Apps                            91
Multi-Track Recording Apps                            93

MIDI Considerations when Choosing
Instrument Apps                                          95
Controllers and Control Surfaces                         96
Sequencers and DAWs                                     100
MIDI Utilities                                          102

4   *Recording MIDI*                                    *104*
Different Entry Methods                                 105
Live Performance                                        106
Troubleshooting MIDI Inputs                             107
Project Settings                                        109
Key Signature                                           109
Exercise                                                111
Tempo                                                   111
Conductor Track                                         111
Click Track                                             114
Exercises                                               117
Sounds                                                  118
Exercises                                               120
Latency                                                 120
Keep the MIDI Path as Simple as Possible               120
Keep Your MIDI Device Drivers Up to Date               122
Use a Reliable Audio Device with
Pro-Quality Drivers                                     122
Use Your DAW's Feature Set to Manage Latency           125
Templates                                               126
Additional Controllers                                  127
Examples                                                129
Downloading MIDI Files                                  131
Alternative Performance Techniques                     133
How Triggering Works                                    134
Percussion Tracks                                       135
Summary                                                 137

5   *Editing MIDI*                                      *139*
Basic Tools and Manual Editing                         139
Quantization                                            139
Notation Editors                                        139

Advanced and Unique Tools                                          140
Basic Tools and Manual Editing                                     140
Survey of Typical Tools                                            140
Typical Editing Workflow                                           142
Example 1                                                          145
Example 2                                                          150
Example 3                                                          152
Additional Editing                                                 154
Quantization                                                       154
Note Value                                                         155
Strength and Sensitivity                                           157
Swing                                                              157
Randomization                                                      158
Groove Quantization                                                159
Examples                                                           159
Notation                                                           160
Working with Notation                                              160
Note Entry                                                         161
Editing                                                            162
Advanced and Unique Tools                                          165
Alternate Storage                                                  165
Transformation Tools                                               166
Making MIDI Musical                                                168
Imitation Is the Truest Form of Flattery                           168
Comparisons                                                        169
Groove Quantize                                                    170
Tempo Changes                                                      172
Envelopes                                                          174
Built-In Envelopes                                                 175
Track Automation                                                   175
Effects                                                            177

6    *Mixing*                                                      179
Level Adjustment                                                   179
Overall Level                                                      184
Placement in the Stereo Field                                      184
Effects                                                            186
Graphic Equalizer                                                  197

Parametric Equalizer                     199
Time-Based Effects                       202
Automation                               208
Example—Sculpting Sound Sources          210
Note                                     212

7   *Using MIDI Live*                     213
Traditional Setups                       213
MIDI Control                             216
DJs and Electronic Artists               217
DAWs and Sequencers                      220
MIDI Mapping                             236
OSC                                      240
Controllerism                            245
Expressive Control                       248

8   *Music Theory Primer*                 251
The Elements of Music                    251
Musical Texture                          254
Music Notation                           254
Ledger Lines                             257
The Musical Alphabet                     258
The Grand Staff                          258
The Piano Keyboard                       259
Sharps and Flats                         260
The Five Accidentals                     260
Note Values                              262
Time Signatures                          263
Notation Protocol                        265
Counting Beats                           265
Ties                                     266
Dotted Notes                             266
Sixteenth Notes                          267
Compound and Simple Meter                268
Duple, Triple, and Quadruple Time        268
Musical Road Maps                        269
Major Scales                             271
Key Signatures                           273

The Circle of Fifths                                 276
Magic Seven                                          277
Interval Summary                                     280
Summary of Triad Construction                        282
Chord Symbol Protocol for Triads                     282
The Harmonic System                                  284
Chord Progressions                                   285

9    *Interviews*                                    *289*
John Swihart                                         289
George Strezov                                       293
Dr. Noize                                            295
C. J. Drummeler                                      298
Jonathan Hillman                                     302
Matt Moldover                                        305
Kenny Bergle                                         308
Jay Smith                                            316
John Staskevich—Highly Liquid                        322

10   *History of MIDI*                               *325*
MIDI—The Early Days                                  326
The First MIDI Instruments                           328
MIDI—Early Computers                                 330
MIDI Interfaces                                      332
MIDI—GM and the Web                                  332
MIDI—Implementation Charts                           334
Drum Machines                                        335
Software Instruments                                 337
MIDI—Mobile Revolution                               338
Sequential Circuits Prophet 600                      339
Roland Jupiter–6                                     340
Yamaha DX7                                           341
Akai S900                                            343
E-mu Virtuoso 2000                                   343
Fairlight CMI (Series I–III)                         344
Akai MPC60                                           346
Sequential Circuits Studio 440                       347

11  *Exploring the Future of MIDI*                          348
    Known MIDI Issues                                       351
    HD–MIDI                                                 353
    HD–MIDI vs. OSC                                         354

12  *Appendix*                                              356
    Introduction                                            361
    All Pages                                               362
    Page 1: Basic Information, MIDI Timing and
    Synchronization, and Extensions Compatibility?          362
    Pages 2 and 3: Control Number Information               370
    MIDI Messages                                           374
    General MIDI 1, 2, and Lite Specifications              393
    General MIDI 2 (GM2)                                    394
    GM2 Specification Update 1.1                            395
    GM2 Specification Update 1.2                            395
    GM2 Features                                            396
    GM2 Developer Information                               397
    General MIDI "Lite" (GML)                               397
    GM Lite vs. SP-MIDI                                     398
    GM Lite vs. GM1                                         398
    GM Lite Features                                        398
    GM Lite Developer Information                           399
    Computer Audio Comes of Age                             400
    MIDI: Let's Share the 'Secret'                          402
    White Paper: Comparison of MIDI and OSC                 406
    Notes                                                   409

    Index                                                   410

# DEDICATION

To my family, for their support during long hours of using and writing about MIDI.

# ACKNOWLEDGMENTS

Thank you to Nathan van der Rest for your hard work; it wouldn't have happened without you! Thank you to Paul Musso and Adam Olson for your contributions. Thank you to Anais, Meagan, and everyone at Focal Press for all your hard work and efforts to get this book published! Thank you to all of my students over the years who have made my professional life a worthwhile endeavor.

# INTRODUCTION TO MIDI 1

*Chapter co-authored by Adam Olson, Shenandoah Conservatory*

MIDI (Musical Instrument Digital Interface) has been around for over 30 years and shows no signs of slowing down or being replaced. MIDI is a control protocol that sends performance data between multiple musical instruments and sequencers. Instead of starting with the history of MIDI in this chapter, let's get right into what it is and how you are going to be using it. The difference between this book and most other books on the subject of MIDI is that we are going to take a very practical approach to using this tool and focus a lot less on much of the underlying data.

Ten things you need to know about MIDI:

1. MIDI is everywhere.
2. MIDI is incapable of making sound by itself.
3. It is possible to successfully use MIDI without knowing anything about it.
4. Famous people use MIDI.
5. MIDI isn't just for music.
6. MIDI's magic number is 128.
7. The key to using MIDI is being a skilled musician.
8. MIDI is a huge time saver/waster.
9. The differences between digital audio and MIDI are fewer and fewer.
10. MIDI has changed very little in the past 30 years.

**Figure 1.1** Notation in
Symphony Pro

**Figure 1.1** Notation in
Symphony Pro

## 1. MIDI Is Everywhere

Chances are that you have held a MIDI device in the past
20 minutes, heard a MIDI performance in the last 12 hours,
and possibly even used MIDI without knowing it. From cell
phones to computers and from television to the movie theater
to the stage, MIDI is used in nearly every situation. It is so
pervasive because it is cheap, reliable, and universal. The
most exciting chapter of this book covers the mobile uses of
MIDI and looks at what the future is bringing.

There has been a really healthy resurgence of television
music being performed by live musicians. A few years ago
only a handful of shows used an actual orchestra, with the
*Simpsons* and *Lost* heading the pack. The majority of shows
use a MIDI-based soundtrack and the viewing audience is
none the wiser. The 30-year-old MIDI protocol can sound
so good because of the programmer in charge and the
sounds she controls, and not because of MIDI itself. Even
when a feature film uses a full orchestra, there is still the

**Figure 1.2** FL Studio 11

likelihood that MIDI was used to layer additional instruments and sounds into the mix.

If you turn on the radio (not taking into account the oldies or classical stations), there is an overwhelming chance that you'll hear the effects of MIDI multiple times each hour. It might be the on-air talent triggering a sound effect or the latest mega hit that was crafted by producers in the studio, but you can't escape MIDI. The next time you play a musical app on your iPhone or Galaxy you might be using some iteration of MIDI. If you go out to a club there is an excellent chance that the DJ will be using Ableton or FL Studio, which means he is using MIDI. It is literally all around us.

The sheer number of implementations of MIDI means that it is a format that is here to stay. The expense involved with a move away from MIDI is prohibitive to say the least, and it works well enough for nearly all situations. This is discussed further in the history chapter, and the ramifications of competing formats are explored when we look at the future.

## 2. MIDI Is Incapable of Making Sound by Itself

An overused analogy for MIDI is the player piano. The paper roll is covered in holes that indicate where the piano should play notes. While a player piano often conjures thoughts of the Wild West and smoky saloons, there are some extremely elegant player pianos. Ampico created a concert grand piano that is controlled by a roll of paper. These pianos were in circulation in the early 20th century and were used by the likes of Rachmaninoff and Debussy. You can still find piano rolls of actual performances of Rachmaninoff, which when played through a grand piano are just like having him in the room. The paper is just a roll of paper until you attach it to a beautiful piano, in the very same way that MIDI is only as good as the sounds you attach it to. If you use the default sounds in FL Studio then it will sound like FL Studio. If you attach it to a MPC, then you have the potential to sound like a hit record.

**Figure 1.3** Ampico Piano and Rolls

MIDI data include a number of pieces of information. When you press a key on a MIDI keyboard, the velocity is tracked along with the note being pressed and any continuing pressure caused by your finger on the key. Once you release the key there is a message transmitted that tells the sound to stop playing. All of this information is transmitted in the MIDI stream and controls the destination instrument. Not only can MIDI not make a sound by itself, but the quality of any sound triggered by MIDI is completely dependent on the quality of the instrument. In a related discussion, a poorly programmed MIDI track cannot make an excellent virtual instrument sound good; both pieces need to be excellent in their level of quality.

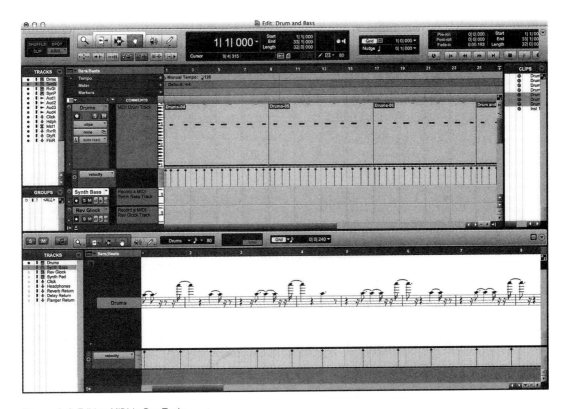

**Figure 1.4** Editing MIDI in Pro Tools

## 3. It Is Possible to Successfully Use MIDI without Knowing Anything about It

Let's look at a user group who needs to know very little, if anything at all, about MIDI in relation to daily usage. For a number of years, GarageBand was released bundled with every new Mac computer. Instead of using much of the traditional recording studio terminology, GarageBand simplified things and barely even used the word MIDI. A musician could hook up his musical keyboard and things would just work. In many cases there was zero setup and everything simply worked. By establishing an interface where digital audio and MIDI essentially looked and functioned in the same way, the end user needed to learn very little about the MIDI spec.

The simplified interface for sequencers is not the only indication that the way we use MIDI is continually changing. Sifting through lists of MIDI data used to be a common occurrence but is not nearly as common anymore. Several things have evolved to help us move in this direction that include more reliable sequencer technology, an exodus away from using external outboard gear, and DAWs that offer much more than basic sequencing.

The reliability of DAWs (Digital Audio Workstations) has decreased the need to be constantly editing and sifting through MIDI data in a numerical format. The more you can trust the visual representations of your data, the less troubleshooting you will have to do. The more frequent use of virtual instruments and the decrease of external sound modules is an example of a fundamental signal flow change that has affected how MIDI is used. Inside Logic Pro you can send three MIDI notes simultaneously to a synthesizer, and all three notes will arrive simultaneously. When sending three notes to a hardware module, the notes are sent as a series of notes and they are not received at the exact same time. Even when you set three notes to start at the same time, they are still received one after another.

**Figure 1.5** Drums in Garageband

In certain situations when using external hardware and with a large number of notes being played together, you might want to make sure certain notes are played earlier than others and so looking directly into the data stream is an important option. The last change is due to the diverse offerings of DAWs. Instead of a simple sequencer, there are now a number of additional expected features, such as a notation editors and piano roll views, that have advanced options. Users have grown accustom to using these alternate view options instead of looking at the text-based views. In 10 years of teaching, I have seen students move away from the actual MIDI data as they rely more heavily on the visual representations. Neither way is right or wrong.

The process for recording and editing MIDI is still the same as it ever was, and you can certainly manipulate the data in a lot of different ways. The point here is that DAWs are now designed to make the process easier and more transparent. As long as your sequencer of choice still has the advanced functionality, simplifying the workflow is probably never going to be a bad thing.

## 4. Famous People Use MIDI

MIDI is not just a format that is used by hobbyists or by basement musicians. MIDI is not some consumer gimmick that has very few professional applications. MIDI is used in every recording studio in the world and by some of the most influential musicians over the years. Later in this book we feature a number of musicians and composers that use MIDI and discuss their individual setups. The prominent theme is that MIDI is accessible to everyone who wants to use it.

Anyone who is willing to work hard and be persistent can program beats and create records that sound amazing. The tools are accessible and quite affordable, but you'll still need a good idea and a catchy hook. In the end it doesn't really matter who uses MIDI except that it is nice to know that MIDI is a tool that has enabled a few generations of musicians to create the music they love.

## 5. MIDI Isn't Just for Music

Our primary focus is using MIDI in the music production process but that doesn't mean it doesn't do more. MIDI plays many different roles: instrument control, control surface communication, time code sync, and lighting control. Each of these uses the basic MIDI format but with varying individual characteristics. The strength of MIDI is that it has a diversity of abilities and is reliable in each situation. The weakness is that MIDI is not the best at any of them.

When considering the non-musical options, MIDI is the older and slower protocol. Control surfaces with newer control implementations, such as EuCon from AVID, can control faders with over 8x resolution and 250x the speed. This type of control is used to control various parameters in your DAW. You can use a physical fader to control the virtual mixer in

**Figure 1.6** Yamaha DM2000 with Control Surface Functionality

your software. You can set panning and control effects. You can also control the project transport and various other tasks through key commands and menu options. However, MIDI is still a viable option and one that is working for thousands of engineers. If you have to make a choice between MIDI-based control and a shinier new format, I would go with the one you can reasonably afford. The new formats often are attached to more costly equipment and that is okay too.

When coordinating sync between gear and/or software you have multiple options. Traditional choices include SMPTE time code and MIDI time code. Newer options include protocol such as Propellerhead's Rewire or Steinberg's VST connection. Timecode is a transmitted positional reference that two or more pieces of equipment can use to sync. Again, MIDI has less resolution than SMPTE but in many cases is enough to provide accurate sync. The biggest issue with timecode is that a "master" has to send the code and then all of the "slaves" have to chase it, which creates a less efficient situation and potential inaccuracies. One of my favorite stories to tell about timecode happened when working on an independent film that started in Nuendo and then an additional team started working in Pro Tools; both sessions were at different sample rates and file formats. Combining the sessions is not as easy as pushing export and then import because Nuendo and Pro Tools don't like to share files. The solution was to sync them together using MIDI timecode, which allowed the sessions to remain separate but it created doubts about sync. It was far from the ideal solution but demonstrates the reliability of MIDI.

Other sync formats are typically proprietary solutions that work with other hardware/software that is designed specifically to work using the same protocol. A solution like Rewire is a much tighter sync option that still requires a master and a slave but which doesn't rely on chasing code and instead locks the transports together for very tight integration. Most sequencers simply do not sync together very easily.

Lighting control is one area where MIDI excels but it doesn't work alone. Lights and stage effects are typically controlled by a DMX capable unit that works well with MIDI. Many

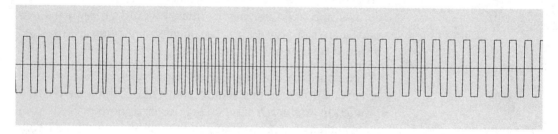

**Figure 1.7** SMPTE Time Code

performers use MIDI output from their instruments to control various lights, or the control boxes are fed from a sequencer timed to the performance. If you have the right equipment it is quite easy to set up a fully interactive music and light show.

## 6. MIDI's Magic Number Is 128

MIDI was invented under a pretty severe set of limitations. In order to keep the bandwidth at acceptable limits and to create an interface that was both efficient and safe at lower costs, MIDI was designed to operate using modest operating parameters. All MIDI data are transmitted serially over a single cable, which means that each piece of datum is sent one piece at a time. The interesting thing about this is that when MIDI is used for relatively small performance needs then it can handle everything really well but when you push it to its limits it definitely starts to fall apart. More of the details of the MIDI specification are described later in this chapter and we look at the math behind the pervasive 128.

**Figure 1.8** MIDI Data Zoomed to See Distinct Steps

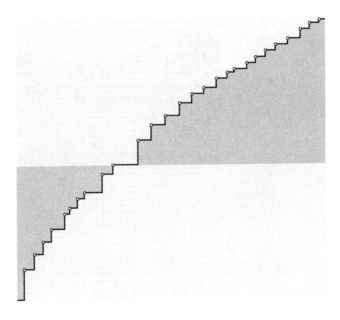

## 7. The Key to Using MIDI Is Being a Skilled Musician

MIDI works well enough that once it is set up you can simply perform. If that hadn't been possible then MIDI would never have survived. While it is possible to create performances without being able to play them, it is highly recommended that you study music and music performance to get the most out of MIDI. Later in the book there is an entire chapter on the basics of music theory, which is a really critical topic for MIDI users to understand. It is not assumed that you already have that knowledge because more and more people are using MIDI without having official musical training but are finding ways to make awesome music. Imagine what you can do once you have all of the tools before you and also have an understanding of the building blocks of music.

Being able to perform on a MIDI controller instead of entering notes with your mouse is something that can make your production sound more natural. Consider for a moment the data that are collected in a performance that would have to be

**Figure 1.9** Data Entry with Track Pad

entered manually without a performance: tempo variations, musical dynamics, additional performance controllers such as sustain pedals or modulation wheels, and the human element. It is possible to re-create all of these by hand but it is not efficient. Working on a score for a film, I worked hours on a single cue, trying to get it just right. I did it all by hand because I had a concept of how I wanted it to sound and thought I could put everything in just the right place. After three to four versions were rejected by the director and under a new deadline, I put away my mouse and just played. After a single take that I never needed to edit but only add additional instruments to, the director approved with great pleasure. The hours I had put into the cue had been eclipsed by a three-minute performance that was "perfect" almost immediately. My ability to play piano and understand theory created an environment where I could compose without MIDI getting in the way.

## 8.  MIDI Is a Huge Time Saver/Waster

Continuing on the previous point, MIDI has the ability to be an enormous saver of resources or a huge waster of them. People get hired because they can create an entire orchestra in their home studio with amazing results, but using MIDI doesn't guarantee a speedier process and can often be a huge drain on the composer who does it all. Using a professional studio orchestra will likely cost more, but you will walk away with an amazing product that isn't in need of another couple days of tweaking. It is also still arguable that an orchestra controlled by MIDI can't sound as good as the real thing, but it is closer now than ever and virtual instruments can sound amazing.

For large-budget projects, the score is going to be produced via MIDI first as a mockup to gain approval before the money is spent on musicians. Some of these mockups could likely pass as final scores by most accounts but serve as a gateway for later recordings. In these cases having a good MIDI mockup can function as a huge efficiency because if the music is recorded and then everyone finds out that they don't like it, then a lot of money will be wasted rerecording it. A mockup hopefully prevents such waste.

**Figure 1.10** Orchestration Using Garageband

MIDI can be a real time and energy sucker for the composer that is still learning the technology. A seasoned expert uses his or her knowledge to move quickly and avoid potholes in the process. If you want to see MIDI used in an amazing fashion, then ask a television composer if you can watch him or her compose. Between session templates and an intimate knowledge of their sound banks, a seasoned composer can plow through cues as if he or she is on a tight deadline, probably because they are.

## 9. The Differences between Digital Audio and MIDI Are Fewer and Fewer

One of the things that preserved MIDI is the ability of DAWs to treat audio and MIDI in the same way. When you change your project tempo, then both the audio and MIDI change their speed. When using loops, it barely makes a difference whether it is audio or MIDI because they both react the same way. Before audio caught up to the flexibility of MIDI, and MIDI caught up to the sonic quality and reliability of audio, most production systems kept them relatively separate. Early sequencers didn't have any audio capabilities, and audio software didn't have any MIDI features. The unification of both technologies has finally reached congruence and DAWs integrate them equally. New technology will continue to make the differences between audio and MIDI fewer and fewer in the way we edit and manipulate our music.

## 10. MIDI Has Changed Very Little in the Past 30 Years

The more you learn about MIDI, the more you'll begin to understand that MIDI has a substantial amount of history and 'baggage'. You can use MIDI hardware that was designed at the very beginning of MIDI with a certain amount of success because a lot of the basics of MIDI haven't changed but be prepared to run into issues. MIDI is surprisingly robust yet implemented MIDI designs are riddled with issues and inconsistencies. MIDI is still a valuable tool that has reached maturity over the years but the more you use it, the more likely you are going to be aware of the issues. The lesson to be learned is that you need to develop patience when using MIDI and you'll need to use your MIDI tools enough to get to know them just as you would get to know any musical instrument. Not every piece of MIDI equipment is designed with the same level of quality and precision and so you should purchase equipment that has reviewed well and has a proven track record.

### MIDI Data

Understanding the details of MIDI data is important because it helps us understand the limitations and challenges while offering insight in how to achieve the most from a limited system.

MIDI data are composed of binary bits, which are combined in groups of eight to form bytes. Bytes are the basic building blocks of MIDI Messages and are organized into a standard format to communicate between devices. MIDI Messages are made up of three essential pieces of data. Each portion is assigned a specific role such as triggering notes, setting velocity, and adjusting other controllers.

The first piece of datum (byte) is known as the Status Message, which communicates the controlling parameter to the receiving device. For example, to trigger a note you would use a Note On Status Message assigned to the corresponding MIDI Channel. The Status Message always begins with the number zero.

The second and third portions of the MIDI Message are Data Byte 1 and Data Byte 2. These are used to transmit a variety of information based on the individual Status Messages. When using a Note On message, Data Byte 1 is used to indicate the specific note being triggered and Data Byte 2 is used to indicate the velocity of the note. Different Status Messages use the Data Bytes in different ways, and some even combine the Data Bytes together.

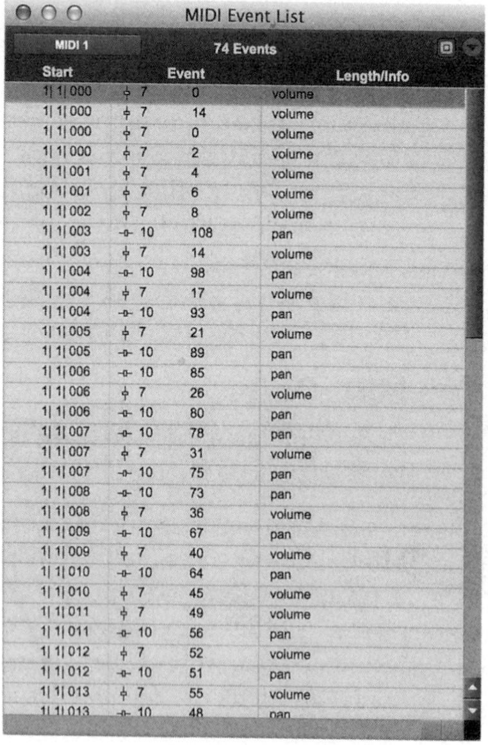

**Figure 1.11** Pro Tools Event List

## Types of MIDI Messages

The Status Message at the beginning of each MIDI Message indicates which parameter is to be controlled. Here is a summary of the available Status Messages, and a chart listing each message and their corresponding Data Bytes is included in Appendix Table 12.2.

### 1. Note On and Off Messages

Note On and Off messages are used to trigger note playback. Not all controllers send Note Off messages and instead they substitute it with a Note On messages with a Data Byte 2 value (velocity) of zero. This message is sent when the key is released and effectively turns the note off because the new note is set to silence.

Another consideration is that MIDI note number 60 is always middle C (C3 is the Yamaha common naming and C4 is the common Roland naming). While note number 60 is always middle C, most MIDI software allows you to change the visual preference for how MIDI On and Off message 60 is referenced. Changing this affects the way the rest of the notes are displayed.

### 2. Polyphonic Aftertouch and Channel Aftertouch

Aftertouch allows a controller to send additional control messages correlating to the pressure placed on the MIDI keyboard. These messages are created by varying the pressure of keys that are held down. Sound modules need to be configured to respond to these messages and can use these data to adjust the depth of vibrato, tremolo, or how bright a sound gets.

The difference between Polyphonic Aftertouch and Channel Aftertouch is that Polyphonic Aftertouch responds on a per-note basis, which means that it transmits a lot more data but it is dependent on how hard each individual note is pressed. Polyphonic Aftertouch is also more expensive to implement since individual sensors are needed for each note, and that makes this option cost prohibitive for many manufacturers.

On the other hand, Channel Aftertouch sends out MIDI messages based on the overall key pressure and only requires one sensor for all of the keys.

Many keyboard controllers don't offer Channel Aftertouch, and you'll want to consult the MIDI implementation chart in the back of the keyboard manual to see if your device sends and responds to these messages. Channel Aftertouch only uses Data Byte 1 for this information and leaves the second byte empty.

### 3. Program Change

This message is used to change what sounds are being triggered on the sound module. This is another example of a message that only uses Data Byte 1, which equals 128 different program changes that can be sent per channel. Had both data bytes been implemented for Program Change, then the total possible program changes would have been 16,384. Sound modules are not limited to only 128 sounds, and it is possible to combine two Control Change messages (CC 0 and CC 32) to give us what is referred to as banks of sounds for a total possibility of 2,097,152 different sounds or 16,384 banks with 128 sounds each. The math behind this is described more below.

There are foot switches on the market that are dedicated to sending out Program Change messages. These are very helpful in situations requiring a switch between loaded sounds, changing settings on an amp, adjusting lighting cues, and switching between preset levels on a digitally controlled mixing console.

### 4. Pitch Wheel Change

Most controllers include a pitch wheel or a joystick to control pitch changes and are used to adjust global pitch. Very few controllers have the ability to control pitch for individual notes and only a select group of software sequencers can do so either. One way of bypassing this is to map Polyphonic Aftertouch to pitch control, which allows pitch control of every note by adjusting the pressure applied to each key.

Data Byte 1 and 2 are combined to provide the resolution of 16,384 steps, but smooth pitch bend is reliant on both hardware and software design. Even in a limited format such as MIDI, high-quality bending can be extrapolated through intelligent design.

### 5.   *Control Change or Continuous Controllers (CC)*

These are often referred to as performance controllers and are used to communicate with the knobs and sliders on many MIDI controllers. CC messages usually win the "cool" factor when it comes to MIDI because of the wide range of parameters that can be adjusted by them.

The controllers listed in the chart below are parameters that have been declared over the years by the MIDI Manufactures Association (MMA) for specific functions in controlling sound modules. In practice what this means is that if you have a control knob assigned to send CC 73, under the General MIDI 2 specification it adjusts the attack time of a sound module (the length of a fade from zero to full volume at the beginning of each note). Alternatively, this could also be mapped to adjust other parameters such as the threshold on a compressor, the send level to headphones, or the volume level of channels in your DAW. This is why CC messages are so popular: they give you tactile control over hardware and software parameters that otherwise might take a lot of scrolling around to find and adjust. See the appendix for a full list of CC messages.

## Channel Mode Messages (Subset of Control Change Messages)

Channel Mode messages are used to change how a device responds to MIDI messages that are received. These messages are part of the Control Message spec, are limited to numbers 120–127, and are used to control global parameters on a device instead of channel specific parameters. These messages will only be received on the device's "basic channel" (one of the 16 channels) that is sometimes predetermined by the device or otherwise programmable. This means that if you simply send one of these messages, it may not change the way the module behaves if not sent on the specific device's "basic" channel number. You should consult the devices manual to find out what channel this is and if it can be changed. A description of each of these messages follows.

## All Sound Off (CC 120)

When the All Sound Off message is received, all oscillators are turned off and their volume envelopes are set to zero.

## Reset All Controllers (CC 121)

When this message is received by a device, all values are reset to the default values set by the manufacture. The Data Byte 2 value should always be set to zero unless other values are supported by the device.

## Local Control (CC 122)

Local control is used for devices that have a controller that is also a sound generator. The local control parameter switches the destination of MIDI output from the keyboard between the "local" or built-in sounds to "non-local" or external MIDI destinations. When used in conjunction with a computer sequencer, it is usually the best practice to turn local control off so that the hardware doesn't trigger the internal sounds and also send out MIDI simultaneously. This keeps notes from being double triggered and causing a hollowness to the sound due to the close phase relationship to the double triggered notes.

While working this way, the user can edit in the computer sequencer and then press play and have the edited performance played on the sound module. This is very analogous to the way a word processor works versus using a typewriter. All the editing can be done in the computer before printing.

When using a keyboard in a concert setting, local control should be activated so that when the keys are played the sounds will be triggered. Data Byte 2 should be set to 0 for Local Control off and 127 for Local Control on. Usually this parameter is changed on the device itself rather than sending a Channel Mode message.

### All Notes Off (CC 123)

Send a Data Byte 2 message of 0 to turn all oscillators and notes off.

### Omni Mode Off (CC 124)

This parameter switches the MIDI Input to respond only to specific channels. Activating Omni Mode Off is used to setup a MIDI device chain and have each respond to only one channel. You could use this for key splitting notes on a keyboard by setting the lower keys to play out a different channel than the upper keys.

An example is setting one module to receive on channel 1 with an acoustic bass patch and a second module connected to the first module's Thru port triggered on channel 2 with a piano patch. There are many other similar uses for Omni Mode Off.

### Omni Mode On (CC 125)

This sets a MIDI device to respond indiscriminately to all incoming MIDI channels that it receives. This is often helpful for troubleshooting, and most DAWs default to receiving from all channels (and, in many cases, all ports).

Data byte 2 should be set to 0. Note: The MMA could have used two values on CC 124 to switch between Omni Mode On and Off but instead decided to use two different CCs.

### Mono Mode On (CC 126)

Mono sets the sound generator to play only one note at a time, which is useful when emulating monophonic instruments such as many wind instruments that can only play a single note at a time.

Pressing and holding a note while playing and releasing other notes on top of the first creates a trill-like transition between two notes (your sound module should be set to re-trigger for this to play the first held note). This is how many synth players are able to get lightning-fast lead lines between successive notes in conjunction with a short portamento time (glide or transition time between notes).

Keep in mind that you could have 16 notes played at the same time in Mono Mode if every note played is on a different channel. Data byte 2 should be set to 0.

### Poly Mode On (CC 127)

This mode allows more than one note to be played at a time on a given channel. The amount of polyphony is up to the sound module, and if it is General MIDI compliant it must have up to 24 notes of polyphony simultaneously for all channels combined (not 24 per channel at the same time). Data byte 2 should be set to 0.

## System Messages

The last status message is the System Message and is divided into three categories known as System Common Messages, System Real-Time Messages, and System Exclusive Messages (SysEx). These messages transmit other miscellaneous information such as synchronization, positional data, and information relating to setup. Sometimes all of these messages are incorrectly referred to as SysEx message when they are discussed, but System Common and System Real-Time Messages have various control parameters that are not "exclusive" to one manufacturer.

## System Common Messages

System Common messages do not have MIDI channels assigned to them, and all devices in the MIDI chain should respond to these messages if they are capable and are properly configured.

1. MIDI Timecode (MTC) allows for location within a song by absolute position timing using hours, minutes, seconds, and frames. Frames are a further division of seconds based on how many pictures frames pass when syncing to picture and is determined by the project frame rate.

Common frame rates are 23.976, 24, 25, 29.97, 29.97 drop frame, and 30 frames per second. When using MTC to sync two devices together, and when the picture is not involved, it is recommended to use the highest frame rate. When video is involved then you should be using the frame rate associated with the video file.

Unlike its analog counterparts, SMPTE timecode (Society of Motion Picture & Television Engineers) and LTC (Longitudinal Time Code) MTC is not contiguous and is broken up with one message transmitted every quarter frame. This means that MTC is less accurate and prone to timing inconsistencies.

2. Song Position Pointer sends the song start position so that two sequencers can start playback at the same point. Positional data are measured using 16th notes with 0 being song start. So a value of 4 would be the second quarter note and 8 the third quarter note from the start and so forth. You have a total of 4,096 quarter notes or 1,024 measures in $\frac{4}{4}$ as possible location information.

3. Song Select is used to jump to a particular song or sequence.

4. Tune Request is used to request that the receiving device retune its internal oscillators, is used mostly for analog oscillators, and is generally not needed for digital synthesizers.

## System Real-Time Messages

1. System Real-Time messages support transport control (start, stop, and continue), also referred to as MIDI Machine Control (MMC).

2. Beat clock is 24 pulses per quarter note (PPQN) that allows two devices to sync in tempo. So as the tempo increases, so does the beat clock allowing the "slave" device or the device following the master to follow tempo variations. This is important because even if two devices have the same tempo, they will eventually drift apart without continued synchronization.

3. Active Sensing allows a receiving device to know the sending device is still attached even when no MIDI data are sent by the user. This is helpful because unplugged cables stop the active sensing messages and the receiving device stops playback, which prevents stuck notes.

## System Exclusive Messages

System Exclusive messages allow manufactures a proprietary way to be able to update files, firmware (software running on hardware), fix bugs and enhance usability, and control parameters. Each manufacture is provided a unique SysEx number assigned by the MMA that is used to identify messages designed specifically for each manufacturer's devices.

When a SysEx message is recognized on the receiving end, it will respond in whatever way the manufacture has programed for it to respond. This may be a system restore, new samples in a sampler, or a change of software menus. If the manufacture's number is received by a device that is from another manufacture or another piece of hardware from the same manufacture, it will not respond to any of the data sent until a closing SysEx message is sent, otherwise known as an EoS or End of SysEx message. This allows for both a universal protocol and the ability for companies to still have a unique way to program and interact with their own equipment. SysEx messages are also used when there are not enough CC values to control all of the parameters within a device and gives the flexibility to change parameters with single proprietary SysEx messages.

## MIDI Controllers and Subprotocols

Subprotocols or standards such as HUI (Human User Interface), Mackie Control Universal, CS-10, and many others have been created to give further control over a DAW and standardize how MIDI messages are used to control a workstation. Keep in mind that the MIDI messages are not changing, but how these messages are being responded to is changing. For instance, pressing play on a control surface often sends a MIDI Note On message, but rather than playing a note it activates the sequencer transport. Sequencers set up to be controlled by these units will know not to use the messages from these controllers to play a note.

A fun experiment if you have one of these controllers is to assign them to a MIDI instrument and press buttons, move faders, and turn knobs and listen to the results. The standard MIDI messages are being sent but not being received as originally intended. It is important to make sure that these controllers are not set up to work as intended in the DAW's setup/preferences or this experiment will not work since the workstation will know not route messages from these controllers to MIDI instruments.

A continued back and forth connection or "handshake" is required with many of these substandards in order for them to communicate with DAWs. An early controller called the CS-10 uses channel 16 when communicating with DAWs. The assignments for the CS-10 are listed below, and if you compare CC assignments you can see that they do not line up with the MMA's standards that would be used to control a MIDI instrument. For example CC 77 is used for pan instead of CC 10.

## CS-10 Controller Assignments

All Continuous Controllers must be sent on channel 16.

Controller # and Name

0. Mute 1
1. Mute 2
2. Mute 3
3. Mute 4
4. Mute 5
5. Mute 6
6. Mute 7
7. Mute 8
8. Mode
9. Shift
10. F1
11. F2
12. F3
13. F4
14. F5
15. F6
16. F7
17. F8

18. F9
19. REWIND
20. FAST FORWARD
21. STOP
22. PLAY
23. RECORD
24. LEFT WHEEL
25. RIGHT WHEEL
26. UP CURSOR
27. DOWN CURSOR
28. LEFT CURSOR
29. RIGHT CURSOR
30. FOOT-SWITCH
64. FADER 1
65. FADER 2
66. FADER 3
67. FADER 4
68. FADER 5
69. FADER 6
70. FADER 7
71. FADER 8
72. BOOST/CUT
73. FREQUENCY
74. BANDWIDTH
75. SEND 1
76. SEND 2
77. PAN
96. WHEEL

## Understanding Parts per Quarter Note

There are 960 parts per quarter note (PPQN) represented in most digital audio workstations; some will even let you adjust what the base value is. PPQN are referred to as ticks, which is the smallest resolution you will work with in MIDI timing. Ninety-six PPQN or less will generally start to have a noticeable quantized feel. This, of course, will depend on the music played and the tempo it was played at. Keep in mind that the display resolution may be different from the actual internal resolution of the recorded MIDI in a sequencer.

As you speed up the tempo, the recorded resolution per second increases since the resolution of the ticks stays the same per quarter note. There is a trick that manipulates the resolution on sequencers by doubling the tempo but halving the speed of the parts providing more resolution in the quantization of the played part.

Some sequencers even limit the time that could be recording in them based on what the tempo of the music is. By lowering the tempo it is possible to get more time to record, since the limitation of the max PPQN is expanded.

## Binary Numbers

Since binary numbers play a role in the fundamental functionality of MIDI, let's take a look at how to count with them. Binary is a base 2 counting system with only two numbers to deal with, which are often referred to as on or off being a 1 or a 0.

MIDI messages are 24 bits, which means there are 24 binary number slots that make up each message. Let's start with a 4-bit number to see how this works. Binary numbers count from right to left instead of left to right.

```
0 = 0000
1 = 0001
2 = 0010
3 = 0011
4 = 0100
5 = 0101
6 = 0110
7 = 0111
```

At this point you should be able to guess what the rest of the sequence is. See if you can write it down next to the numbers above and then check the answers that follow.

```
 8 = 1000
 9 = 1001
10 = 1010
11 = 1011
12 = 1100
```

13 = 1101
14 = 1110
15 = 1111

As you can see in a 4-digit binary number, there are 16 possible values. If it were base 10, there would be a total of 10,000 (0,000–9,999).

Every time we add a number in binary we get a doubling of the previous max position:

- 1 binary number can represent two numbers: 0 and 1
- 2 binary numbers can represent 4 numbers: 00, 01, 10, and 11
- 3 binary numbers can represent 8 numbers: 000, 001, 010, 011, 100, 101, 110, and 111

The pattern of doubling continues as you add more binary numbers in the sequence.

So now let's think of MIDI in relation to a piano keyboard. If we wanted to have a full-size piano with all 88 keys, how many binary places would we need as a minimum to get 88? The answer is 7.

1 binary number = 2
2 binary numbers = 4
3 binary numbers = 8
4 binary numbers = 16
5 binary numbers = 32
6 binary numbers = 64
7 binary numbers = 128

One hundred twenty-eight is the value that we see represented over and over again with MIDI. You may have started to recognize that pattern in relation to other things you have often seen in computers with such things as RAM 128, 256, 512, 1024, 2048, etc. Computers are making the slow transition from 32-bit processing to 64-bit processing, which would be 2 to the 64th power or 1.84467440737096 E19 (a really, really big number).

The extra 40 (128 MIDI values minus 88 keys) can be used to trigger an extended range of notes, but in many cases the extra 40 numbers aren't used. Extra notes are also used for additional trigger information such as key switches, which allows you to play one note and cause other samples to be performed in a different style. These alternate performance styles might include staccato, legato, arco, and ponticello.

While 128 is a common number in MIDI, there are 24 numbers in a MIDI message broken up into groups of 8, which has a max value of 256 for each word. The reason for this discrepancy is that the start of each byte is reserved for indicating positional information. The Status byte always starts with a 1, and the start of Data byte 1 and 2 always begins with 0. As a result, the number is cut in half for the values of each that we are able to use because we have 7 free bits from every 8-bit word.

| Status Byte | Data Byte 1 | Data Byte 2 |
|---|---|---|
| 1 001 0000 | 0 1000000 | 0 1111111 |

The Status Message has bytes and nibbles (half of a byte.) The first nibble of the status byte has a maximum value of 8 (3 bits) because the first bit is always reserved for a 1 to indicate the start of a MIDI message. This number is the most significant bit (MSB) because it is the bit which has the most value. These status messages and their corresponding data byte function are listed in the appendix.

## Reading Binary

Reading binary beyond 16 is really not all that difficult, though it's generally not needful to read since most event lists will show these data often as text for their values where

Table 1.1

| Number to Add | 128 | 64 | 32 | 16 | 8 | 4 | 2 | 1 | | |
|---|---|---|---|---|---|---|---|---|---|---|
| Place Holder | 8 | 7 | 6 | 5 | 4 | 3 | 2 | 1 | | |
| | 1 | 0 | 0 | 0 | 0 | 0 | 0 | 0 | = | 128 |
| | 0 | 1 | 0 | 0 | 0 | 0 | 0 | 0 | = | 64 |
| | 0 | 0 | 1 | 0 | 0 | 0 | 0 | 0 | = | 32 |
| | 0 | 0 | 1 | 0 | 0 | 0 | 0 | 1 | = | 33 |
| | 0 | 0 | 1 | 0 | 0 | 0 | 1 | 0 | = | 34 |
| | 0 | 0 | 1 | 1 | 0 | 1 | 0 | 0 | = | 52 |
| | 1 | 0 | 0 | 0 | 0 | 0 | 1 | 0 | = | 130 |

possible. See the following table to see how you read the numbers simply by remembering their placeholder values and then adding them up based on whether or not they have a value of 1 in their place holder.

In the first example, the first 1 is in the 128 slot and all the rest are 0, so $128 + 0 + 0 + 0 + 0 + 0 + 0 = 128$. Follow that pattern and you are all set to convert a binary number into a base 10 value.

## MIDI Files

MIDI can be stored and passed around as small files and are much smaller in size than digital audio files would be. As you know by now, MIDI is not the audio itself but information much like music on a page. MIDI files can be found all over the Internet, many of which are free. There are several companies that sell performance-based MIDI files to be used in songs that

Table 1.2

| *Channel Numbers | |
| --- | --- |
| 0 | 1 |
| 1 | 2 |
| 10 | 3 |
| 11 | 4 |
| 100 | 5 |
| 101 | 6 |
| 110 | 7 |
| 111 | 8 |
| 1000 | 9 |
| 1001 | 10 |
| 1010 | 11 |
| 1011 | 12 |
| 1100 | 13 |
| 1101 | 14 |
| 1110 | 15 |
| 1111 | 16 |

have the time and feel of real musicians because they are played by real musicians. A few companies worth noting are Twiddly Bits, ToonTrack, BFD, and MusicSoft. Many companies' MIDI files are meant to be used inside proprietary players but at the foundation are MIDI files that trigger the performance.

These MIDI files have the advantage of using real musicians and in many cases using their performance to trigger real sampled or recorded audio rather than step entering or programing in music as you might read it on a page, which would feel stiff and robotic. This gives the ability to both transpose and change the tempo while still maintaining the feel of the performance.

Standard MIDI files (SMF) with the extension of .mid* are time stamped and stored in a simple file format. Before files formats became available, MIDI was purely a real-time protocol and were played sequentially as they were performed.

Standard MIDI files today are stored in two file types: Type 0 and Type 1. All major digital audio workstations on the market support both formats and can also export these formats. Type 0 stores all sequenced track as a single track, meaning that if you exported 12 tracks of MIDI or instruments in your notation software and chose File Type 0, it will be combined into a single track. There was also a third format that never really caught on, which was Type 2 and it allowed for a combination of Type 1 and Type 2.

When exporting Type 1 files, all of the tracks retain their individual/separated track information with all of their notes, controller information, and program changes. Standard MIDI files also support track names though these may not be exported with your file when saved since it is up to the DAW how the names are retained in the Type 1 files.

Tempo maps and other controller information are stored in the SMF, and when exporting these files you may choose to also send out initial messages at the start of each channel to insure that your sounds and performance will be played back as expected. Importing these files into many sequencers will likely still play back with the wrong triggered sounds despite your efforts to record proper patch change and other such messages at the start of the sequence. As a result these have to be assigned on the receiving device/virtual instrument.

Pitch bend range is adjusted on the sound module or virtual instrument; though there is an MMA standard RPN (Registered Parameter Number) for setting pitch bend range, this is often not adhered to. If the pitch bend information is intended to bend over a range of a whole step and you have your instrument set to bend over an octave, things might sound a bit strange. This information is not stored in the MIDI file as intervals but rather as relative range values based on your sound modules settings.

Messages that you may want to consider including at the start of your MIDI files to ensure accuracy in performance in your sequencer are the following:

Program Change # (status message)
Modulation (CC 1)
Initial Volume (CC 7)
Pan (CC 10–Center = 64)
Expression (CC 11)
Hold pedal (CC 64–0 = off)

Reset All Controllers (CC 121) (not all devices may recognize this command so you may prefer to zero out or reset individual controllers).

## General MIDI

In 1992, General MIDI (GM) expanded on the MIDI 1.0 spec and further defined what could be expected from compatible devices. The reason behind the GM standard is that though there were standard ways of sending messages such as notes, pitch bend, etc., there was nothing in the specification that dictated which instruments would sound when a note was played. Sending a program change to one sound module may trigger an overdrive guitar, while the same program change on another module might trigger a vibraphone. Worse yet, you could also end up triggering drums or sound effects when you were expecting a pitched-based instrument instead. See the appendix for a list of GM instrument assignments.

In addition to defining what sounds will play, it also assigned a dedicated channel to percussion instruments where each note is assigned to an instrument such as a kick drum, snare drum, or ride cymbal.

Table 1.3

| Note | Drum Sound |
| --- | --- |
| B0 | Acoustic Bass Drum |
| C1 | Bass Drum 1 |
| C#1 | Side Stick |
| D1 | Acoustic Snare |
| Eb1 | Hand Clap |
| E1 | Electric Snare |
| F1 | Low Floor Tom |
| F#1 | Closed Hi Hat |
| G1 | High Floor Tom |
| Ab1 | Pedal Hi-Hat |
| A1 | Low Tom |
| Bb1 | Open Hi-Hat |
| B1 | Low-Mid Tom |
| C2 | Hi Mid Tom |
| C#2 | Crash Cymbal 1 |
| D2 | High Tom |
| Eb2 | Ride Cymbal 1 |
| E2 | Chinese Cymbal |
| F2 | Ride Bell |
| F#2 | Tambourine |
| G2 | Splash Cymbal |
| Ab2 | Cowbell |
| A2 | Crash Cymbal 2 |

*(Continued)*

Table 1.3 (Continued)

| Note | Drum Sound |
|------|------------|
| Bb2 | Vibraslap |
| B2 | Ride Cymbal 2 |
| C3 | Hi Bongo |
| C#3 | Low Bongo |
| D3 | Mute Hi Conga |
| Eb3 | Open Hi Conga |
| E3 | Low Conga |
| F3 | High Timbale |
| F#3 | Low Timbale |
| G3 | High Agogo |
| Ab3 | Low Agogo |
| A3 | Cabasa |
| Bb3 | Maracas |
| B3 | Short Whistle |
| C4 | Long Whistle |
| C#4 | Short Guiro |
| D4 | Long Guiro |
| Eb4 | Claves |
| E4 | Hi Wood Block |
| F4 | Low Wood Block |
| F#4 | Mute Cuica |
| G4 | Open Cuica |
| Ab4 | Mute Triangle |
| A4 | Open Triangle |

In order to be considered compliant with the GM standard, a device has to meet a list of requirements:

1.  Voices: It is required to be able to produce 16 simultaneous voices (notes) on pitched-based instruments. Every voice must be able to individually respond to its received velocity message. Eight voices are required for percussion instruments.
2.  Instruments: A minimum of 16 instruments, all with their own unique sounds based on the GM instrument table (see appendix) need to be able to sound simultaneously.

Percussion sounds also need to map to the correct instruments based on the MIDI note number received.

3. Channels: All 16 MIDI channels must be supported and if a message is sent on channel 15 then there needs to be a sound that can respond to that message. Every channel also needs to be able to change to the assigned program instrument defined by GM on channels 1–9 and 11–16. Drums are reserved for channel 10.

4. Channel Voice Status Messages: Must use Note On, Channel Pressure, Program and Pitch Bend.

5. Control Change Messages:

   - 1 for modulation;
   - 7 for volume;
   - 10 for panning or placement of the sound in the speakers;
   - 11 for expression (this is generally used to change the volume and can be used as a trim control);
   - 64 pedal on or off, and is almost always used for sustain;
   - 121 and 123 RPN (registered parameter number) numbers 0 for pitch bend range, 1 for master fine tuning in cents (100 cents in a half-step), 2 for master course tuning in half-steps;

6. Other Messages: Respond to the data entry controller 6 for coarse adjustment when using the RPNs, and data entry 38 for fine adjustments for pitch bend range and master tuning, as well as all General MIDI Level 1 System Messages.

## GS and XG

Both Roland and Yamaha came up with their own standards to further unify compatibility across their products. Roland came out with General Standard (GS) in 1991 and Yamaha has three versions of XG (doesn't stand for anything but is an extension of the GM format) known as "levels" that started in 1994—each with higher standards of voices, drum kits, and channels required to be XG 1, 2, or 3 compliant. They also defined how continuous controllers would be used on products that were listed as GS or XG. Keep in mind that this did not in any way alter the original MIDI spec, but rather further defined requirements of the hardware or software that bore these labels. Some of the messages that hadn't been defined were now required to follow a standard of what they were controlling. This serves much the same purpose as General MIDI does.

## GM2

As a result of this in 1999, General MIDI Level 2 was passed by the MMA, which like the various Yamaha XG levels introduces further requirements while maintaining the requirements of GM 1. Thirty-two simultaneous voices became required rather than the 24 previously required. It also raised the number to 16 simultaneous voices vs. the 8 in GM1 for percussion instruments. Also similar to the GS spec that allowed more than 1 channel for percussion (channel 16 in GS), channel 10 and 11 became dedicated for use of percussion tracks. Several other control change and Universal SysEx messages were standardized.

## Running Status

Running status is the process of sending MIDI messages without the Status Message to be more efficient. This relies on the most recently sent Status Message and keeps it stored in memory and applies all subsequent Data Bytes to the same message type. The advantage of running status is that since all MIDI messages are transferred serially, it means every note or message has to wait its turn to be played and omitting repetitive data can keep things efficient. MIDI is transmitted at a data rate of 31.25 kilobits per second with 10 bits total transmitted for every 8-bit message or, in other words, 30 bits for a single MIDI message. There is a start bit that has a value of 0, 8 data bits, and 1 stop bit that has a value of 1. This means that a single MIDI message takes slightly less than 1 millisecond (a thousandth of a second) to be transmitted.

This all is not much of a problem until you start getting into many chords all played at once. Having upward of 30 notes that are supposed to all start at the same time would cause almost 30 ms of difference between the first note and the last note, and this causes a smearing in the sound, especially when those notes are to be played in unison. To help alleviate this problem Running Status only transmits the data byte messages until the status changes. What is even more exciting is that a Note On message of zero can be sent in place of a Note Off message. As you would expect, there are many Note Off messages that are expected to be sent to stop the notes from playing, which would mix and mingle with Note On messages requiring the status byte to be sent again and again. This reduces the effectiveness of running status by sending Note On messages with a value of zero in place of Note Off messages; there is no need to send a new Status Message and all of the notes are played with less delay than would otherwise be possible.

## Summary

Some of you may have gotten exactly what you wanted from this chapter and others may still be scratching your head about why MIDI Messages are important to understand. The truth is that understanding the basics of MIDI will not make your music better, but it can help you when troubleshooting and getting the most out of your sequencers. Let's move to the next chapter and explore MIDI hardware.

# MIDI HARDWARE 2

Making MIDI connections is deceptively simple. While most setups have benefited from the integration of USB as a MIDI carrier, there are six common ways to connect MIDI devices. Each method has similarities and differences, but none have been able to fully escape the low bandwidth of the original MIDI design. What this means is that you can't look to a single format as being better than the rest and instead you have to look at each individual interface and workflow. The six connection types are the 5-pin DIN MIDI cable, USB, FireWire, Ethernet, PCI cards, and WiFi. In this chapter we explore the practical side of hooking things together.

## Five-pin DIN MIDI Cables

Five-pin DIN MIDI cables have been around since the earliest MIDI days and are still used in most studios. With data only moving in one direction through cables, a complete connection between two devices requires two cables with an optional third cable. A synth will typically have a MIDI In, a MIDI Out, and a MIDI Thru. The input accepts control data from a MIDI control source. The output can send a copy of the input and/or separate MIDI data, if the synth has generation capabilities. The THRU port sends a direct copy on to other gear and is the recommended option for passing data on to other gear, especially since the output isn't required to send an exact copy of the input.

**Figure 2.1** Prophet 600—The First MIDI Instrument

The connectors on this type of MIDI cable are the same on both ends and can be used for any of the three ports. As a result of the cost effective design there are several quirks when using this connection type. The first is that there is always voltage present and the MIDI data are transmitted by turning it off to form data words. To protect equipment from stray current, light resistors convert the transmitted signal to usable levels. This step, while deemed necessary to protect equipment and prepare the signal for further use, creates a very short delay in the signal. Combine this delay with a full data stream, and it means that you can only chain three to four units together using MIDI Thru before the delay becomes audibly obvious. The more complex the setup, the more trouble that using MIDI Thru becomes.

It is possible to have a single control source that sends MIDI out to various destinations using a single chain of cables attached to the In from each Thru. As an example, let's look at a possible setup. The source is Logic Pro via a single MIDI interface. The MIDI Out attaches to the first MIDI In on an old Proteus 1, which in turn connects to a Proteus 2 via the first's

**Figure 2.2** Proteus Modules Connected in Series

MIDI Thru. This is repeated with four different Proteus devices so that we can use a variety of different sounds. If you only connect each device like this without adjusting other settings you will end up with each unit playing the exact same part because they will respond to the same MIDI information. Using the 16 available MIDI channels is the solution and will allow you to assign different MIDI parts to each Proteus while still using a single cable. The source track for each part needs to be assigned to an individual MIDI channel, and then the corresponding Proteus needs to be set to accept data on the same channel. All of the MIDI will be sent to every unit, but each unit will only respond to the data that are on their channel. You can use all 16 channels to create a medium-sized arrangement, all starting with a single output from the sequencer.

The biggest problem is that the MIDI is still sent serially, which means that if all 16 channels are used and each is playing a 3-note chord, then you are looking at 48 simultaneous notes that must be transmitted one after another. Add in any other controllers (such as pitch bend, modulation, and aftertouch), and you are going to be stuck in the middle of a MIDI traffic jam. Timings will all be off and the system performance will deteriorate. In our example with the 4 Proteus units, we should be fine most of the time as long

**Figure 2.3** Yamaha MIDI Expander Box

*Source:* Photo courtesy of www.perfectcircuitaudio.com

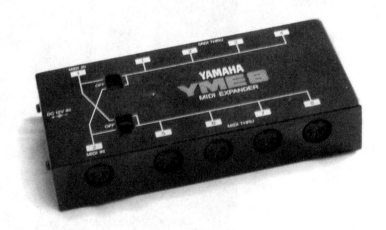

as not every part includes complex chords and/or rapid timed sequences.

An alternate to using a single chain of instruments is to use a Thru box that takes a single In signal and sends it to multiple Thru ports. This doesn't fix any issues caused by MIDI traffic because everything still travels down the same cable, but it will help minimize the effects of using multiple Thru ports on all of the devices. It also helps with connecting devices that don't have Thru ports.

The last of these options is to make connections using an interface with multiple MIDI Outs. This minimizes the risk of overloading the bandwidth when using multiple devices. If your sequence uses 48–64 tracks, then you are going to need an interface with quite a few ports and then still use multiple channels on each feed. Finding a balance of individual outputs while utilizing multiple channels is one of the more realistic options when working on large productions.

The three types of MIDI ports are included on most MIDI-capable devices, but in order to connect to a computer you need to have a MIDI interface. All of the other connection types have the option to include 5-pin MIDI cable ports. While there are a number of dedicated MIDI interfaces, most MIDI ports are available as a part of audio interfaces. No matter which type you use, you are still at the mercy of the serial MIDI format. Let's look at each of the connection types with examples of specific hardware offerings.

**Figure 2.4** MOTU MIDI Express XT

## USB

USB (Universal Serial Bus) is the most common MIDI connection option outside of the 5-pin cables. When USB-MIDI was originally developed, it revolutionized how MIDI was transmitted. In addition to increasing the speed and bandwidth of the format, USB-MIDI also allowed devices to be bus powered, which means a keyboard controller can be attached to your computer without needing a separate power supply. A single USB connection can send multiple MIDI streams over a single cable, which translates into a more efficient system. There is little doubt, based on the successful adoption of USB-MIDI in the music industry, that this format is very usable. However, there are a number of considerations for getting the best performance when using USB-MIDI.

In the document titled *Universal Serial Bus Device Class Definition for MIDI Devices* (1999), the team that developed the specification used in USB-MIDI listed the essential components required for use. Modern operating systems include software drivers that permit USB-MIDI devices to work without needing additional software. Hardware that is designed to be class compliant works immediately upon being connected. Not all MIDI devices are class compliant and those that aren't require additional software drivers to be installed separately. These drivers might work very well or they might not work at all. An example of an interface that is not class compliant is the

**Figure 2.5** M-Audio USB MIDI Interface

MBox from Avid. You are required to install software in order to use the device. Some devices require additional software and achieve better results than devices that are class compliant because of the quality of the design and programming.

USB requires more care when dealing with the operating system because of the way that USB data are shared among competing sources. If you have multiple devices connected to your computer that are sharing the same USB bus and the MIDI device is not given priority, then you are at risk of timing jitter. Jitter is defined as variations in timing based on environmental or design issues. Be cautious when using a hub or having too many USB devices connected at the same time because jitter will likely be at higher levels, and your recorded performances will not be accurate to the original performance.

## FireWire

There isn't an accepted class compliant standard for FireWire. In fact, this is a format that is in steep decline and is rarely an option for MIDI interfaces. The primary relationship between MIDI and FireWire is through audio interfaces that use FireWire but which add a MIDI IN and OUT as an additional, but not primary, feature offering. The primary trend away from FireWire interfaces happened because Apple stopped adding FireWire ports to their successful lines of MacBook Pros and no other computer hardware developers adopted FireWire for their machines. At the time of writing, a major music company had 9 FireWire interfaces available with MIDI and 177 with USB-MIDI. FireWire offers more in terms of timing and isolation from bus sharing than USB does, but it only matters what is adopted by instrument and interface manufacturers.

**Figure 2.6**
Focusrite Firewire Interface with MIDI

## Ethernet

This format saw some very interesting developments starting in the late '90s. Yamaha released its mLan spec, which seemed very promising because of the speed of the format and the ability to avoid the shortcomings of USB. Instead of becoming a widespread format, it has all but died off with no new mLan products in the past few years. Other Ethernet formats have been developed such as EuCon, which is a replacement for MIDI when connecting to control surfaces. Its speed and resolution is very good, but it is not an open format that can be used by other companies, leaving Avid to control its usage.

Ethernet connectivity is currently making a resurgence and has the potential to become a solid player in the MIDI connection business. The only problem is that the development is happening at a time when mobile devices are in high demand and everything is moving to wireless. However, let's look at an example of a new product that seems to fit the needs of every MIDI market. The iConnectMIDI4 is a device that can attach via Ethernet, USB, and MIDI 5-pin DIN. The Ethernet option can be hooked to a wireless router and shared with multiple devices. The USB option can attach to MIDI-enabled mobile devices. The devices can work with 64 MIDI ports (1024 individual MIDI channels), which is more than most people will need. The device is class compliant and will work without needing additional drivers.

Roland has also incorporated Ethernet functionality into equipment with MIDI functionality using a protocol called RRC2. Roland's FC-300 foot controller has both MIDI ports and an Ethernet port, which is only compatible with a small selection of other equipment.

**Figure 2.7** Roland FC-300

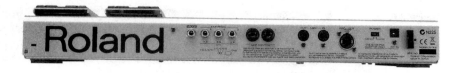

## PCI Cards

This is another area of MIDI connectivity that is dying out because laptops and mobile devices are solidly taking over. Even for studios that have desktop computers, quite a few people want to have an interface that can be taken with them, but a PCI option lives inside the computer as an expansion card and so many are seeking USB options instead. Because of the size of PCI cards, MIDI cables typically have to be attached using breakout cables.

## Wireless (WiFi)

The wireless option is described in the chapter on mobile devices because this is the area that has pushed wireless MIDI into the forefront. Using the same essential communication as Ethernet, connectivity over WiFi is not only good enough for most connection needs, in some cases it is the only option. The promise of WiFi is hardware simplicity, which

**Figure 2.8** Lemur Network Connection

means that multiple devices can connect without needing adapters, cables, or anything extra. The iPad is an example of a device that benefits from connecting via WiFi because it has very limited ports to use for connecting peripherals. You can use the Apple-designed Camera Connection Kit to attach class compliant USB-MIDI devices but are limited to operation on battery power while in use.

The primary consideration with a wireless connection is the same as with all of these connections; bandwidth is shared with other operations and so it is recommended that you reserve the wireless connection to just MIDI information. If you are downloading a large file from the Internet over WiFi and are also trying to record MIDI wirelessly, then you will run into a bandwidth issue.

Another MIDI connection that uses wireless technology involves similar technology to wireless microphones, which is a direct box-to-box connection used primarily in live performance. Unlike using WiFi, this wireless connection requires a specific hardware broadcaster and receiver, and it does not use network connections at all.

## Hardware Devices

Hardware options are a vital part of the MIDI production process and are grouped into three categories: controllers, sound generators, and control surfaces.

### Controllers

A MIDI controller's primary function is to control other devices via MIDI. These controllers can take many different forms such as a piano keyboard, a set of drums, a guitar, or a mobile device. The key elements of a controller are an interface that you interact with and a method of transmitting the performance data. Some controllers imitate traditional musical instruments such as pianos or drums, other controllers are brand new inventions that don't resemble anything, and some involve equipment that is added onto musical instruments.

**Figure 2.9** AKAI MPK88

*Source:* Photo courtesy of Roland.

Keyboard controllers rarely just include the musical keys and will often have drum pads, faders for controlling your DAW, and various buttons. This style of controller is an example of a device that is both a controller and a control surface. Many synths/samplers are controllers, control surfaces, and sound generators. The keyboard controller is most likely to be class compliant and work without additional software, but controllers with additional control surface features often need or benefit from additional software provided by the manufacturer.

Drum controllers come in several varieties. The first is designed to look like an actual drum kit, with pads instead of drums, snares, and cymbals. The next type is a set of percussion pads, which come in a much more economical shape. The last type is the drum machine, which is similar to the percussion pad but often has additional features such as sampling and sequencing. Many drum machines are entire workstations while percussion pads are just pads.

Controllers based on nontraditional designs can take any shape or form and be designed to accomplish any MIDI tasks that you can think of. There aren't that many available for purchase online because most of them are custom creations that aren't commercially viable for large-scale release. However, you can find several DIY kits online that provide the core electronic components so you can create your own controller. There are also some options that include equipment like Microsoft Kinect to control your DAW using motion capture but these are not using MIDI. In the chapter on live performance and alternate formats, we look at developing formats

**Figure 2.10** Roland
V-Drums

*Source:* Photo courtesy of
Roland.

like OSC. Some devices, like Ableton's Push, use a custom scheme to control its software but make MIDI available for connecting to alternate DAWs.

A MIDI guitar is an example of an instrument with MIDI functionality added to make it a controller. Some guitars have special pickups built in, and others are guitars with a special MIDI pickup kit that is added after market. Guitar players often use this functionality for live performances but it is useful for all phases of music production. The notes are converted into MIDI, and they can be used to control sounds from synthesizers and samplers, which provide an alternate way of performing other instrument sounds. Melodies performed on a guitar and a keyboard are typically phrased much differently and so there are different applications for each.

**Figure 2.11** Livid
Instruments Brain 2
*Source:* Photo courtesy of
AKAI.

**Figure 2.12** VRoland VG Series
350 with MIDI Capabilities
*Source:* Photo courtesy of Roland.

Keyboard instruments are sometimes converted from solely acoustic instruments to instruments with MIDI capabilities. The Moog Piano Bar is a product that fit onto acoustic pianos and translated key movement into MIDI data. While a great idea, it never worked well without an unusual amount of setup and was pulled from production. The concept of using a quality grand piano as a MIDI controller certainly has its merits, and perhaps additional products will pop up in the future.

## Controller Accessories

Accessories are categorized as controllers that send non-note MIDI data. This group contains sustain pedals, expression pedals, and breath controllers. Each of these have to be connected to a controller to be used but not every controller has the appropriate accessory inputs. Seeking a controller that uses accessories should be a consideration during the purchase phase unless you are absolutely sure you won't ever need them.

## Example Controller Installations

Let's look at the installation of three different controller options. Each of these scenarios demonstrates a different issue that you might face during the installation process.

### Example #1—Akai MPK88 (Pictured Previously)

This large keyboard has 88 hammer action keys, drum pads, knobs, and faders. There are two MIDI connection options, USB, and 5-pin MIDI cables. The MPK88 is class compliant and so you can plug the USB into your computer and use it without additional software. You can also plug it into any mobile devices that work with compliant controllers such as an iPad, even though it looks a little odd attaching a huge keyboard to a small tablet.

You can also install the Akai software that adds additional functionality; but without plugging in the keyboard using an external power supply you cannot use the 5-pin MIDI ports. Controllers that attach to computers via USB and that have 5-pin ports usually have the ability to act as a MIDI interface. Playing the keyboard sends MIDI data to the computer and/or to the MIDI Out port. MIDI from the computer is sent to the keyboard and then distributed to the Out port. Without being connected to a power supply, the MPK88 does not have enough power to use the Out port and the MIDI won't be sent anywhere.

If you use a powered USB hub, you can connect the keyboard and a USB microphone simultaneously to an iPad for recording both the keyboard part and a vocal performance.

*Example #2—Roland SPD-SX*

This controller is labeled as a sampling pad by Roland and has many of the features of a drum machine and percussion pad. The primary difference between the SPD-SX and a traditional drum machine is that the SPD doesn't have a built-in sequencer to store patterns and songs. USB and MIDI cables are the two methods of attaching the SPD to your computer. When using USB there are two pieces of software you need to install to be able to achieve full connection. The first is the driver, which allows the SPD to connect as a MIDI and audio interface. The second is the manager software, which allows you to connect to the SPD and share sounds and patches.

The SPD-SX has the ability to connect to the computer via USB in two distinct ways. The first is as a USB drive that allows the manager application to connect and exchange files and backup settings. The second is as an audio/MIDI interface that allows the SPD to control software via MIDI but also can pass audio as an interface, which means you can choose the SPD in your DAW's settings to make it the primary audio output. This means that a drummer could have this in his rig on stage and use it to trigger samples on a laptop. The SPD not only acts as the trigger but also as the audio interface for the laptop, which means that the drummer can minimize the

**Figure 2.13** Roland SPD-SX
*Source:* Photo courtesy of Roland.

**Figure 2.14** Yamaha
DX-7

*Source:* Photo courtesy of
www.perfectcircuitaudio.com

gear required. The only thing required to change between the
USB modes is a preference option that switches between
them on the SPD-SX.

### Example #3—DX-7

One of the original keyboard success stories, the DX-7 is a
FM synthesizer with great sounds and solid MIDI capabilities. There is only one option when using the DX-7 as a controller, and that is to use a MIDI cable and connect it to some
other MIDI interface. When the DX-7 was originally designed,
USB had not been released and so it doesn't have that option.
Some people prefer to have multiple controllers in their
studio because one might have beautifully weighted keys
and another might have feather light keys, and both are used
in very different ways. It is nice to have both.

## Sound Generators

MIDI is used to control samplers and synthesizers. While most
sound sources are now of the virtual variety, there are many
hardware synths and samplers that can be used in the production process. In particular, synthesizers still have more
character and sometimes unique features that can't be found
in a software version. Let's take a look at the common types
of sound generators that you'll be using with MIDI and some
considerations when using them.

### Samplers

Samplers use detailed recordings of musical instruments mapped
onto specific MIDI notes to re-create a virtual version of the

instrument. There was a point in the 1990s when hardware samplers were still more powerful than software samplers, primarily due to slower processors, limited RAM, and hard drive seek times. As computer power increased, sampling was moved into the software realm, and for most purposes samplers have never returned to popularity with hardware. This is primarily because it no longer made sense to use a hardware digital sampler when a computer could do the same exact thing but better and more easily. The only exception to this is when it comes to drums and other modules used in live performance, although that is something that has changed with the reliability of laptops and mobile devices. Drum modules, both MIDI drums and drum machines, are not on the decline because they are used in both the studio and on the stage, but the sounds they offer are commonly available as virtual instruments.

Musicians still use hardware samplers and sampling has come back a little with the introduction to sampling on mobile devices, which makes it extremely easy to do. One of the keys to getting the most out of samplers is understanding their basic architecture so you can program accordingly. The five things to consider are velocity layers, zone ranges, round robin triggers, loops, and key switches.

### Velocity Layers

In order to create realistic sounding samples, the source instrument is recorded at different levels of loudness and then mapped so that different samples are triggered at different velocity levels. This creates an instrument that actually sounds like it is being played louder when the MIDI triggers it at higher velocities. Otherwise you would end up with a soft sounding sample that is simply louder. If you are using an early sampler then there are likely fewer velocity layers for each note due to the limited resources available. If there are three to four layers, you will need to be careful when sequencing to make sure you don't jump from one layer to the next at inappropriate times. Nothing makes it obvious that you are using a sampler like a timbre change when moving from one layer to the next when

**Figure 2.15**
Mapping in Logic
Pro's EXS-24

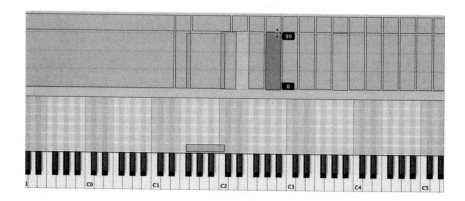

only a minor level increase should have occurred. Either edit the MIDI data to prevent such switches or use quantization to automatically control the velocity ranges.

Other times the velocity layers are used to create alternate performance options. An example is a bass patch that has a pitch bend on the highest velocity layer to imitate what a bass play might do at loud levels. A guitar patch might have a glissando at the highest layer or a pickup note to give variety to the virtual instrument. You should get to know your sampled instrument enough to see what is included in each layer so that you can get the most efficient performance possible.

### Zone Ranges

Sampled instruments rarely have a recording for each note of the chromatic scale. While it is now possible, it still is less efficient than creating shared resources. One note might be recorded and then used for three to four other pitches. The sampler shifts the pitch up or down for the adjacent notes and saves on loading additional samples. The easiest pitch adjustments occur with a speed-up or slow-down technique and this is what samplers use. For small changes this works fairly well but not when large changes are required. Instruments with individual samples for every note are the most realistic but you can achieve good results using both techniques. You should be aware of the number of samples used and discover if there are any breaks in the sound as you move through the octaves.

### Round Robin

Some samplers trigger different samples each time a note is played. An example would be performing a single note, and each time you press the key a different sound is played. It will sound very similar but is a separate recording that makes the resulting instrument closer to a real instrument, which rarely sounds exactly the same. Round robin is very useful when you desire to have an instrument which does not sound robotic or repetitive. However, the round robin function can be an issue when it comes to system resources and performance consistency. The latter means that you might record a MIDI track just how you want it but it has the potential to sound slightly difference each time you press play. Depending on the quality of the instrument this may be acceptable or something you want to turn off because you want to have complete control; it really depends on how the feature is implemented.

### Loops

Another feature of samplers that is important to consider is the looping of notes. Each sampled note can play back exactly as the original file or can be looped to give the appearance of a note that can sustain indefinitely. If a note is set to loop then you will have a sustained sound when a key is held. If the loop function is disabled then a held note will only sustain the length of the sample. Some sounds such as a sting patch can be looped easier than others, such as a snare drum. The difference is in the natural sustain and decay of the recorded sample; if there is a section of the sound that sustains, then it has the high probability of being successfully looped.

### Key Switches

Since most real instruments can be performed using a variety of attacks and releases, a sampled instrument should be able to accomplish the same thing. Key switching allows additional

**55**

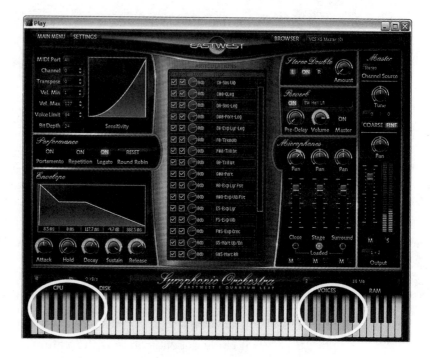

**Figure 2.16** Key Switching in Symphonic Orchestra

mapped instruments to be combined into a much larger instrument. Consider the instrument that has a short attack, an accented attack, a legato articulation, and a very soft entrance. Instead of loading a difference instrument for each, key switching means you can load them all at once and then switch between them using a MIDI trigger.

The most common trigger is a note in an unused range such as the bottom octave. Another option is to tie the switching of layers to the modulation wheel. Both options mean you can perform using various articulations and performance styles in real time or by adding the triggers after the fact.

## Synthesizers

Using hardware synths can be a rewarding experience because you get the great sound and tactile experience while benefiting from the precision and power of MIDI. Not all synthesizers have keyboards attached, but almost all of them have MIDI inputs and so you can control them from your sequencer or another controller.

If you want to connect a pre-MIDI synthesizer to your sequencer, then you'll need a MIDI-to-CV converter. There are several available for purchase and many have the ability for advanced control data conversion. Here is an example configuration to demonstrate how this might be accomplished.

### Example—Oberheim MIDI to CV Connected to ARP 2600

The MIDI controller that is at the heart of this example is the MPK88, which is attached via USB to Logic Pro. Logic sends

**Figure 2.17** Oberheim MIDI to CV

tomoberheim.com

out MIDI from the MPK88 to the MIDI-to-CV converter via a MOTU MIDI interface. The CV (plus gate and envelope) is sent to the ARP 2600, which is triggered and plays the performed notes. Logic can also arpeggiate the incoming MIDI and create a very technical performance that is replicated on the ARP 2600 exactly as programmed.

## New Synths

There are still active synth makers that are innovating and reworking traditional synthesis. In fact, because of the care that is taken when designing new synths, it often correlates to care in designing the MIDI components. New synths often have the best designed MIDI capabilities and should be used as your controller.

## Other Considerations

Depending on the synthesizer, you may discover other typical performance limitations. The first is triggering a monophonic synthesizer, which means that the synth has a single voice and cannot play multiple notes. This is a function of the design and is not necessarily to be considered a flaw. Another consideration is that many vintage synths don't have a full MIDI spec implementation. Velocity might not control level, and there are likely no after-touch features. Each synth should be treated as an individual specimen.

While an analog synth will likely have enough faders and knobs to craft their sounds without needing a digital display, many hybrid synths and digital synths are harder to control because of the size of the included screen. Some synths (Yamaha TX-816) have no controls at all and must be controlled via a sequencer or library manager.

## Local MIDI Settings

When working with any hardware there are a few additional settings that you will often need to adjust when setting up a studio. These are the Global Settings, MIDI Mode, and Local Control.

## Global Settings

The pitch and transposition of hardware units can be set separately from the incoming MIDI, which can be used for good purposes but can also be a source of problems if you change the setting but forget to change it back. If you send a Note On for C3, the unit might play something entirely different if the transposition settings are engaged. Familiarize yourself with the global settings for each unit you are using and keep track of the settings you are using. Here are some potential uses for each setting.

### Example #1—Alternate Tunings

In a situation where an audio recording is made of an instrument that is not tuned to the standard A-440, you can add MIDI tracks that are in tune if you adjust their global intonation. The primary thing to figure out is the difference in tuning so that you can set the hardware device to the correct amount. It may take some trial and error to get this right. If the tuning isn't consistent over the course of the song, then it becomes substantially more difficult to compensate for without using the tuning capabilities of a sequencer.

### Example #2—Transposition

If you are sending a MIDI part out to a sampler and want to create a simple harmony, you can use the Thru port and send a copy of the MIDI to a second unit and then transpose the input. This solution will create a simple harmony that is always the same interval apart and cannot create an intelligent harmonic progression.

### MIDI Mode

The MIDI Mode sets how MIDI inputs are treated in relationship to channels and the triggering of multiple patches. The primary options are Omni, Mono, Poly, and Multi. Modes can sometimes be combined for specific uses but several are rarely used.

### Omni

When Omni Mode is active, MIDI on all channels will be accepted for triggering notes. When Omni is turned off, then only the specified channel can be used to trigger notes. This is very important when using the Thru port to control multiple devices because each device needs to be set to an unique channel that matches the channel on its corresponding MIDI tracks.

### Mono

In Monophonic Mode only a single note can be played at a time. This is one Mode that is rarely used but does have a place when working with bass parts or melodies played by instruments that can only play one note at a time. Mono and Omni can typically be set simultaneously.

### Poly

Polyphonic Mode is the opposite of Mono Mode and allows multiple notes to be played at the same time. You are still limited by the maximum number of voices that the device can access simultaneously.

### Multi

In Multitimbral Mode the device can play back using multiple patches that are either Omni and accessed with the same MIDI regardless of the channel or non-Omni and each accessed with specific MIDI channels. If a device can load more than one patch such as bass and drums, then controlling them individually becomes more important. Channel 1 might control the bass, and the standard percussion channel 10 would control the drums. Multi Mono Mode is often used with MIDI guitar parts so that you don't have multiple notes per string and can control the output more efficiently.

## Local Control

When using hardware that has both sound generation capabilities and an attached MIDI controller, you will often need to set who can control the sounds. If Local Control is turned on then the attached keyboard will be able to control the sound. If the Local Control is disabled then the sounds can be controlled via external controller or from an attached sequencer. One of the most common ways to operate is to use the keyboard as a controller for a software sequencer and have the output of the sequencer control the sounds of the device. It is a little bit of a roundabout way to get the MIDI from the controller back to itself, but it means you can control much more than just your own sounds and you can take advantage of the power of the sequencer.

### Control Surfaces

The last group of MIDI hardware units consists of control surfaces. A control surface is used to adjust mixer parameters and other functions using a tactile device with buttons, faders, and knobs. Due to improvements in control technology, MIDI is being used less and less for new control surfaces and is being replaced by other protocols such as OSC and EuCon. For the surfaces that still use MIDI, HUI (Human User Interface) is still the most prominent. Devices that use this protocol use a series of System Exclusive messages to adjust fader levels, panning, and transport functions.

### Hooking Up a Control Surface

When attaching a MIDI-based control surface, there are certain steps to follow in order to make the connection. Start by installing any drivers that are provided by the device manufacturer. Attach the device and confirm that it is being recognized by your DAW. The device will show up as a MIDI interface and then you will need to tell the DAW that it is a control surface. If the control surface is designed to be HUI compliant, it will likely work with every DAW that is capable of using surfaces. The elements that need to be set are the MIDI ports for the surface, the type of protocol, and the DAW channels it will control.

Non-HUI controllers can also be used but need additional setup and in some cases cannot be used. Pro Tools doesn't have the ability to use faders and knobs that are designed to work with HUI. Logic Pro can take any MIDI input and assign its data to control various parameters just as a control surface would do. Most DAWs can create custom control maps based on devices that have pads, knobs, and faders. While Logic can create a custom map, the way its sequencer is designed is to accept MIDI from all sources, and so a control surface output can actually affect the other tracks if not set up properly.

### MMC

MIDI Machine Control is not part of the control surface spec, but it is a feature of MIDI that is closely related. MMC is designed to allow a device to send transport controls to other hardware. A keyboard with transport buttons generally connects as a control surface and directly activates the sequencer's

**Figure 2.19** Pro Tools MMC
Dialog

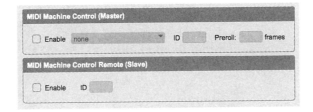

transport instead of sending MMC, but when non-DAW recording systems such as ADATs and DA-98s were used it was more common to use MMC. The sequencer could send out a start signal and the tapes would engage playback. In play mode the tape machine would send out time code and the sequencer would chase it and start to play back as well. MMC is easy to set up, and all you need to do is turn it on in the sequencer and on the tape machine and then connect time code between the devices. You could also set the tape machine to chase time code and then send time code from the sequencer, but for a long time the time code on tapes was more reliable and meant that the sync would always stay with the recording medium instead of in the sequencer. The solution then is to take control of when the tape starts and stops and let everything else chase its time code.

## Hardware Configurations

This final section explores several configurations to demonstrate the power of MIDI-capable hardware. The examples illustrate various ways to use hardware in your production process, with a particular focus on ways to incorporate "vintage" gear into the modern production process. While it is possible to do everything inside your DAW there are reasons to use external gear. Reasons include availability and affordability of older gear, interesting sounds that aren't commonly used anymore, freeing up your computer resources, and "just because you can." These examples are launching pads for finding solutions that work for you.

### Configuration #1 — Simple

DAW: Logic Pro
MIDI Interface: Roland UM-ONE
Synth and Controller: Kawai SX-240

Setup:

The UM-ONE attaches to the computer via USB and to the Kawai SX-240 via MIDI cable. The SX-240 acts as both the controller and the sound source. While you could just play the synth and record the outputs into Logic Pro, using the MIDI capabilities allows you to record and edit the performance in a Logic MIDI track.

Strengths:

The simplicity of this setup creates an environment that takes advantage of the synthesis power of the SX-240 without compromising the sequencing power of Logic Pro. The SX-240 has rich sounds and most of the synthesis tools that you might want, but adding Logic's sequencer provides additional features such as an arpeggiator and chord memorizer. An additional benefit is that you can have the sound of a

**Figure 2.20** Simple Configuration

vintage synth intermixed with the virtual instruments in Logic without excessive costs or configuration.

Weaknesses:

Keeping everything inside Logic has its advantages for the sake of low delays and simple connections. In order to record the output of the synthesizer you will also need an audio interface that has inputs to record the sound. Creating a system with a single synth has relatively low risk.

### Configuration #2—Medium Complexity

DAW: Pro Tools
MIDI Interface: MOTU MIDI Express XT
Audio Interface: Focusrite Saffire 40
Controller: AKAI MPK88
Sound Modules: KORG Wavestation SR, KORG 01R/W, ENSONIQ
    SQ-R Plus, E-MU Proteus/1, Proteus/2, Proteus/3

Setup:

There are enough MIDI outs on the Express XT to connect each sound module without using the MIDI Thru ports.

**Figure 2.21** Medium Configuration

None of these devices use USB and so you will need a MIDI cable for each unit. The audio outputs can be connected into the Saffire. Attach the MPK88 via USB to the computer.

Strengths:

Using a dedicated MIDI interface such as the Express XT is a way to manage a large number of MIDI devices. The reliability of the MIDI output and the ability to feed dedicated MIDI data to each module helps maintain a clean system with little worries of MIDI log jams.

This variety of modules will enhance any production, but they are certainly still not replacements for the virtual offerings in Pro Tools. In particular are the percussion sounds that the ENSONIQ offers and quite a few of the sounds in the Wavestation. The others offer some nostalgia for records from Vangelis and Enya, and others are less useful in many cases.

Weaknesses:

The biggest weakness of this system is that there are not enough audio inputs on the Saffire to match the outputs of the various modules. This means that you will either need to use a mixer to combine the outputs into less channels before inputting them into Pro Tools or you need to get an interface with more inputs. Both options cost money and add complexity but are necessary for using all of them at once. If you do not need to use them simultaneously then you can use a patch bay to switch between the sounds that you want to record at any given time.

### Configuration #3—Complex

DAW: Logic Pro
MIDI Interface: MOTU MIDI Express XT
Audio Interface: Focusrite Saffire 40
Mixer: Ramsa WR-S4424
Controller: AKAI MPK88
Sound Modules: 15 External modules/3 Synths
Control Surface: PreSonus FaderPort
Mobile Device: iPad

**Figure 2.22** Complex
Configuration

Setup:

There are a lot of similarities between configurations #2 and
#3. Since the MIDI Express XT only has eight MIDI outputs,
the rest of the modules will need to be connected via MIDI
Thru ports, MIDI Thru boxes, or a MIDI patch bay. In this
setup we are using a MIDI Thru box made by Yamaha
many years ago to connect six of the Proteus units to two
MIDI ports. Two other modules share MIDI using MIDI
Thru ports.

Concerning the modules that are attached via MIDI Thru, it is
necessary to assign the MIDI outputs from the Express XT so
that you can control each unit individually. This requires a
MIDI Mode of Poly or Multi. Use Poly if you plan on only
using a single patch on each unit and then set the MIDI channel
to match the desired output from Logic. In Logic you'll need
to set the output port and channel for each track to keep them
separate. If you are planning on using multiple patches on
each module, then use Multi because this will allow you to
assign multiple MIDI channels to each module. The difference
is important when it comes to mixing the outputs using effects

and processing. Different units have different tools and this will affect your decision on how to use them.

Here is a list of possible scenarios:

1.  Modules can typically load a minimum of 16 patches but often only have 3 stereo outputs. More than one patch can be assigned to each output, but that limits the processing that can be used on individual sounds.
2.  Some modules have internal effects that can be used to sculpt the sounds. Effects such as EQ, compression, and reverb can be used to get the exact sound you are looking for but are better served in your DAW or on an audio console where you can more easily create a consistent sound between modules.
3.  Create the MIDI production that you want without effects and then record each individual instrument into your DAW as audio tracks so you can process them there with all of the tools that DAWs offer.

Connecting the synths requires some specialty items because not all synths are able to be controlled via MIDI. In this case one of the synths is an expander module from Oberheim that has a built-in MIDI-to-CV converter. The synth portion is 100% analog and can only be controlled with a control voltage source. With the CV converter, built-in Logic can be used as control for the synth. There is also a CV and Gate output that is used to control an Arp 2600 vintage synth. The MIDI source for all of this comes from the Roland SPD-SX, which is attached to the computer using a USB cable. Since the SPD-SX also acts as a MIDI interface, Logic is set to send MIDI to that device but is intended for the synths. The Thru port on the Oberheim is attached to the Kawai SX-240.

All of the outputs are attached to the audio mixing console, except for the synths, which are attached directly to the additional inputs on the Saffire. The master out of the console is also attached to the Saffire. If you want to capture the entire MIDI production into Logic, then you'll want to set levels and add effects on the console because Logic will only receive a stereo output of everything and not individual parts. The mixer can use inserts and sends to add hardware effects and is used for panning and setting levels.

The FaderPort is a single fader control surface that is pretty handy in terms of space on the desk when a bigger console is already there. The biggest issue is that this controller is connected using USB and there is already a substantial number of connections using USB.

A typical list of attached USB items is as follows:

1. Mouse
2. Keyboard
3. Software keys
4. MIDI Controller #1
5. MIDI Controller #2 (percussion)
6. MIDI Express XT
7. External hard drives
8. Control Surface
9. iPad

The problem with such a long list is that USB buses are typically limited to two or three on most modern computers so each bus will be overloaded and you will not even have enough ports available. To help with the situation, attach a powered USB hub and attach additional devices to it. It's important to use a powered hub because it will help relieve the power drain caused by attaching so many devices. It is possible to attach more than one hub. Some sources say that USB only works as fast as its slowest connection, which means that attaching a USB 1.0 device will slow down USB 2.0/3.0 devices. It's easy enough to test this by attaching a hard drive to a bus along with a really basic 1.0 device. Copy files to the hard drive and see how fast they are transferred. Reconfigure your USB connections until you are happy with the copy test, but in most situations you'll find that you are getting mediocre speeds from your USB anyway. In terms of MIDI, it's not the speed that matters as much as the making sure there aren't any log jams of MIDI data.

In this configuration, the iPad plays several roles. It connects to Logic Pro as a controller but using OSC instead of MIDI. It also connects wirelessly using MIDI in an app named Lemur. This app can use OSC but it struggles when working with Logic and MIDI seems more straightforward. The wireless connect bypasses the need for MIDI cables but has issues all of its own. See the chapter discussing mobile MIDI for more information.

Strengths of Configuration #3:

Having a diversity of modules means you have access to many more sounds than your DAW offers by itself. With 15 available units it is likely that you could create an entire song without using any virtual sounds but it is more likely that you would be using them side by side and not instead of them entirely.

Weaknesses:

Having 15 sound modules is going to make it hard to keep track of everything and to troubleshoot when something goes awry. If you don't take the time to create a map of where everything is and which channels are which, then good luck getting anything connected properly. As much as possible assign MIDI ports in the order of hardware in the racks; that should help substantially in everyday operations. Another weakness is that you are bound to have more noise present in the system because of the console and the analog outputs of all of the units added together. Using high-quality gear will help minimize this, as will doing everything in the "box." The other option is to not be afraid of a little noise and use the units and patches that you like and then focus on the music instead of the technology.

## Summary

Using MIDI hardware is a rewarding challenge because it can be difficult to get everything set up and working together, but once it is you can enjoy the additional sounds and MIDI experience. If you are set on creating a MIDI studio with a lot of gear like configuration #3 above, then be prepared to think creatively and spend a lot of money on cables. Configuration #3 could easily cost you $500 in cables alone to do it right.

As technology continues to change, more and more of this will move to wireless. In the chapter on mobile devices we look into how to connect your device into a setup like the ones above. It's already possible to use your iPad to control an Arp 2600, which is actually pretty amazing considering the two were invented 40 years apart. The unifying factor between the two devices is MIDI—and some patience in trying to get it all connected.

The other area of MIDI hardware is live performance, which is covered in a later chapter. The truth is that modules as discussed in this chapter are rarely used on the stage anymore, except controllers, because it makes so much more sense to use a laptop with virtual instruments. Not only is it difficult to connect external sound sources to a laptop that has one or two USB ports, but software such as Ableton Live is reliable enough so that you don't need much else. There are even custom control surfaces created to aid in live performance, which can trigger files and make a show go very smoothly. The new trend in computer offerings includes touch screen monitors, and this is certainly starting to become a live performance addition because you can trigger sounds and loops without having to do anything but touch the screen.

Devices such as the iPad have created an expectation of high power in a small design. More and more performances use devices such as iPads as replacements for other instruments. More and more people are using mobile devices in the recording studio and in the preproduction phase of record making. As you'll see in the following chapter, mobile technology is going to continue changing everything about how we make and enjoy music.

# MOBILE MIDI

When the iPad was released in 2010, it was a personal computing breakthrough for viewing media, surfing the Web, and sending e-mails. Its elegant interface, ease of use, and access to the App Store quickly gave it the edge in the tablet market. In addition to the thousands of apps already available through its compatibility with the iPhone, new iPad-specific music apps began to quickly appear. These apps took advantage of the iPad's multi-touch interface and followed the trend of visually elegant designs made popular on the iPhone and iPod Touch.

**Figure 3.1** Arturia iMini

## iPad Apps

The potential for professional-level music creation is becoming a reality with high-quality instruments, controllers, and semi-full-featured digital audio workstations. In current usage, apps from each of these categories use MIDI on some level, and each plays an important part in the continuing evolution of MIDI as a musician's tool. Perhaps more significantly, the mobile device revolution is bringing MIDI, for the first time, to millions of new consumers and expanding its relevancy, which is remarkable considering the fundamentals of MIDI as a format are over 30 years old.

## iPad Instruments

The range of available musical instrument apps for the iPad includes everything from drums and guitars to orchestral instruments and synthesizers. Nontraditional, exotic instruments are also being released, and it is possible that any given instrument you are looking for will eventually be developed and released.

**Figure 3.2** AKAI iMPC

**Figure 3.3** iSequence

Musical instruments on the iPad can be categorized as MIDI enabled and not-MIDI enabled. Instruments that don't have MIDI functionality cannot be controlled via an external MIDI keyboard. This distinction is important because having access to MIDI input/output means you can more easily use the iPad as a musical instrument in a professional studio environment or in a live concert setting. If you have to rely on the multi-touch interface for performing, then for some instruments it can inhibit full access to the performance requirements you might need.

For example, some instruments have a piano-style keyboard on the screen to play the instrument, but the keys are too close together, which makes it difficult to play. However, some instrument apps take full advantage of the multi-touch interface, and a MIDI keyboard would lessen the efficiency of using your fingers on the iPad screen itself. It really depends on the individual app and varies from case to case.

**Figure 3.4** Korg iMS-20

One example of an effective touch screen experience on the iPad is the Korg iMS-20. You can play this analog synth replica app via the iPad's on-screen keyboard, but it is limited because you have a very compact playing area. The iMS-20 also has a feature called the Kaoss Pad that consists of two squares acting as controllers for pitch and loudness on one side and filter control on the other. Using your thumbs you can create some very interesting and sonically dynamic sounds that would be significantly more difficult to create using a traditional keyboard. The best of both worlds is a combination approach that involves using an external MIDI controller and the iPad's touch interface.

## Making Connections

The iPad as a stand-alone musical creation tool is very capable, but some of the most powerful collaborative options rely on connecting the iPad to your computer or MIDI-enabled keyboard or controller. Setting up a MIDI studio with an iPad as the central unit or as a peripheral can be complicated and in some cases very frustrating until you get a handle on the connections involved. The most common setups are explained here to help you get started. Keep in mind that because of the ease of updating apps for the iPad and the rapid growth of iOS, there are going to be bumps along the way due to the rapid progression of technology. An app that works perfectly well one day may receive an update and then no longer work at all. Does that sound exaggerated? It has happened at least once to everyone who frequently uses and updates apps.

## Connecting Wirelessly

One issue with the iPad having such a young but rapidly developing operating system is that programmers are taking different approaches to implementing MIDI connectivity, and so not every app will provide the same functionality. There are two typical ways to set up your Mac so you can connect your iPad wirelessly. The first is through the Audio MIDI Setup utility, and the other is through specifically designed software installed separately.

## Audio MIDI Setup

The Audio MIDI Setup utility in OS X is the control center for everything surrounding audio and MIDI. By default, only the audio portion of this utility is visible when you first open it. Open the MIDI window by navigating to Window > Show MIDI Window. This view shows all connected MIDI devices and is the gateway to establishing network connections. The Network icon (with the purple heading) is a default part of

**Figure 3.5** OS X MIDI Studio

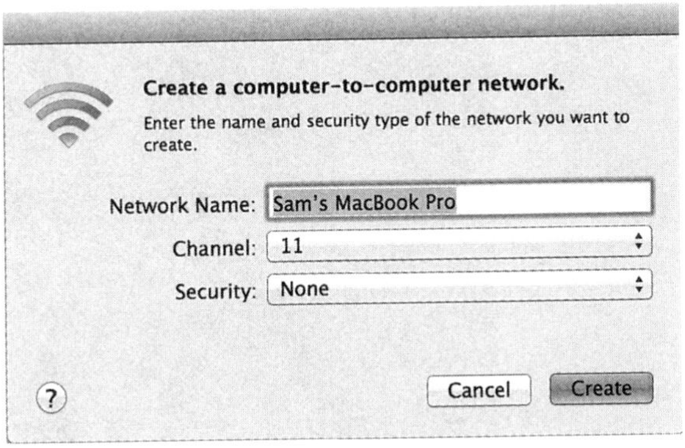

**Figure 3.6** Ad Hoc Network

the MIDI Studio utility and is automatically active when loaded. Double-click the Network icon to open the MIDI Network Setup dialog. This dialog contains all of the necessary options to connect your iPad to any software sequencer on your Mac.

The easiest way to connect is by setting up your computer and your iPad on the same wireless network or by creating an ad hoc computer-to-computer network. Creating an ad hoc network is recommended for the lowest latency interaction but will limit your ability to connect to the Internet (which is partly why the connection is better). When connected, the iPad should automatically be displayed in the Directory window of the MIDI Studio utility. You can also add a nonlocal connection but you'll need to know the web address of the device, and you'll likely need to open the specific port to be accessible through any existing firewalls. Most of the default settings in the MIDI Network Setup will suffice to create a basic connection.

## Example App/AC-7 Core

An affordable app that you can use to control a variety of DAWs is the AC-7 Core, which uses Mackie Control/HUI. These control protocol are transmitted natively through MIDI and so a wireless connection makes for a good choice. Here are the

**Figure 3.7** AC-7 Core

**Figure 3.8** iPad WiFi Settings

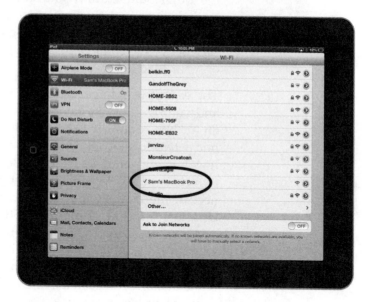

steps for a successful connection that should be followed closely to avoid failed communication:

1.  Install the AC-7 Core App.
2.  Make sure the app is not running in the background.
    a.  Double-click the home button while on the home screen.
    b.  If the app icon is present, hold it until it wiggles.

**Figure 3.9** MIDI Network Setup

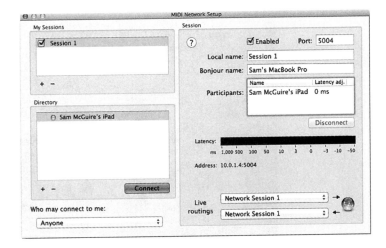

   c.   Click the x to close the app.

   d.   Connect your iPad and computer to the same wireless network or create an ad hoc network on your Mac.

3.   Open the MIDI Network Setup by double-clicking the Network icon in the MIDI Window of the Audio MIDI Setup utility.

4.   Open the AC-7 app and watch your MIDI Network Setup window for the iPad to show up.

   a.   Troubleshooting:

      i.   If it doesn't show up, then close the app as described above and restart the iPad.

      ii.   If it doesn't work and you are on a separate wireless network, then try using an ad hoc network.

5.   Assign the Live Routings to the input and output that align with your active MIDI Network session name.

6.   Select your iPad from the Directory list in the MIDI Network Setup and then click the connect button.

7.   Inside Logic Pro opens the Control Surface Setup window.

8.   Create a new control surface connection using the Scan All Models option.

9.   A connection is now made to the AC-7 app with full transport control and fader control. If at any time you run into problems you should restart the app or iPad. This technology is stable once it is set up, but it often takes a few tries to get there!

**Figure 3.10** Logic Pro Control Surface Setup

**Figure 3.11** Scan All Models

## Third Party Software

We are going to look at connection solutions that don't rely directly on the Audio MIDI Setup utility. A popular and powerful controller app called V-Control relies on MIDI to communicate between your iPad and your DAW but it does not rely on the Audio MIDI Setup capability. Instead you are required to download an app called Ney-Fi, which creates a virtual MIDI port to connect everything together. Once Ney-Fi is installed and running you can set up V-Control in your various DAWs with very little hassle.

Another popular alternative to MIDI is OSC (open sound control), which allows for a connection between compatible iOS apps and your computer. This is a protocol that is capable of much more than simple controller connections for DAWs but that is outside the scope of this particular section. TouchOSC is a controller app that is very much like V-Control but perhaps less traditional with a more creative interface. The implementation is just as easy as with Ney-FI and is

**Figure 3.12** V-Control Pro

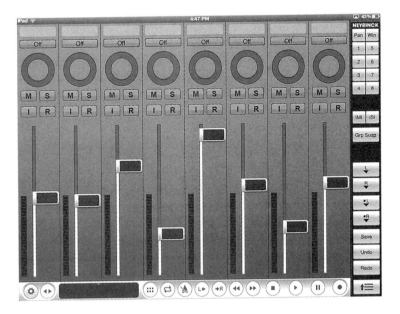

**Figure 3.13** TouchOSC App

accomplished through a simple installation on your computer of an app called the TouchOSC Bridge. You can also use the Audio MIDI Setup for this when using MIDI, but I have found the OSC option to be much more reliable in certain situations, such as working with Logic Pro, which has OSC support built in starting with version 9.1.2.

Certainly there will be more options available as time passes, but one thing that seems to be certain is that MIDI is still one of the most prominent connection options for iOS/DAW communications.

## MIDI on Android

When dealing with MIDI on a mobile device, Apple seems to hold the monopoly. That is not to say that other devices and operating systems do not support MIDI, Apple just seems to dominate the market. That being said, there are many useful and innovative apps that deal with MIDI for Android that differ quite substantially from their Apple counter parts. Before we dive into the various app and device combinations available to Android users, it is important to note some drawbacks and benefits of using MIDI on the Android platform.

Up until recently, Android users were stuck with only using MIDI over WiFi and Bluetooth. Due to Android devices not supporting the USB-Host protocol, MIDI could not be transferred via USB. This proved to be an immense problem due to the unreliable nature of both WiFi and Bluetooth connections, as well as the various latency issues with the two connections. Even today, there are only a limited number of Android devices that are capable of transferring MIDI over USB: The Asus TF101, Acer A500, Galaxy Nexus, and the Nexus 7, to name a few. To combat the vast majority of Android devices not allowing MIDI over USB, many users have designed "hacks" in order to attain pseudo-MIDI over USB. A quick Internet search will yield a wealth of schematics and tutorials on the various "hacks" available to Android users.

Although all device and app combinations vary on how they transmit MIDI over WiFi and/or Bluetooth, a generic setup is as follows:

## WiFi

First, the user will most likely (although not always) have to download a third party software such as "MIDI Bridge" to the host computer in order to relay MIDI messages sent from the device to the particular DAW in use. Next, the user must ensure the device is connected to the same WiFi network as the host computer. Finally, the user must map the input and output of the third party software to the mobile device and DAW respectively. Oftentimes, the user will be required to manually type in the host computer's IP address into the app's setup window as well as the third party software. Last, it is important that the user read all documentation pertaining to the app and third party program in order to ensure everything is routed correctly.

### Bluetooth

Like with the WiFi setup, transmitting MIDI via Bluetooth will usually require a third party software installed on the host computer in order to relay MIDI messages between the device and the computer. The user must then ensure Bluetooth is enabled on both the device and host computer. Next, the user must pair the device to the host computer, which is accomplished in the Bluetooth settings of the device and computer. Often times, the user will have to manually type in Bluetooth names into the app's settings window as well as the third party software's setting window. As with MIDI over WiFi setup, it is important that the user read all relevant documentation to ensure proper set up as all apps and devices call for different configurations.

The apps available on the Android platform that utilize MIDI can be organized into a few categories: MIDI/OSC control apps, Musical Instrument apps, Loops/Sequencer/Sampler apps, and Multi-Track Recording apps.

## MIDI/OSC Control

MIDI/OSC control apps are used to control external gear and programs via the MIDI or OSC protocol. MIDI/OSC control apps can be extremely powerful in both studio and live settings as they allow for extreme creative control. Many of the apps in this category tend to have similar interfaces to the "Lemur" by Jazz Mutant—a highly advanced touch pad controller that used the OSC Protocol; the Jazz Mutant Lemur has since been discontinued due to the much lower cost iPad and subsequent tablets taking over the market.

One of the most popular apps in this category is Touch OSC. Touch OSC is a cross-platform (for use with both iOS and Android devices) customizable control interface app. Users are free to customize the layout and controls on the interface to suit their particular needs. Touch sends and receives MIDI data over a WiFi network and can be used to control hardware units as well as functions inside of many DAWs. One

**Figure 3.14** TouchOSC App

**Figure 3.15** TouchOSC App

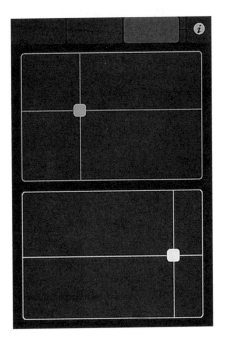

**Figure 3.16** Control App

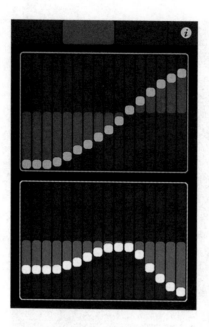

of the main reasons for Touch's success is its compatibility with open source coding programs such as Max/MSP, Max for Live, and Pure Data. By using Touch in conjunction with one of the aforementioned coding programs, the user cannot only create an extremely custom user interface, but can also determine how his DAW responds with almost limitless options.

A similar cross-platform app is Control (OSC + MIDI). Like Touch OSC, Control allows users to make their own interfaces for controlling their gear and software. The ability to create user-specific interfaces allows for extreme creativity. Despite its name, in its current state, Control only outputs "Open Sound Control" (OSC). Users can, however, share their customized interfaces with other users via JSON files, making for an intuitive creative community.

In the same vein, the app MIDIDroide not only communicates with the user's computer via WiFi-transmitted MIDI

**Figure 3.17** Control App

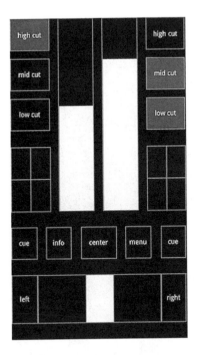

**Figure 3.18** MIDIDroide App

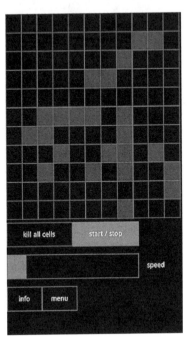

**Figure 3.19** TouchDAW App

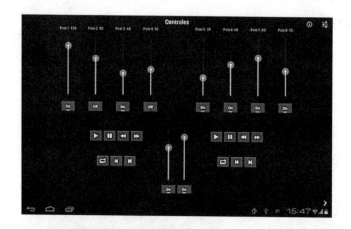

**Figure 3.20** TouchDAW App

but is multiclient, allowing an endless number of devices running MIDIDroide to communicate together.

Although Touch OSC, Control, and MIDIDroide all allow users to create templates in which they can control virtually any parameter in their given DAW, a dedicated app might be beneficial when wanting to control a DAWs workflow and mixing capabilities. One such app is TouchDAW.

TouchDAW sends MIDI information via WiFi or through USB if the Android device is USB-Host compliant to both PC and

Apple computers in order to control set parameters inside of a DAW. TouchDAW, in essence, acts like a stand-alone control surface. In its current state, TouchDAW works with Cubase/ Nuendo, Ableton Live, Pro Tools, Logic, Sonar, FL Studio, and Digital Performer, among others. Some DAWs have apps of their own to do this same task, but having the flexibility to work in most major DAWs as well as being able to customize the interface makes apps like TouchDAW the better option.

## Musical Instrument Apps

Many apps are available on the market that can simulate musical instruments—both in the novelty and professional range. These apps can be determined novelty or professional based not only on their price but also on their abilities. For example, a professional app will typically not only have a variety of customizable features, but will also allow for external control from a dedicated MIDI device, whereas novelty apps will typically not offer any of this functionality.

By far the most common types of musical instrument app available to mobile devices are those that simulate piano and keyboard instruments. One such app is "Grand Piano Pro." Grand Piano Pro is one of the only musical instrument apps for Android at the moment that allows for MIDI over USB (considering your particular device can handle MIDI over USB). Using Grand Piano Pro, the user has access to a variety of different high-quality samples for various keyboarded instruments.

**Figure 3.21** Grand Piano Pro App

With a traditional keyboard app, the user is left to play the notes on the virtual keyboard on the touch screen. This type of touch screen keyboard is extremely difficult to play and typically does not yield good results. Therefore, by allowing MIDI over USB, the user is free to play on an external MIDI keyboard controller yielding much more realistic results.

Next to piano and keyboard simulations, the next most common type of musical instrument app is that of synthesizer recreation. Like piano and keyboard recreation apps, most synthesizer apps have a virtual keyboard or touch surface for the user to play on. There are also a few apps on the market that utilize the new USB-Host protocol and allow for MIDI over USB control.

One of the most popular synthesizer app on the market is the "Animoog" by Moog Music. Animoog is a polyphonic expressive synthesizer that uses Moog's patented Anisotropic Synth Engine. The user moves his or her finger over an X/Y pad in order to create an ever-changing musical landscape. Although Animoog was originally only available to Apple users, it has now been introduced for the new Blackberry Z10, and speculations are forming that it will soon be available for the Android platform.

**Figure 3.22** AniMOOG App

**Figure 3.23** Caustic 2 App

**Figure 3.24** Caustic 2 App

Another popular synthesizer simulation app is "Caustic 2." Caustic 2 is an analog synthesizer simulation app that allows users to control the typical parameters of an analog synth via the device's touch screen as well as a devoted bass line synthesizer and PCM Synthesizer. The app also features an onboard sampling drum machine. Finally, the app has onboard effects like delay and reverb to further craft the end sound.

## Loop/Sequencer/Sampler Apps

For a long while, non-Apple devices didn't have much in the form of music-making apps. Thankfully that is starting to change. One app for Android that is on the rise is "Audiotool Sketch." Audiotool is a synth and drum machine combo app with the ability to save, organize, and edit patterns making for

**Figure 3.25** Audiotool
Sketch App

**Figure 3.26** Audiotool
Sketch App

an intuitive and musical app. One major benefit of Audiotool is
the high-resolution audio that it is capable of outputting.

Another good option for a sampling/sequencing app is the
"Electrum Drum Machine/Sampler" app. One extremely
beneficial feature Electrum has to offer is the ability for users
to load in their own .WAV files to use in conjunction with the
app. Once the user loads in his .WAV files, he is free to assemble them in any which way he pleases as well as editing his
samples. Inside of Electrum, the user can also import MIDI
drum files for quick programming—an extremely beneficial
feature in today's programming world.

**Figure 3.27** Electrum Drum Machine/Sampler App

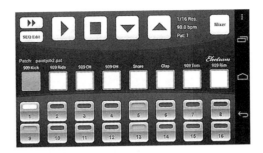

**Figure 3.28** Audio Evolution Mobile App

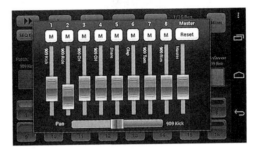

## Multi-Track Recording Apps

When in a studio setting, a multi-track recording app might be beneficial for the modern mobile savvy musician. One of the most popular apps on the market for multi-track recording is "Audio Evolution Mobile." Audio Evolution is completely cross-platform and is available on Apple, Windows, and Android. Besides simple multi-track playback and audio recording during playback, Audio Evolution allows users to import .WAV, .AIFF, .FLAC, .OGG/VORBIS, and .MP3 files. Audio Evolution also provides users with an unlimited number of tracks and groups as well as a wealth of real-time and off-line effects. Finally, Audio Evolution allows users to bounce down to stereo .WAV, .AIFF, and .FLAC files. Users are also able to customize settings inside the program such as changing grid options for aligning audio and selecting from different buffer sizes for each particular project.

**Figure 3.29** Audio Evolution
Mobile App

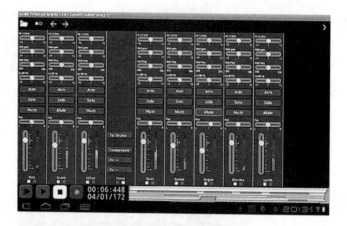

**Figure 3.30** J4T Multi-Track
Recorder App

Unlike Audio Evolution, the vast majority of multi-track
recording apps available are more geared toward creating
quick demos. Apps like "J4T Multitrack Recorder" and "Four
Tracks Pro" give users the ability to record four separate
tracks and also offer some basic effects and processing. These
types of apps, however, should not be omitted from consideration because they are oftentimes cheaper and could be
exactly what the user needs. Similar demo-creating apps are
available for strictly MIDI use. One such app is "MIDI Mixer."
MIDI Mixer gives the user complete multi-track MIDI recording and comes with over 100 virtual instruments. At the
moment, MIDI Mixer is only available to Android and does
not currently utilize the USB-Host protocol so the user cannot
use MIDI over USB.

## MIDI Considerations When Choosing Instrument Apps

When deciding on an instrument app, you'll need to ask yourself the following questions to ensure satisfaction in your particular situation:

1. Does the app have MIDI functionality? Some apps are designed more as a gimmick to showcase the multi-touch functionality of the iPad. If you are paying 99¢ for an instrument app, then keep your expectations of a professional quality app with full MIDI capabilities to a minimum.

2. How functional is the app without an external MIDI keyboard? An app that doesn't have MIDI capability might still have a great interface that is easy to use and provides the performance functionality you want. If the app interface is cramped and difficult to use, then you might reconsider purchasing the app.

3. How does the instrument sound? Just because your brand new app has an amazing interface and has full MIDI functionality, it still might not sound good. If it doesn't sound good it can often function as a creative tool that helps you in the songwriting process or as a musical notepad. If you want to use the instrument in the production process, then listen more closely because the quality will make a huge difference. Listen for noise in the sound and also for clicks/pops at the beginning and end of notes.

4. Have you seen the app in action before buying? Quite a few developers will post videos/sound examples of their apps on the Web, and you should seek these out before buying. A lot of videos are also posted on YouTube.com, and these are invaluable because not only do you see the instrument in action but you are likely to hear some positive or negative feedback by the video creator. If there aren't any videos posted, then take note that no one cares enough about it to make a video. There are quite a few videos online demonstrating MIDI connections with iPad apps, and these are also very useful because they verify that MIDI works with the specific app and they can help you troubleshoot if you are having problems with your setup.

**Figure 3.31** Non-MIDI Congos

**Figure 3.32** Product Video on YouTube.com

## Controllers and Control Surfaces

Before the iPad was released, a revolutionary product named the Lemur from JazzMutant was the most popular multi-touch controller available. The Lemur demonstrated close software integration with Digital Audio Workstations and provided audio engineers with a true multi-touch experience. The iPad changed everything with its incredibly affordable

**Figure 3.33** Lemur App

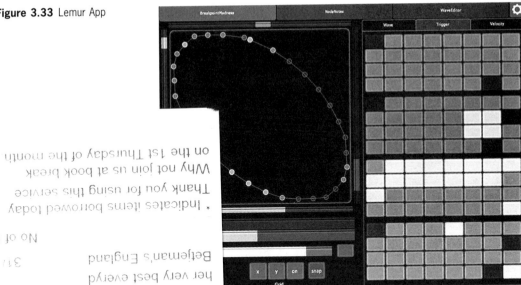

...mparison to very expensive products like the ...d its inexpensive apps. You can now purchase a ...from the app store for under $10, which has much ...e functionality of the Lemur. The primary issue is ...emur was designed by some very talented pro-...who understood music production and perfor-...d the iPad was designed with a much broader set ...ions in mind. This made the Lemur an excellent ...atively manipulating music, while the iPad is only ...the apps that individual developers create. The ...nly has the potential to surpass the Lemur, and ...on the app developers, there will be some excel-...l options available.

...l Lemur is no longer available but a new Lemur ...lable for iOS. Priced at $49.99, it is still a hard sell ...ad users because it's difficult to compete in a marketplace that has grown to expect 99¢ apps.

## Controllers vs. Control Surfaces

The distinction between a controller and a controller surface is that a controller controls a musical instrument/musical performance, and a control surface is used by audio engineers to control the mix/mixing software during the production process. Both types often use MIDI to accomplish their tasks and rely on either wired or wireless connections. Apple made using iPad apps as control surfaces possible and then set the bar extremely high with the release of Logic Remote alongside Logic Pro X. This app can act as a MIDI controller, a control surface, and as a full DAW interface.

Control (OSC + MIDI) is an example of a controller. As a free app it is less polished than some other apps but it deftly allows you to control instrument parameters using MIDI over a wireless network. Its open structure allows you to control much more than just musical instruments and therein lies its true power. With Control you can manipulate multiple parameters of your DAW's instruments without having to

**Figure 3.34** Logic Remote

use your computer's mouse or track pad. Once you get past the initial setup of the controller, you will achieve greater flexibility and efficiency.

AC-7 Core is an example of a control surface. While this app is not free, it is very affordable at under $10. It connects to all of the most popular DAWs via a network MIDI connection and controls a variety of parameters including transport, channel levels, panning, and basic editing functionality. Using a mouse or track pad you can only control a single channel's volume at a time, but with the AC-7 you can control up to eight channels at a time (although only three–four are realistically manageable). The primary benefit is that you can work more efficiently with a greater sense of tactile control.

### *MIDI Considerations When Choosing Controller and Control Surface Apps*

1. Do you have proof that it works with your instrument/software? I've seen reviews for various apps that claim they work universally, but no one can seem to make them work as advertised. The app store is very good at helping you weed out poorly designed apps with its user rating and review system. The trouble comes when a new app is released and you jump on the wagon before anyone else has a chance to provide feedback. If you decide to be an early adopter, then provide feedback to help others along the way. Post your results for better or worse. Keep in mind that you rarely get your money back if you purchase an app that doesn't work properly.

2. Does the app require a wireless or wired connection to work? If you are planning on using this app in a studio without a freely accessible wireless network, then using an iPad app that

**Figure 3.35** Reviews on iTunes

1. **Doesn't work with GarageBand 11** ☆☆☆☆
by Donald Short - Version 1.2.0 - Nov 6, 2010

Really like the app but now can't use it pending GarageBand 11 support. Probably just the plugin. Great idea and well implemented though.

2. **GB 11?** ☆☆☆
by Brent Huber - Version 1.2.0 - Nov 9, 2010

This is going to be a cool but I have moved to GB 11 and, unlike advertised above, the app and the plugin still seem to be only for GB 9. Had to crash my software to get out. Let us know when it is really ready. Support site is only mentions iLife 9.

requires a wireless connection is going to be more difficult. If the studio has tight security on their wireless network, it might prevent the iPad from connecting to the studio computer correctly. There are options available that are described in the section on connections, but it can be a tricky situation.

3. Is the app really going to help you be more efficient? The AC-7 Core is an excellent example of an app that might seem to be the right price and have a good feature set, but for some people the design is actually prohibitive. The color scheme creates difficulty seeing all of the buttons, especially if you have poor eyesight. Some of the buttons themselves are less useful and that creates wasted space. There are several better control surface options, but they cost $50 and above, which creates a situation that requires compromise. Do you want to pay the premium cost for a better app or does the less expensive app have enough of what you are looking for? Unfortunately you can't try before you buy so you'll need to make a careful decision based on your situation.

4. Is there an app that is better suited for the job? If you want to buy a controller app to work with a specific DAW, then you should see whether there are any that are dedicated for the job. There is an app that is designed to control Ableton Live, and if that is what you want to do then you shouldn't even consider the other options. If you want to keep your options open, then perhaps one of the more universal apps would be a better fit. That way you could get the most out of an app even if you decide to switch to a different DAW.

## Sequencers and DAWs

The distinction between a sequencer and a digital audio workstation had become more and more irrelevant over the years since almost all music production software could function as both a MIDI sequencer and a digital audio editor and mixer. In some ways we have regressed with the release of the iPad because of its limited computational resources and the forced return to square one in terms of programming new apps. Since it isn't possible to transfer applications like Logic Pro and Pro Tools directly onto the iPad, developers have to start from scratch. Initially this created a situation where an app would focus on either recording and mixing audio or sequencing MIDI but not both.

**Figure 3.36** Editing in GarageBand

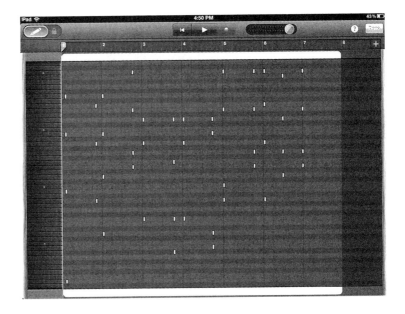

With the release of GarageBand for the iPad, an app existed that could both record audio and MIDI. While GarageBand was light years ahead of every other music production app, it still had major limitations when compared with industry-standard music production software. These limitations include only allowing eight tracks, limited MIDI editing (none at first), and limited audio effects. However it is possible to transfer your project to Logic Pro or GarageBand for the Mac, which allows you to take advantage of the portability of the iPad with the power of your laptop or desktop. Most of the iPad DAWs do not have MIDI capabilities and so our focus is on the workstations that provide MIDI functionality.

## MIDI Considerations When Purchasing Sequencer Apps

1.  Does the app allow MIDI editing? Some apps allow you to record and fully edit MIDI data, while others only allow you to record with minimal MIDI data editing. One powerful MIDI recording and editing app is called Music Studio, which allows

fairly detailed editing and quantization capabilities. Advanced MIDI editing features are still only available in full-featured DAWs outside of the iOS environment.

2. Can the sequencer app send out real-time MIDI data to control external computers or hardware? I think you are better off focusing on an app that has the recording and editing capabilities you need, but you may want to send out MIDI data from your sequencer app to control external equipment. If you want to create a larger setup with the iPad at the core or if you want to use the iPad in a live performance situation with some sounds originating on the iPad and some originating from other gear, then a sequencer that can transmit MIDI would be a critical element.

3. How does the app export MIDI data? This might be a small decision point but it can make a difference in efficiency. Most sequencer apps have some method of getting the MIDI data onto your computer but some are easier to use than others. Some let you e-mail the MIDI files while others require that you transmit the files wirelessly on the local network. A few of the apps need the iPad to be attached to iTunes in order to copy MIDI onto your computer. It is only a matter of time before you'll be able to save MIDI files on the iPad itself for transfer to other apps or transfer directly to your computer via an AirDrop-type file structure.

## MIDI Utilities

There are a number of useful MIDI utilities available that you can use in your MIDI studio. The apps in this group are categorized as such because they have MIDI functionality but do not fit in the other categories above. These apps do a variety of things such as monitoring, organizing, and storing MIDI data. One incredibly useful MIDI utility is the MIDI Monitor. This app allows you to see incoming MIDI data and is very useful when diagnosing problems with external hardware. It is also useful when verifying compatibility between MIDI gear and your iPad. The best part is that it is free! Until iPad apps are programed to communicate with each other internally, the utilities are only useful for dealing with external

**Figure 3.37** MIDI Monitor

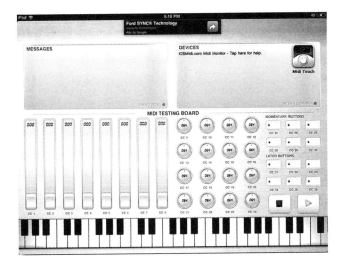

MIDI equipment and signals. Some programmers are finding ways to achieve inter-application MIDI communication, but there is still no global standard for implementation between different apps.

# RECORDING MIDI 4

Now that we've covered hardware, it's time to explore a variety of topics surrounding MIDI recording. You don't have to be a proficient musician to achieve your desired musical results, but it is still important to emphasize musical training. The reason that musical training is recommended is because it will save you time and make the editing/mixing process much more efficient. The more you get right during the recording phase, the less you will have to fix later.

**Figure 4.1** AKAI 88 and Laptop

The piano style keyboard controller is perhaps the most common way to record MIDI data. The second most common controller is the percussion pad. It's not surprising that software equivalents mimic their hardware counterparts in controller apps. iPad controller apps, for instance, are most often designed to look like a piano keyboard even when they could be designed with a much more intuitive and efficient interface. Some very innovative designs do exist and are covered in chapter 3.

The first step of recording MIDI is to ensure your controller is connected to your computer as is discussed in chapter 3. The majority of MIDI controllers work without installing additional software, but searching out the manufacturer's website may provide access to software with additional functionality. This is especially true if the controller has additional hardware options such as faders and knobs. (see figure 4.1) Make sure you install software that matches the operating system you are using; otherwise, incompatibilities may arise that range from less efficient operations to completely not working.

## Different Entry Methods

There are three common ways of entering or recording your MIDI data. You can record live using a MIDI controller, enter notes manually with a mouse or computer keyboard, or use a variety of other methods such as importing loops, converting audio to MIDI, or scanning sheet music. Each has its own strengths and limitations, but in this chapter we are going to look exclusively at live performance. The other entry methods are explored in the next chapter, which focuses on editing and related topics.

**Figure 4.2** Knobs and Faders

## Live Performance

Although you may immediately think of performing on a stage, recording a live performance describes the process and not the location. If you push "record" in your basement studio and perform a song "real-time" then it is a live performance. This method is very similar to the traditional audio recording of acoustic instruments. First, you create a MIDI or instrument track in your DAW, record arm the track, and then begin recording.

Horizontal tracks that hold MIDI regions are the norm when it comes to DAW design. Some also have alternate methods of storing MIDI regions and playing them back but we'll get to that in a later chapter. For now let's go through the process of recording MIDI.

The first step to recording is to engage the track's "record" button.

With this button engaged you should be able to play your MIDI controller, and the track should be receiving MIDI information. The MIDI will only be stored in the track as a region once you activate the global transport into record mode.

Most DAWs have a single button record process in the transport, but there are still a few that rely on a two-button process mimicking the transport on a tape machine. After pressing the record button in Pro Tools you also have to press the play button. This helps prevent accidental recording but is no

If you are new to recording, the multi-step recording process is often confusing. Almost all of the steps and terminology have grown out of the nearly extinct process of recording to analog tape. If you come across a term or process that doesn't seem to make sense, then it possibly comes from the world of analog recording.

**Figure 4.3** Instrument Track

**Figure 4.4** Record Armed Track

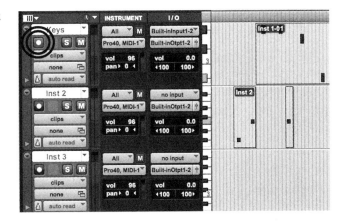

**Figure 4.5** Logic Pro Transport

**Figure 4.6** Pro Tools Transport

longer necessary due to the ease of undoing and redoing actions. It is even easier when using keyboard shortcuts because you can bypass the two buttons on the transport for a single key stroke.

## Troubleshooting MIDI Inputs

If you record arm the MIDI track and play on the controller but receive no input, then there are few steps you can follow to figure where the problem is in the system. Many of these tips also apply to external MIDI hardware.

1. Symptom: USB controller not receiving power/lights aren't active.
   a. Check all cables to make sure the equipment is properly connected. Cables can go bad and might need replacing.
   b. Plug the controller into a different USB port in case you have overloaded the original bus.
   c. If you have attached too many devices the bus might be low on power. Use a powered USB hub to add additional power or use a power supply for the controller.
2. Symptom: DAW isn't recognizing the controller.
   a. If the controller doesn't work automatically as a class compliant device, then search out drivers on the manufacturer's website and follow their installation instructions. If a device is considered legacy (drivers are no longer updated), then an alternate connection is required. Consider using a MIDI to USB interface and powering the controller with its own power supply.
   b. Each DAW has a set of preferences and most have the option to activate or deactivate MIDI devices. Verify the controller is activated in the DAW.
3. Symptom: Device is recognized and powered but MIDI is not being received.
   a. Make sure there are no active MIDI filters in the DAW. Filters can be used to remove parts of the incoming MIDI, including notes and velocities.
   b. Check the controller to determine if there are key ranges set that are outside of the range you are trying to play. Many controllers can set the range of MIDI output and even split the controller into multiple channels, but if the range is accidentally set too narrow, then no output is available. Check the manual for the controller for how to change the range or for a factory reset so you can restore all of the standard settings.
   c. If the controller has an output level control, then make sure it is not set to zero.
4. Symptom: The wrong notes are received in the DAW. Both controllers and DAWs have transposition controls and will cause different notes to be sent and recorded.
5. Symptom: No matter how hard or soft you play the sound is the same level.
   a. The controller may have velocity functionality turned off.

b.  The instrument in your DAW might not have velocity functionality. Some instruments mimic real instruments that do not have velocity action such as organ instruments and some synthesizers. In these cases you might not have the option for velocity, and it doesn't mean your controller is malfunctioning.

## Project Settings

Before recording any MIDI data it's a good idea to establish the key signature and tempo of your song. Both are settings that will impact the editing and mixing process and that are recommended to be set before you record. The next few sections take a closer look at each of these and the impact they have on your projects.

## Key Signature

Music theory is something that is outside of the scope of this book but it plays a very important role in understanding why setting a key signature is important. There are two primary functions that rely on the key signature so they can work properly. The first is to ensure your notes display properly in your DAW's notation editor. Not all DAWs have notation editors but they are certainly more common than not. The other set of functions that rely on the appropriate key signature is a variety of editing tools that include things such as transposition, arpeggiation, looping, and any number of other loosely related functions. None of these "require" a properly set key signature to work but all benefit from it.

Figures 4.8 and 4.9 demonstrate the difference between a MIDI sequence that has the wrong key signature selected (fig. 4.8) and the correct signature (fig. 4.9).

While both show the same notes, the accidentals that are there when the key signature is wrong provide confusing and unnecessarily complex information to a performer. Setting the key signature is not something that absolutely has to be set in advance of recording, but it is considered good housekeeping.

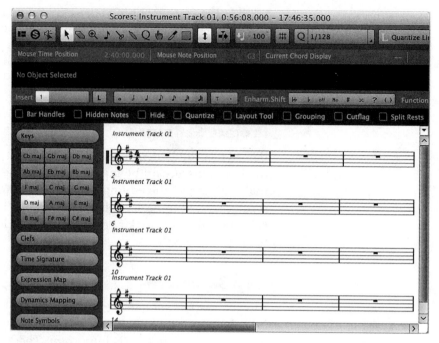

**Figure 4.7** Key Signatures in Nuendo

**Figure 4.8** Incorrect Key Signature

**Figure 4.9** Correct Key Signature

In most DAWs, when you change the key signature after recording, it automatically transposes the MIDI and so you will want to know how your DAW handles this. An example of this is Logic Pro where a key signature change will transpose all used Apple Loops (MIDI regions with tempo and key information embedded). In this particular situation it is possible to convert the Apple Loops into non-loop regions, but then you will lose the really useful functionality provided by the format. Instead, it makes more sense to set the key before recording MIDI information. If you don't set it initially and need to change it later, these special loops will transpose but not necessarily any other MIDI data that you recorded, and that results in the various portions being in different keys.

## Exercise

1.  Set the key signature to Bb Major. Enter a Bb Major chord. Change the key signature to any other key and see what happens to the MIDI data. This will tell you about your sequencer but you will also probably be able to change how your sequencer handles key changes.

## Tempo

Establishing the tempo before recording is another highly recommended process. Every DAW has a click track and it provides an aural cue for the performer to know the tempo and to perform in time. Recording in time provides access to a lot of editing and manipulation tools that are covered in subsequent chapters, but there are a few things to set up that are discussed here.

## Conductor Track

Conductor tracks provide global control over the project tempo. Just like a conductor controls the tempo when leading an orchestra, the conductor track (also referred to as a tempo track) can be set to one tempo or have multiple tempos throughout your project. Most conductor tracks look similar to automation, and you can use a variety of tools to manipulate the tempo.

**Figure 4.10** Conductor
Track in Pro Tools

You should explore your specific DAW's tempo manipulation tools to discover what it has to offer. For example, using a pencil tool you can draw in various tempos and tempo transitions. You can likely enter your tempo information into a dialog window that subsequently makes the changes to the project tempo. You will use this very little in most genres of popular music production but quite often when scoring for film.

A lot of DAWs allow you to sync recorded audio to the tempo along with MIDI. Once the sync connection is made, a tempo

**Figure 4.11** Tempo
Operations in Pro Tools

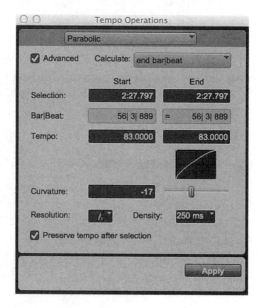

change in the project changes the speed of the audio. Due to imperfect audio stretch algorithms and differing levels of quality in each DAW, you may find a feature like this useful or not. The times that you are most likely to use it are when you are writing/composing and you need a quick fix without rerecording audio. For example, when writing a song you can record vocals and guitars using microphones along with MIDI tracks using your keyboard and then try the song at various tempos without rerecording any of the instruments. Adjust the tempo until you like what you hear, keep the recorded MIDI, erase the temporary audio tracks, and then rerecord the final audio parts at the new tempo.

The conductor track is easiest to use when you set the tempo prior to recording but it can also be adapted for use after a free tempo recording is made. Under most circumstances, changing the tempo will also change the speed of the existing MIDI regions. When you record without a click, you will want to create a custom tempo map that matches the performance, and this requires changing the tempo while leaving the MIDI in place. Most good sequencers will have a set of tools and functionality to make this task easier but it is never an automatic task. Expect to spend a good chunk of time setting this up and creating the custom map. However, there are a lot of reasons for creating a custom tempo map when recording

**Figure 4.12** Flex Time in Logic Pro

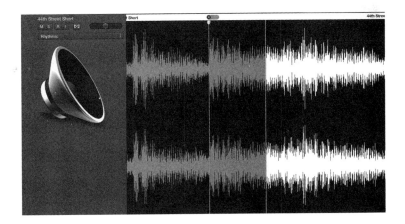

**Figure 4.13** Tempo Before and After

without a click, and it is something you will get better at the more you practice it.

Creating a custom tempo map is helpful when recording keyboardists that are not at a professional level and who can't seem to play to a click in time. One solution is to record the keyboardist playing without a click. Hopefully this will encourage a better performance from a musician who is not skilled enough to play with a click. Next, create a custom tempo map using your DAW's tempo tools. Essentially you are taking the musical grid of the project and telling it which notes are downbeats and you'll determine where each measure starts. After a custom map is created, you will then change the tempo of the entire section to the desired tempo, since your MIDI is now set to follow the tempo.

## Click Track

A click, often referred to as a metronome, is an audio sound that is used to provide the tempo to musicians and the producers. There are three typical click setups that you'll see in different DAWs. The first is a built-in click that follows the tempo of the project and is often activated by a single button on your interface.

For this type you wouldn't need to create a new track, and the audio from the click would be sent out with your main

**Figure 4.14** Click in Logic

**Figure 4.15** Click in Pro Tools

audio channels automatically. Logic Pro has a click like this and it can be turned on independently for playback and/or recording. The next type is a click that has to be added as a plug-in on a track. The click in Pro Tools works this way and you have to add a click into the project to use it.

The last type is not an audio click at all but is a MIDI click. The DAW sends out MIDI note information that is used to trigger an instrument in your DAW or an external sound module. Most DAWs still have this functionality even if they primarily recommend the use of one of the other two types of clicks.

The MIDI option is typically used less frequently but is still a viable option for studios that have a lot of MIDI gear in use. It is also nice to be able to trigger a separate software instrument instead of using what are often terrible default click sounds.

Many musicians prefer to use an alternate metronome solution such as an audio drum loop. This creates a time keeper that is much closer to performing live with other musicians and can have excellent results. The drum loop needs to be a

**Figure 4.16** MIDI Click

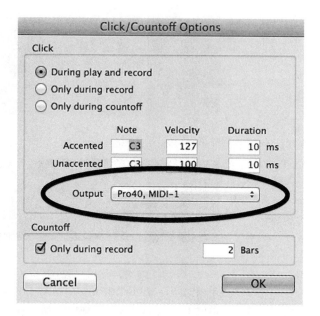

**Figure 4.17** Drum
Loop Click

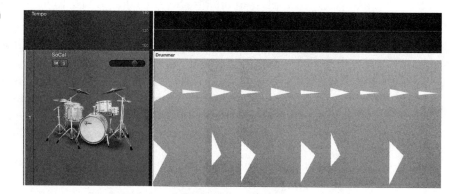

file that follows the project tempo or it won't make things
easy when you change the tempo. Import the loop into an
audio track before recording the MIDI data, and it will serve
as the time keeper. Pick a loop with a grove that you want
because it will set the feel for the song and it will be difficult
to change later.

**Figure 4.18** Activating Count-In on Nuendo's Transport

Regardless of the type of click you use, you will also have the option to use a count-in. Typically set between one–two bars, the count-in provides time for you to internalize the tempo before recording begins.

While most DAWs provide a specific count-in feature it is also possible to start your song in the third bar of your project and let the first two bars act as the count-in. If you start at the very beginning of the project and use the count-in, then you run the risk of playing a note just before the start, which might result in it not being recorded. Missing the first note can happen anytime your DAW doesn't record while the count-in is playing if you strike the note early, and in some DAWs this is not an adjustable setting.

It takes skill to record using a click track and you will need to practice with one often. One good thing about recording MIDI with a click, as opposed to recording audio, is that you can use your speakers and not have to rely on headphones. When using a click and recording into microphones you have to be diligent in your efforts to prevent bleed because the sound of a click easily finds its way onto recordings but not with MIDI. You can crank the playback up and not worry about bleed at all.

## Exercises

1. Create a tempo track with three tempo changes. Make the first one an abrupt change. Make the second one a gradual change that speeds up over four bars. The last change should be a subtle retardando.
2. Create a project with an audio file and a MIDI recording. Change the tempo after the clips are on their tracks and see what happens with the MIDI and audio. Does the audio change tempo along with the MIDI?

## Sounds

Your tracks will only sound as good as the sounds you have access to. Picking the right instruments during recording is critical because it clearly affects your performance and the quality of the resulting MIDI data. For example, two different bass patches would have different sample detail and the nuances of performing each might be drastically different. While an obvious strength of MIDI is that you can change patches at any time, you will discover that it never translates as seamlessly as you want. The velocity layers and sample choices will often be different for sampled instruments, and synthesizers are all much too different for simply switching patches. It is recommended that you find the right sound in the beginning.

Another common technique is to layer tracks together to create increasingly complex sounds. Whether you want a thicker drum sound or want to add bass to a synth patch, layering is a useful technique and almost always easy to accomplish. One

**Figure 4.19** Auditioning Bass Patches

**Figure 4.20** Layering Using Tracks: The Bottom MIDI Track Feeds Both of the Instruments

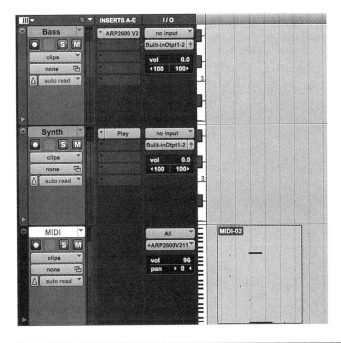

**Figure 4.21** Layering Using a Multitimbral Instrument: Three Patches Loaded into a Single Instrument

option is to load the various sounds into separate tracks and set the input to the same MIDI input. Once you record arm all of the tracks, they will all play layered together.

Another option is to use a multitimbral instrument and load different sounds simultaneously. The MIDI input for each sound should be set identically, which may or may not be the default.

## Exercises

1. Mix two similar sounds in order to make a more impressive and larger sound.
2. Try mixing sounds that are completely different. How different can they be and still work as an effective instrument?

## Latency

There is no such thing as instantaneous when it comes to MIDI. There are potential delays in several stages of data transfer and DAWs provide additional difficulties. In order to minimize the delay you have to make an active effort to understand your DAW and adjust its settings. Every effort to decrease delay and increase efficiency will make a difference when working with MIDI.

Following some best practices will create an environment where you can manage the timing weaknesses that are inherent to MIDI.

## Keep the MIDI Path as Simple as Possible

USB is not an ideal transfer protocol when dealing with MIDI although it is the most common connection. A single controller hooked straight to your computer will create the fewest opportunities for delay. Timing inaccuracies are often unnoticed and mistaken as imperfections in the performance but become more exaggerated when communicated through multiple stages. An example would be connecting a keyboard

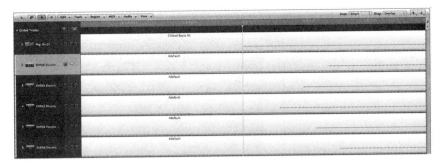

**Figure 4.22** MIDI Timing on a Saffire Pro 40 in Logic Pro: Note the Inconsistent Timing of Recorded Data All Sent from the Same Initial Note

through a 5-pin MIDI to USB interface and then to a computer. With each additional connection you will notice greater inconsistencies in timing.

A simple test of the timing of MIDI is to take the output and input of your device and connect them with a MIDI cable. Send a simple pattern and record it back in. If you record a few of these in a row and then analyze the results you will see slightly different timing in each iteration. These timing variations can be minimized in software and hardware that are designed properly and are often exaggerated with poor designs. There is nothing you can do in the recording phase to fix this, but you can compensate for poor timing in the editing phase.

If you are using external MIDI hardware, then try not to use MIDI Thru. Buy a MIDI interface that allows you to have enough MIDI ports for each device or set up a MIDI patch bay. MIDI Thru adds additional delay and is messy in terms of sync. Another test you can do to see how well your device is designed is to record MIDI Out and its audio out at the same time. Compare the two side by side in your DAW to see just how tight the timing is; you may be surprised.

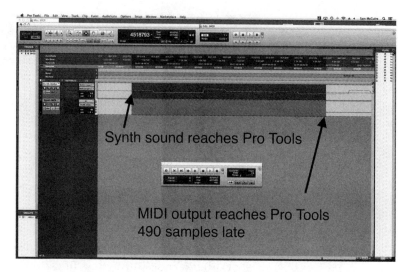

Synth sound reaches Pro Tools

MIDI output reaches Pro Tools
490 samples late

**Figure 4.23** A Comparison of Audio and MIDI Data from the Same Synthesizer:
Three Different Notes Produced Three Different Delays and Were Unpredictable

## Keep your MIDI Device Drivers Up to Date

Quite a few modern MIDI controllers are class compliant,
which means that you can plug them in and your operating
system will automatically recognize them for use.
Downloading and installing any specific drivers from your
controller's manufacturer may increase stability and decrease
latency. If your DAW allows you to choose any MIDI inputs
that your operating system automatically recognizes, then
you'll need to seek out any available documentation from
your system to help you understand the correct settings to
put in place. Working with Windows is often more complicated than working with Mac OS but if you can fine tune your
settings, then both are very suitable for working with MIDI.
See chapter 3 for more information about drivers.

## Use a Reliable Audio Device with Pro-Quality Drivers

In the early days of sequencers you could have a system
without audio input/output because all of the sound sources
would be external synths and samplers and none of the

**Figure 4.24** Saffire Pro 40

sound would come from the sequencer itself. With the proliferation of software synths and the combination of audio
and MIDI into high-powered DAWs, having a high-quality
audio interface is critical to having low latency in your MIDI
chain. Any delay added by your audio device translates into
a delay with all of your MIDI input/output.

There are two basic settings in every DAW that affect the
overall latency of the system: buffer size and sample rate.
The buffer size is the most important setting when optimiz-
ing your system for low latency. The buffer is a mechanism
that is designed to provide your DAW flexible processing
power to handle large numbers of plug-ins, instruments,
and things like automation and high track counts. You are
able to change the buffer size depending on the needs of
your project.

**Figure 4.25** Buffer Size
in Pro Tools

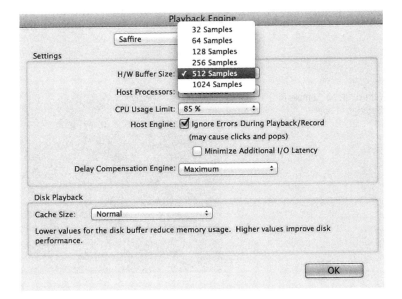

A small project with a small processing load can handle the smallest buffer sizes while a large project requires a large buffer. Get in the practice of changing the buffer in different situations because having it set too high when you are recording will create a delay and, whether you can tell or not, it affects your ability to create a great performance.

If you are seeking the lowest latency environment, then use higher sample rate settings. This is tied closely to the buffer size because higher sample rates mean that each sample is shorter and so the same buffer size in two different sample rates will have different lengths. The difference between 48 kHz and 44.1 kHz is minor but you will notice more when using 96 kHz.

There are no "free" ways to achieve lower latency when working in your DAW and it always comes at the price of processing power. Using low buffer sizes with high sample rates will cut into available power needed for other tasks later in the process, and so you'll need to be constantly aware of your settings and fine tune them for your needs. Once you finish the recording portion of your project and begin mixing then you will set your buffer to a higher setting to free up power for adding effects and automation. The more power that your computer has then the less adjustments you will make.

**Figure 4.26** Sample Rate Settings in Logic

## Use Your DAW's Feature Set to Manage Latency

Some DAWs have low latency modes to help manage system delay. Logic Pro is an example of this and has latency considerations integrated into its operations.

You can adjust how low it needs to go in the settings and push the button to engage for recording. This is extremely useful for those of you who like to be actively mixing your music while still recording additional parts. Once you start adding a lot of effects and automation you will likely have a high buffer setting and delay compensation engaged (see chapter 8), which means there will be more delay than appropriate for performing new recordings. Engaging the low latency mode adjusts effects and timing so your system has less delay while you record, but you'll only want to use this when recording or you won't have access to all of your mix.

**Figure 4.27** Logic's Low Latency Mode and Associated Settings

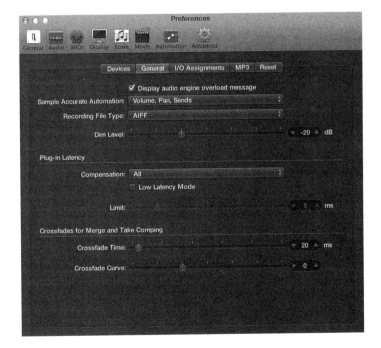

**Figure 4.28** Freezing
Tracks in Nuendo

Freezing tracks is another way to help keep the latency and timing issues to a minimum. Most DAWs have a freeze function that takes the audio output of your MIDI/instrument tracks and records them into an audio file. Once the audio file is created then the MIDI, sound bank, and any associated effects are all deactivated until needed later. This creates the potential to use as many "synth" tracks as needed up to the limit of your DAW and hard drives for audio tracks.

## Templates

In situations where you use the same outboard gear and/or virtual instruments it may be more efficient to create template sessions. The typical process for creating a template is to start a new project and set it up just as you want the template to look. Set all of the tracks and I/O as needed and then save the project as a template. Most DAWs allow for the creation of a template and when you subsequently start a new session and choose the template it will open it up and ask for you to save it under a new name. This preserves the original template while saving you time.

A practical example of a template in use might be a sound palette for a composer. You can recall your virtual orchestra with all of your favorite instruments pre-loaded. Setting up a new session each time you want to start a new project with 20–30 tracks can suck up a lot of time for each project, or you can use a template you created once and then tweak it as

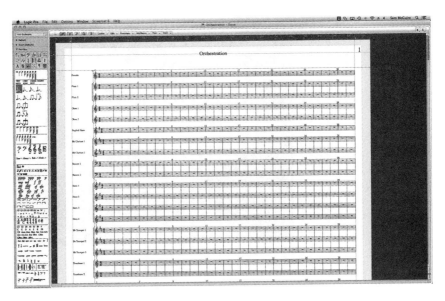

**Figure 4.29** An Orchestral Template in Logic

needed. Templates can often store tracks, I/O settings, effects, instruments, and system settings. There is no universal template format and so each DAW will have its own offerings.

## Additional Controllers

One of the keys to creating realistic sounding MIDI parts is to use additional performance control. The three most common sources for this are pitch bend, the modulation wheel, and the sustain pedal. You can perform using one hand to play the keys while the other adjusts the wheels, or you can record the wheel separately and merge the data with previously recorded performances. The sustain pedal is much easier to operate simultaneously while playing the keyboard and is often considered a requirement by musicians who are trained piano players.

The pitch bend knob is most often a spring-loaded wheel that returns to its center position when released. This allows you to bend up and down but always easily return

**Figure 4.30** Controllers: Modulation Wheel and Pitch Bend

to zero. The modulation wheel is not spring loaded and is used for a variety of control tasks that are programmed either on the keyboard or in your software. The mod wheel often controls instrument timbre, key switching between sample banks, or other instrument specific parameters. The sustain pedal is used to keep notes playing after you release their keys. You can use it to sustain chords while moving your fingers to prepare for the next set of notes. A developed sustain pedal technique allows you to play in a sustained and legato style without having to keep the keys pressed in a sustained manner. All of these controllers can also be edited using the MIDI functionality of your DAW and are covered in chapter 5.

Faders, knobs, mobile devices, foot pedals, and joysticks are also examples of controllers that can be used to send MIDI control data. MIDI data created from these controllers need to be combined with Note On/Off messages in order to trigger sound from a module either recorded simultaneously with note data or after the fact. If control data are recorded separately, then consider merging the data into a single clip for efficiency in the editing and mixing process. The methods

**Figure 4.31** Additional Controllers: Foot Pedal

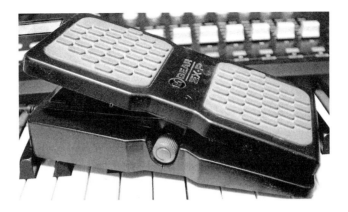

**Figure 4.32** Merge MIDI in Pro Tools

of doing this vary from DAW to DAW but often include glue tools or menu options. In Pro Tools you can set the transport to merge mode for recording incoming MIDI and there is a similar option in Logic.

## Examples

Let's explore several scenarios that include recording MIDI.

1. A band is producing a new single but is having a difficult time recording the bass player, who is always late to rehearsals and hasn't learned the parts. The keyboard player offers to record the bass part using a virtual instrument. The drum parts and guitar parts are already recorded and since the rhythm is established by the drums, you do not need to turn on a click. Typically at this point the key signature and tempo are set because they should be set before any recording happens. Load the bass patch and record arm the instrument track. Engage record and then perform the part. Rerecord and punch in as needed.

2.  A singer/songwriter is starting from scratch on a song that is going to be produced entirely in MIDI. The first step is the pick the right key signature and tempo. The artist is unsure about these and proceeds to record the first verse and then change both the tempo and the key until it is determined that they are correct. Once they are set, the song is recorded and then mixed.

3.  A film composer is writing a new score in sync to picture. He starts with a steady tempo and then after recording the parts he begins to adjust the tempo to match the film. It may sound right for a slightly quicker tempo at the beginning of the cue, but then a gradual retardando is put into the score to help the section end at the right before it transitions into a different cue. You can create a tempo map before or after recording, but when recording audio is involved the tempo needs to be set firmly before recording. Changing the tempo when scoring is not a simple manner and needs to be carefully considered because timing is everything and changing it affects sync with the video.

**Figure 4.33** Example of Downloaded MIDI File in Pro Tools

## Downloading MIDI Files

Even though the production of MIDI files online has slowed over the past 5–10 years, there are still thousands of MIDI files available for download. These are useful for a variety of reasons during the recording phase but are especially good for providing ideas, rhythm sections, and "sampled" material.

Nothing is worse than "writer's block" when writing music and downloadable MIDI files are one way to push through it. This isn't a recommendation to pass off someone else's music as your own but seeing a song in MIDI form can provide some inspiration for programming in ways that perhaps you haven't considered. If you find a file that has a great performance, then look at the data and see where the groove is and look at the conductor track. Use the following questions to guide you when looking at the data:

1. Do the notes start precisely on the beat or do they start earlier/later?
2. How much velocity variation exists?
3. What CCs are being used and for what purpose?
4. What is happening in the conductor track?
5. Are there any program changes? Which GM program numbers are being used?

If you want your production to sound similar to a track that you like, then it should look similar as well. This isn't to say that you need to perform a scientific analysis but a quick look over should tell you a lot. Also don't mistake looking at MIDI data as a replacement for listening to it since your ears are the only judge that matters in music. There are countless examples of sequencing MIDI, editing the data to what you think will be better, and subsequently finding out that the edited version sounds worse than the unedited version. Similarly there will always be the case when something that looks completely wrong on the screen will sound perfect. Usually this happens because of the sound source it is controlling and not because of the data. An example is one of the original Rhodes instruments in Reason, which could be triggered with a quick series of short notes that resulted in a very unique, gated sound on the output.

For non-drummers or those of you who are rhythmically challenged, downloading MIDI files with rhythm parts that you like can be an excellent way to get the percussion that you need. Using these types of files is very similar to using audio drum loops, and since drum parts can't be individually copyrighted it is possible to use MIDI drum sequences indiscriminately. Sometimes you can find drum tracks/MIDI loops online but more often you will find full songs. The full songs can still be used but you'll need to strip away all of the other parts. Depending on your DAW it is likely better to import the MIDI file into a brand new session so that the tempo and key signature are maintained from the file without having to compete or adapt to the tempo and signature of the existing project. Once you have it in a new project then you can adjust, edit, and prepare the parts you want before copying it into the destination project. Consider preparing the drum track before recording other parts because then the grooves will likely be different and it won't sound good.

There are several ways to incorporate other people's music in your project, with the most common being a straightforward use of a sample from the song. While mashing things up is fairly common, it is also the most legally protected. If you want to pay homage to another song you can accomplish it also using MIDI. Even if you don't find the song online in the MIDI format you can still incorporate identifying parts of the song's harmonic progression, rhythmic structure, or melodic content. If you can find a MIDI version of the song online, then download it and use portions of the song in your project. Using recognizable parts of the song can still require caution so that you don't infringe on copyright, but it's possible to use elements without crossing any lines. The benefit of doing this is that you can more easily incorporate the music of others without having to use their master recording. The downside is that there is very little chance of sounding exactly like the original and unless you are careful there is a chance it will sound hokey. It can also be informative to look at the way the sequence layers instruments together to achieve the resulting sound. If nothing else, looking at the MIDI of other songs will teach you about the arrangement and production process. Hundreds of years ago the great composers learned to write music by literally copying the masters of their era. As they copied the music they learned about harmony, melody, counterpoint, and all of the structure considerations. This way of learning is still just as valid and the more you look at the music of others the more you will learn.

## Alternative Performance Techniques

The chapter on performing live covers more about techniques for the stage but it is possible to use some of those in the studio as well. Several sequencers have alternate MIDI and audio storage mechanisms that can be used to create songs in a much different fashion than traditional keyboard performance. While the implementation is different in each DAW, there are several key similarities:

1.  MIDI and audio files are used as loops that are triggered as desired instead of being placed in linear tracks and played back at a set time.
2.  All of the elements of a song are prepared in advance and then are combined via triggers.
3.  Effects and processing are manipulated with controllers to create variations in the loops, often including real-time recordings of the song as it is being performed, played back immediately with time and pitch warping.

All of the individual elements and effects are placed in a palette to be triggered and combined in creative ways. Because of the nontraditional performance technique involved, a keyboard is not usually enough and a controller with buttons, faders, and touch options is more efficient. Several DAWs are designed to work with multi-touch screens and you can trigger loops by using the screen and not have a controller at all. When working with loops and triggering files there are some options that you'll need to master so you can get the performance you desire. These options are entirely dependent on the capabilities of your software and are not options in some of the most popular options. Pro Tools, Logic Pro, and Cubase are not considered great options for live performance. Each of these has some tools that are similar, but other DAWs such as Ableton Live, Fl Studio, and Sonar have specially designed interfaces and options for this alternate type of performance.

## How Triggering Works

Each file needs to be assigned as a trigger-able loop. Once it is set apart in your DAW's performance area you'll need to know which MIDI note is the trigger and map it to your controller. Since MIDI and audio still need to sync to a tempo and other global settings, you'll want to make sure those are set appropriately. Most of the time the transport will need to be put in play mode before the triggers are activated and synced together. The good news with this is that DAWs that

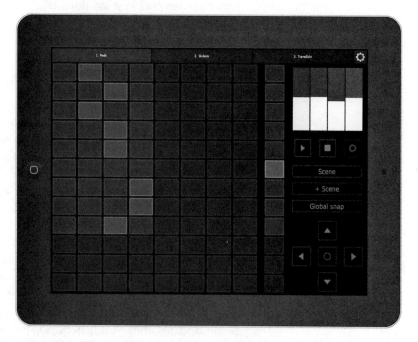

**Figure 4.34** Controlling FL Studio with Lemur App on an iPad

are designed for live performance will typically include templates for syncing with popular controller modules. This relieves the task of manually mapping triggers to functions, except when you want to make special connections to effects and processing.

The trigger mode of each loop should be set and will vary depending on the function in the song. Some loops might need to play immediately when triggered and others will start on the next cycle. This means you could trigger a file any time during a bar and expect to have it start on the next loop or press a trigger and have the loop join right away but still be in time. You can also set loops to play continuously after being triggered and to stop only when the loop is triggered a second time. This latch functionality is useful for layering sounds and makes adding/removing sounds from the song very easy. As an alternate you can assign a loop to only play when the key is pressed, which allows you play loops to create melodies and interesting rhythms. Sometimes you can set a sequence of loops to play and trigger the entire chain by choosing any of the loops as a starting point. A loop can be as simple as a single note or a full mixed audio file.

The important thing is to learn what your DAW does for the triggering of loops and to master the technique. While you can immediately see the strength of this type of system for live performance, it is also very useful for studio productions. You can either use your DAW to capture the "performance" of triggering loops and effects or record the output of your DAW into an audio track/file. The chapter on live performance explores this topic in more depth and looks at additional technology used on the stage.

## Percussion Tracks

MIDI drums and percussion parts need to receive a little extra consideration because using a keyboard is often the least effective way to get the groove you want. Invariably the drums sound like they were performed on a keyboard, which is not what you want people to think when listening. Using percussion pads or full MIDI drums can provide a much more desirable result but comes at the price of additional gear and is often quite expensive. Here are three examples of scenarios that are typically used when recording percussion parts.

1.  Percussion Controller—Pads can be used to create very natural sounding groove and are used by many musicians because they are more affordable and economically sized. The pads can be triggered using drum sticks or by hand. When using your hands you'll need to set the sensitivity differently than when using sticks because the sticks can be used to hit harder without hurting. A very light and sensitive feel will provide the touch needed for soft taps and gentle hits without sticks. To get a good groove you'll still need to practice and become proficient using the pads. Use a metronome or click when practicing so you can get used to playing in time, which is an important recording skill to have.

2.  MIDI Drums—This option is only practical when you are a drummer or often work with drummers who have used this type of instrument before. Using a full "kit" resembles an actual drum kit more than the other options but is still different than hitting actual drum heads. The primary similarity is in the placement and general size of the pads, which make it a natural fit for drummers but you should count on a decent chunk of time for a drummer to adapt to a MIDI kit if he hasn't used one before. Each kit has a master module that has sounds that are triggered and also MIDI outputs. Record the MIDI into your DAW and assign the notes to your drummer sampler of choice. Even with a track recorded through a MIDI kit, you will still likely need to edit the MIDI to sound just how you want it.

3.  Drum Replacement Technology—The most natural sounding MIDI drums tracks come from audio recordings of drums. The option to replace drums means that each audio track from a drum recording is analyzed by your DAW, and then the hits are converted to MIDI with included velocity and pitch (when applicable) data for use with any sound sources that you have. Because you have to record the drums acoustically first, this option adds a lot of work but in situations

when the room used for recording doesn't sound very good, this is a good compromise. You can leave the acoustics of the room out of the equation by replacing each drum with any number of different samples. If you like the basic sound of your acoustically recorded drums then you can also layer in samples to make the drums sound bigger. Another tool is Drumagog, which can replace and/or layer acoustic drums with samples in real time. This is useful for live performance and efficient studio usage.

There isn't a right or wrong way to record drums, but there are results that are not good and this is what you need to avoid. Explore the options and pick one that has consistently professional results for your playing technique. If none of them seem to help, then get used to using audio drum loops and not making your own.

4. Alternate Recording Methods—There are always going to be alternate controllers that can be used when recording your MIDI performances. Wind controllers that rely on pressed keys and the power of your breath are strong options for those who have woodwind instrument backgrounds. Several vintage Yamaha keyboards have breath controller inputs that involve placing an accessory in your mouth while playing the traditional keyboard. You can also use a volume foot pedal for a similar effect but nothing can quite mimic the volume of certain sampled instruments like actual breath. This thread again begins to encroach on the instruments and controllers used in live performance, but neither one has the right to claim alternate controllers as just for live or just for use in the studio. The mantra for this chapter is to find the solution that works for you, and then go and make some crazy music.

## Summary

Recording MIDI using a controller is just one way of getting the performance you want. In the following chapters we are going to explore editing and mixing with MIDI, and these include looks into alternate entry methods for both notes and control data. The key to recording with MIDI is to understand the strengths and limitations of your system. Test out your latency and research hardware so you can buy the best MIDI devices you can afford because not all of them are designed with the same quality. Decide which type of controller makes sense for the music you create and never feel like you have to use a tradition keyboard. Take a page out of the book written by modern controllerists who use very nontraditional instruments to create very interesting music. The sooner you can break down the boundaries of traditional musical expectations, then the closer you are to realizing that it is the creativity and music that matter and not the means by which you record it. However, once you have your recordings, then it's time to begin editing and crafting your performances.

# EDITING MIDI 5

Much of the power and flexibility of MIDI exists in the ability to edit and manipulate its data. DAWs offer a wide variety of tools and functions designed for working with MIDI.

There are four general areas to consider when discussing MIDI editing and these are explored in depth in this chapter.

## Basic Tools and Manual Editing

DAWs provide comprehensive MIDI editing capabilities and there are some common features that are universal. In this section we'll focus on the basics of MIDI editing and will explore some practical scenarios that you will likely encounter.

## Quantization

Quantization is an option that is used to clean up or purposely change the timing of recorded notes and when used appropriately can make your MIDI performances sound tighter. In this section we'll look at how to use quantization, when to use it, and when to avoid it.

## Notation Editors

Bars, notes, and score markings all show the same information that you might see in a piano roll editor with MIDI data, but for musicians reading a score is a completely different experience. In this section we'll explore how to use a notation editor to work with MIDI and look at how the different views can be used in the production process.

## Advanced and Unique Tools

This section explores MIDI features that are unique to specifidc software and/or are more advanced in nature. There is also a guide to making your MIDI sound musical after the editing process is complete.

## Basic Tools and Manual Editing

Gone are the days of looking at numbers or long lists of MIDI data when editing, and now we use easy-to-understand visual interfaces. It is simple to adjust the start and end of notes with a simple click and drag. It is just as easy to transpose notes. There are tools that help in these procedures and some common practices that will help you make changes that are both accurate and musical.

## Survey of Typical Tools

MIDI is represented in three ways: rectangles on a grid, notation in a score, and as numbers in a list. In this section we are looking at MIDI as rectangles and in regions as used in piano rolls and MIDI sequencers. The use of "boxes" to visualize MIDI data is

**Figure 5.1** Different Editing Tools in Logic Pro

| ✓ | ↖ | Pointer Tool | T |
| | ✎ | Pencil Tool | 2 |
| | ◣ | Eraser Tool | 3 |
| | I | Text Tool | 4 |
| | ✂ | Scissors Tool | 5 |
| | ◥ | Glue Tool | 6 |
| | S | Solo Tool | 7 |
| | M | Mute Tool | 8 |
| | Q | Zoom Tool | 9 |
| | > | Fade Tool | 0 |
| | ↖ | Automation Select Tool | Q |
| | ↖ | Automation Curve Tool | W |
| | ⊣⊢ | Marquee Tool | E |
| | ◂▸ | Flex Tool | R |

simple to understand with the start and end points the left and right edges of the box. The vertical placement of the note determines the pitch. Velocity is also typically shown and edited as a part of the note with color or other visual indicator. All other MIDI data are controlled and edited separately.

The basic tools include a pencil tool to "draw" notes, a mover tool to adjust the placement of the notes, a trim tool to adjust the length of the notes, and a velocity tool to adjust the velocity level of the notes. All of the other controller data is edited and manipulated with a variety of tools that we'll cover later in this section. Basic editing is typically intuitive but getting the results you want can be more difficult.

The first rule of editing MIDI is to use a tempo-based project. Everything relies on utilizing the session grid appropriately. Vertical lines represent musical bars and beats and these provide both a visual and "physical" reference for your editing needs. Learn how to set the snap-to-grid function in your DAW so that you can edit with the grid guiding your moves.

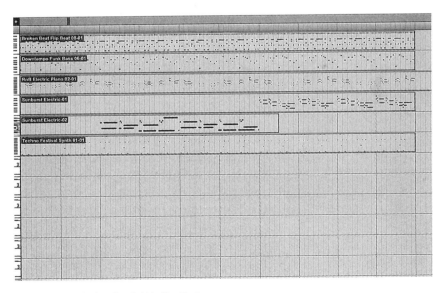

**Figure 5.2** MIDI Session Grid in Pro Tools

## Typical Editing Workflow

After your MIDI part is recorded then the editing can begin. If the recording has room for improvement that you feel can be obtained through additional recording attempts, then it is recommended that you rerecord because it is much easier to obtain a natural performance through a solid performance. Editing can provide excellent results but requires additional time and effort.

This section assumes that you have at least some musical experience, but there is an entire section later in the book devoted to music theory basics that is designed to help any of you that are new to the topic.

Listen through what you have and make notes about the sections that need editing. You can either dig in and fix each part as you come across them or you can use your DAW's marker feature to makes notes for later. When you are in a creative zone, you may want to put off detailed editing until later, and in those cases you will want to have as much information saved as possible about what needs to be fixed later.

There are two types of editing that you'll be engaged in. The first is to fix mistakes that are limiting your performance, and the second is to take a solid performance and switch things up as a creative tool. Once you have cleaned up the data then you can begin to use the editing process as a creative process.

Start by adjusting the start times of notes that don't start at the right time. How do you know what the right time is? This depends on a lot of factors that include style of music, feel of the music, and the instrument in question. Sometimes you'll want to have the notes start right on the beat and be exactly in time, and other times you want the notes to start a little early or a little late. Most of the time the editing process is aligning notes that were missed during recording and just need to be moved to match the other notes. If you know a song that has the feel you are looking for, then import it into your project and line up the notes with the audio peaks (check out groove quantize later in this chapter).

After adjusting the start time you will often then need to change the note length to compensate for the change in placement. When recording using a keyboard that has a sustain pedal, the length of the notes are often recorded as shorter

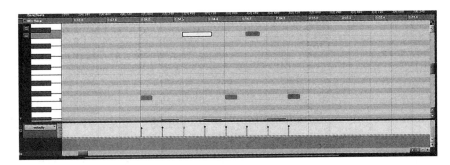

**Figure 5.3** Adjusting MIDI Note Length in Pro Tools

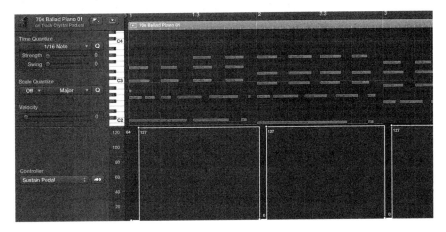

**Figure 5.4** Sustain Pedal Adjustment View in Logic

notes but held due to the sustain control data. In this situation, changing the note length will not change how long the note actually holds. If you need to change the length you will need to change the note and the sustain control data. Be aware of you sustain data when shortening and lengthening notes to avoid crossing over a break point because it could drastically affect the note length.

Additional editing might include adjusting velocity to set the level of each note. You can also engage in splitting notes, which is a technique used to take a long note and turn it into shorter notes to form a pattern. You can transpose notes up and down

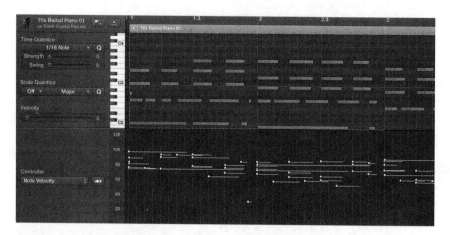

**Figure 5.5** Individual Note Velocity in Logic

to change chords and melodies. Copying and pasting MIDI is another basic editing technique that is used to repeat phrases of melodies, bass lines, and general rhythm section parts. This is different than looping because it is edited as individual notes and looping typically happens at the region/clip level.

As the notes begin to fall into place, then it's time to start considering the additional control data and performance capabilities that you have access to. Whether it is pitch bend, sustain, or other modulation data, all sequencers provide the ability to record and edit these data. There are three ways to add these data.

a.  The first method is to record control data simultaneously with the notes using pedals, mod wheels, or another interface. If you are using both hands on the keyboard, it makes it more difficult and using both feet is often a skill that needs practice. When performing leads and solos with one hand it is much easier to add pitch bend and modulation using the free hand.

b.  The second method is to record the data in a second pass. Each sequencer handles this differently, but you will typically have two options for what happens to the new data. It can be stored in a new MIDI region or merged in the existing region. Both options control the sound source, but merging allows for easier editing later on because the data live in the same region.

**Figure 5.6** Drawing in Pitch
Bend Information into Pro Tools

c. The third option is to manually draw in the data after the recording is made. Perhaps the best option is to record as much as you can live, followed by an editing pass to clean up and enhance the performance. Manual editing can be tedious, but it gives you the chance to get it exactly how you want it. By the time you get good at manual editing you will appreciate capturing the performance in real time because of the time and energy it saves.

Editing can (and often does) continue until the very end of production. While it can be a vicious cycle of constant fiddling until "perfection" is obtained, editing is an important part of the process of working with MIDI. To better understand the fundamentals of MIDI editing, let's look at a number of examples.

## Example 1 (Example Files Are Available on ModernMIDI.com)

This example has three tracks that include an audio drum loop, a bass track, and a keyboard track. The drum loop is a fixed element in this example and serves as the foundation for tempo and groove. The bass part is in need of timing adjustments, and the velocities of the notes are inconsistent. There is also room to experiment with some pitch bend as a means to create variety in the part. The keyboard part was recorded quite well but needs some velocity editing, and several chords are in need of time alignment. You wouldn't pitch bend most keyboard parts because it is not a sound that is possible on hardware keyboards.

### Step One: Importing

Make sure that the tempo of the project is set to the same tempo of the drum loop before importing any files. You may find your DAW can handle the import without setting the tempo first but

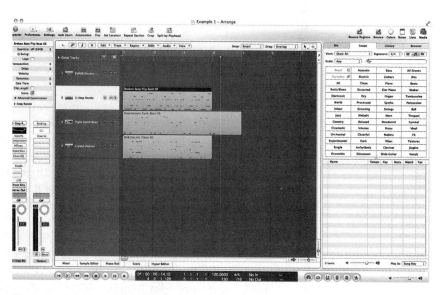

**Figure ex. 1.1** Example 1 Overview

more often than not this is a critical step. The tempo is listed in the name of the sample files available for download on the companion website. Use an audio track for the loop and then use instrument tracks for the MIDI. Assign any bass and keyboard sound that you like to each of these tracks, and adjust as needed as we progress through these steps.

**Figure ex. 1.2** Importing MIDI Files in Logic

| Name ▼ | Tempo | Key | Beats | Match | Fav |
|---|---|---|---|---|---|
| Broken Beat Flip Beat 03 | 123 | – | 16 | 95% | ☐ |
| Broken Beat Flip Beat 04 | 123 | – | 16 | 95% | ☐ |
| Broken Beat Flip Beat 05 | 123 | – | 16 | 95% | ☐ |
| Broken Beat Flip Beat 06 | 123 | – | 16 | 95% | ☐ |
| Broken Beat Flip Beat 07 | 123 | – | 16 | 95% | ☐ |
| Broken Beat Flip Beat 08 | 123 | – | 16 | 95% | ☐ |
| Broken Beat Flip Beat 09 | 123 | – | 16 | 95% | ☐ |
| Broken Beat Flip Beat 10 | 123 | – | 16 | 95% | ☐ |
| Broken Beat Flip Beat 11 | 123 | – | 8 | 96% | ☐ |
| Broken Beat Flip Beat 12 | 123 | – | 8 | 96% | ☐ |
| Broken Beat Flip Beat 13 | 123 | – | 8 | 96% | ☐ |
| Broken Beat Flip Beat 14 | 123 | – | 16 | 95% | ☐ |
| Broken Beat Flip Beat 15 | 123 | – | 16 | 95% | ☐ |
| Broken Beat Flip Beat 16 | 123 | – | 16 | 95% | ☐ |
| Broken Beat Flip Beat 17 | 123 | – | 8 | 96% | ☐ |
| Broken Beat Flip Beat 18 | 123 | – | 8 | 95% | ☐ |
| Broken Beat Shadow Beat | 140 | – | 16 | 71% | ☐ |
| Chilled Beats 01 | 105 | – | 32 | 84% | ☐ |
| Chilled Beats 02 | 105 | – | 32 | 84% | ☐ |

## Step Two: Grid View

The bass part is simple but was played poorly. Compare it with the waveform of the drum loop and see where the loop's downbeats are. Set the grid of your project to a setting that makes sense musically. The grid often follows the primary transport setting and can just as easily show minutes and seconds instead of bars and beats. If the visual grid isn't set to bars and beats during the editing phase then you are likely to lose important functionality. You often have control over the number of grid lines that are visible and they should be set to at least 16th notes.

## Step Three: Adjust Start Times

You have several options when aligning the bass notes with the drum loop. You can place the notes exactly in time on the beat or slightly before or after. Visually lining up the notes with the audio transients is a way to synchronize the bass with the drums. You'll notice that this leaves the notes a varying amount off of the beat but that could be the perfect placement. Listen

**Figure ex. 1.3** Notice the Down Beats Are Not Lined Up between the Drums and Bass

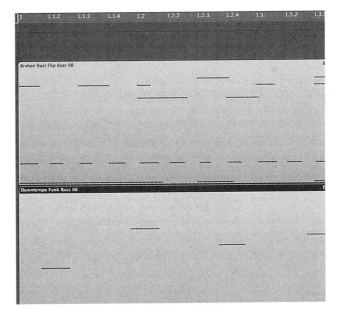

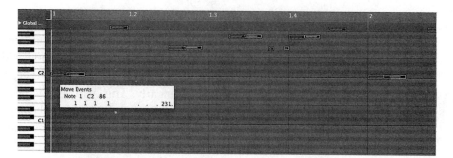

**Figure ex. 1.4** Dragging the Bass Notes onto the Downbeat in Logic

to the notes in a variety of places and find the placement that sounds correct. There are not MIDI editing tools that can make accurate musical decisions better than your ears.

### Step Four: Adjust Lengths

The lengths of the notes will vary depending on the bass patch you assigned. If you picked a bass patch that has a short decay then the length of each note makes very little difference. If you picked a bass patch that has substantial sustain then the end of each note will need to be carefully monitored. It is more important that you have consistent note lengths throughout the clip and could just as easily have them go full length as well as shorter lengths with space in between. Look for the controller data that shows sustain information, and verify that no data exist for the MIDI region.

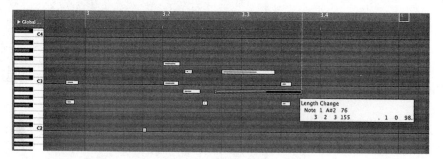

**Figure ex. 1.5** Adjusting MIDI Note Length in Logic

### *Step Five: Adjust Velocities*

There are two typical ways to access velocity data in sequencers. The first is through a special velocity tool, and the second is through a velocity view. Neither method is clearly superior but you will need to discover which method is available in your DAW. Some DAWs even have both options, and in that case you should use the one that works best for you.

There are some things to consider when adjusting note velocities. First, when working with sampled instruments that have inconsistent sound breaks at different velocity levels, you will need to be more careful in your programming. Often this is a process of trial and error as you explore the sounds of the instrument. Second, when working with synths the various velocities can create a much different sound at the extremes. A bass patch might sound more like a lead at higher velocities and dull and muted at lower velocities. This can be used as a creative tool in the sequencing process. Third, not all instruments change their level when triggered at different velocities. This is true when an instrument is modeled after a "real" instrument that has no volume change at different velocities, such as a B-3 organ. To change the level of the sound of the instrument you will need to control the volume at the track or mixer stage.

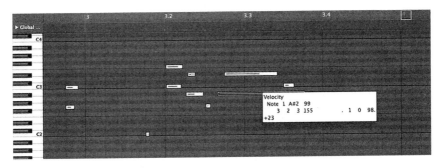

**Figure ex. 1.6** Changing Velocities in Logic

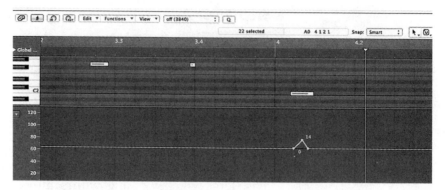

**Figure ex. 1.7** Drawing in Pitch Bend Information into Logic

### Step Six: Add Pitch Bend

Pitch bend information is rarely editable without opening an additional view. Find the view for bend and pick one note to adjust the pitch. You can start it low and bend it up into the correct pitch, or start a note at zero and bend it as a transition out. Experiment with a few different bends until you find something that is interesting. If you find it difficult to obtain natural sounding results then try recording the pitch bend with the pitch wheel on your hardware controller. Make sure your sequencer is set to merge newly recorded MIDI with existing data.

### Step Seven: Repeat Steps 2–6 for the Keyboard Part

The keyboard part has more notes but the editing is the same. The one thing that you need to know is that at least one note in the keyboard file was played incorrectly, and you will need to transpose the pitch. Find it and fix it.

## Example 2 (Example Files Are Available on ModernMIDI.com)

This example has a number of different tracks and is going to require additional audio recording skills. The goal of this example is to teach you about transposition. Each track has been transposed into a different key, and you get to transpose each of them back into a single key. All but two of the tracks are transposed entirely to a new key, and the remaining two were transposed in sections to multiple keys. Your task is to "fix" this sequence.

### Step One: Import and Assign Tracks

After importing the MIDI into a session, assign each track to an instrument. Each track is already labeled but you can be creative in your assignments. There are no percussion tracks that are appropriate because transposition for percussion doesn't make sense in most cases with a sound assigned to each note individually. Transposition of a percussion track won't make it sound higher or lower but will instead change the sounds being triggered.

### Step Two: Analyze the Tracks

For those of you who have a musical background this could be a really easy assignment. Use your score view to see the notes and figure out the relationship between tracks. For the rest of you, trial and error is a supported method of figuring this out. Ideally you will look for patterns between tracks, such as final notes and similar melodies. The two tracks with multiple changes are the biggest challenge but (without being too obvious) there are clues.

### Step Three: Transpose

Start transposing! Select the notes you want to transpose and drag them up or down. Another common way to transpose is to select the notes and activate your sequencer's transpose function. Often found as a menu option, a transpose window offers a number of specific transposition settings to change the notes as needed. No matter the method you use, you will need to listen and follow the clues to find the proper transpositions. There may be several possible solutions to this example because octave displacement and alternate harmonies may sound perfectly acceptable. You can also experiment with alternate combinations and find very creative solutions.

## Example 3 (Example Files Are Available on ModernMIDI.com)

This example involves creating a source MIDI track to be used for triggering an instrument during the sampling process. A sampled instrument is created by recording a wide range of notes and then using a sampler to map the recordings to MIDI input. Acoustic instruments require each sampled note to be played by a performer, but if you are working with an instrument that has MIDI capabilities then you can trigger the notes using a sequencer; the output is MIDI and the recorded input is audio.

### Step One: Track Setup

This example requires a minimum of two tracks: one audio and one MIDI. If you do not have an audio interface with available inputs then you can still complete this example entirely in your DAW. Ideally you should hook an external sound source such as a synthesizer to your audio inputs, using a virtual instrument and buses between tracks as an alternative. The MIDI track should be set to an external port and connected to the external sound source. When you play a MIDI note in your sequencer it should trigger the sound source that you should hear coming into the audio track once it is armed for recording.

### Step Two: Creating the MIDI Sequence

For this step you need to know about the source you are recording. What is its range? Is it velocity sensitive? The

**Figure ex. 3.1** Creating One MIDI Track and One Audio Track in Pro Tools

New Tracks

Create [1] new [MIDI Track ⬍] in [Ticks ⬍] ⊖ ⊕ ↕
Create [1] new [Mono ⬍] [Audio Track ⬍] in [Samples ⬍] ⊖ ⊕ ↕

[Cancel]  [Create]

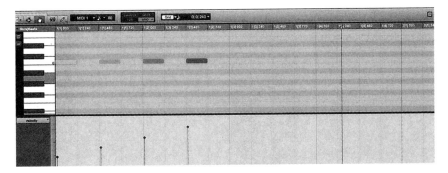

**Figure ex. 3.2** Adjusting the MIDI Note Velocities to 25%, 50%, 75%, and 100% in Pro Tools

reason you need to know the information about the instrument is so that you can add the correct notes for triggering the sounds. The other information you need to decide on is the amount of detail you plan on capturing. Higher levels of detail include things like recording every note at multiple velocity levels while lower levels of detail might include recording only several notes per octave and fewer velocity levels.

For this example, program an instrument with two octaves and four different velocity levels. Draw the first note four times and then adjust the velocity levels so that each has a different level. A good starting place would be velocities at 25%, 50%, 75%, and 100% although the actual velocities should make sense in context of the instrument. If there isn't a difference between the sound of the instrument at 25% and 50%, then there is not a reason to record both. After you finish with the first four then select all four and copy and paste them on the next note level. If you want to expedite the process then copy larger sets of notes and copy and paste them.

### *Step Three: Begin the Recording*

Press record. The MIDI triggers the instrument that is then recorded into the armed audio track. This example demonstrates the ability of MIDI to aid in the preparation of sampled instruments and there are several software offerings that utilize this process.

**Figure ex. 3.3** Recording the Output of the Sampled Instrument into Pro Tools

## Additional Editing

This chapter makes no attempt at listing every single tool and function for every single workstation. It would be impossible to do and immediately outdated even if it was attempted. The key is to understand the capabilities of MIDI so you know what is possible during the editing phase. Knowing the basics will enable you to accomplish basic tasks, appreciate the advanced functions that we will talk about a little later, and ultimately be creative in your solutions to problems.

## Quantization

When inputting MIDI information via real-time performance, small timing imperfections are inevitable. Quantization is used to alter and/or improve the timing. The quantize feature in most digital audio workstations offers a wide variety of

**Figure 5.7** Quantize Window in Logic

options in order to tighten up MIDI performances and move individual MIDI events onto the grid. In essence, the quantization feature shifts selected MIDI events to the closest specified rhythmic point (i.e. bars, beats, or sub beats). By properly using the quantize function, it is possible to take a drastically off-time performance and make it seem as if it was played with perfect timing. Fixing mistakes, however, is not all we use the quantization feature for. We can also add a pseudo-human element back into MIDI clips that are too rigid in the desired style, to make them sound more natural. To better understand quantization, let's take a look at some of the parameters commonly found in most sequencers.

## Note Value

When opening the quantization dialog box of any given DAW, the first parameter that must be adjusted is the note type. Like in musical notation, quantization note types range from whole note, half note, quarter note, and so on. It's important to select the appropriate note type based on your musical content in order for the selected notes to be quantized correctly. For example, if you select the half note setting, all selected MIDI events that happen exactly on the half note markers will be left alone. A MIDI event taking place a little before or after the half note mark, however, will snap exactly on to the half note grid point. Consequently, if there are MIDI events a bit further from the half note mark, they could

**Figure 5.8** Quantize Note
Values in Logic

potentially be moved to an undesirable grid mark. Therefore, it is important to select the appropriate note value when applying quantization. Although quantization usually deals with "note on" events, most sequencers allow the user to maintain performed note duration so the "note off" event is shifted by the same amount as the "note on" event. As a rule of thumb, you should select a quantization note value equal to the shortest note value in the selected piece. When a performance has more complex rhythms involving values such as triplets, section-by-section quantization rather than complete region quantization will yield better results.

## Strength and Sensitivity

Most, if not all, sequencers allow you to control the strength of quantization. The strength parameter is usually displayed in percentage points. If we use the same half note example and apply a 75% strength, MIDI events that take place before or after the half note mark will be moved 75%, or ¾ths, closer to the half note mark rather than exactly on to the half note mark. This strength feature allows users to maintain a "human" type element to their performances. Like the strength parameter, sensitivity also gives the user control over the "human" element of his performance. By adjusting the sensitivity parameter, the user is able to control which MIDI events get shifted to the grid: that is, events happening after the specified sensitivity point will be shifted, while events happening before the sensitivity point will not be shifted. When used correctly, the strength and sensitivity parameters allow users to achieve non-robotic sounding performances while still correcting timing issues.

## Swing

A common quantization parameter is swing, which allows users to apply a specified timing setting to selected MIDI events. The swing feature takes MIDI events at the ⅛th note length and changes the note duration to match a specific timing template. For example, Jazz music typically has a long-short-long-short note pattern. You can adjust how much swing is used and the ratio of the note lengths. A subtle swing can add energy to a rhythm track and is an effect used with

**Figure 5.9** Quantize Strength Control in Pro Tools

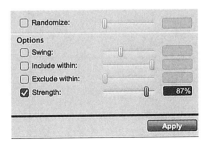

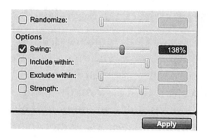

**Figure 5.10** Quantize Swing Control in Pro Tools

successful results on drum machines such as the MPC. High swing settings are rarely used and are difficult incorporate into projects.

## Randomization

You can "randomize" MIDI events inside a selected region. The randomization feature moves MIDI events away from a specified rhythmic position within a selected range. This randomization feature can be extremely successful in "humanizing" MIDI clips that are too "square." Randomization is typically used to transform notes that were entered manually (and thus likely on the grid) or that are first quantized and then need some loosening up. Either way, randomization takes the control out of your hands and this could result in less-than-ideal results. It is never recommended to use a real-time randomization effect because then the results are different every time it is played, and that is rarely desirable. The better solution in this is to craft the part manually to get the perfect feel or to use a groove template.

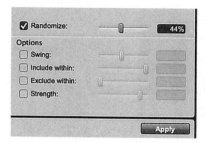

**Figure 5.11** Quantize Randomize Amount in Pro Tools

## Groove Quantization

Standard quantization shifts MIDI events to an absolute rhythmic grid. In more recent years, however, many sequencers offer a different type of quantization called "groove quantization." Groove quantization shifts MIDI events to a rhythmic performance template rather than an absolute rhythmic grid. This allows the user to quantize selected MIDI events to an actual performance in order to better match the song. Grooves can be extracted from a sequenced part or taken from an audio clip.

## Examples

1. After recording a piano player and then a bass player, you notice the timing between the two is not together. Perhaps you can keep rerecording until the timing is perfect but in some cases that may not be practical. Instead, use the original piano part and capture it as a groove template. Apply the groove template to the bass part, trying several strengths until the timing is as desired. If your DAW has flex time or a different audio quantization feature, you can even apply the groove to recorded audio.

2. After spending too long trying to get the feel of a bass line just right, you could use the best take and then use a groove template that has the right feel. Most sequencers have default templates that you can try or if you have a song with the right feel you can import a selection and create a new template.

3. Groove templates not only control the timing but also the velocity. Some sequencers allow you to edit groove templates just as if they are normal MIDI clips, which means you can tweak timing and velocity to exactly what you want. This creates a situation with a great deal of flexibility.

**Figure 5.12** Groove Quantize in Logic

5-Tuplet/4
5-Tuplet/8
7-Tuplet
9-Tuplet

1/16 & 1/16 Triplet
1/16 & 1/8 Triplet
1/8 & 1/8 Triplet

70s Ballad Piano 01

## Notation

MIDI sequencers often include an option to view MIDI data in the form of musical notation. Whether you are a musician that prefers to look at your data in the familiar format of notes on a page or an engineer/producer that needs to print out the parts for session musicians coming into the studio for a recording session, notation is an important part of sequencing and a very useful tool.

## Working with Notation

MIDI notes in the piano roll are directly linked to the notes in the notation view, which means you can work in either view and edit the same performance data. Because the notation uses MIDI as the foundation, it can incorporate all of the

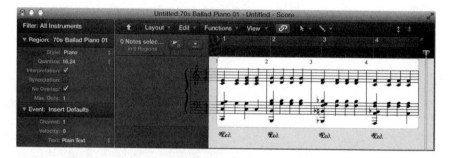

**Figure 5.13** MIDI Notation View inside Logic

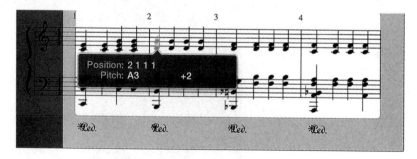

**Figure 5.14** Manually Dragging MIDI Notes in Logic's Notation View

performance markings into as realistic a rendition as is possible with the features of MIDI. While the editing capabilities in the piano roll and the notation editor are very similar, there are some marked differences. There are three phases when working with notation: note entry, editing, and output.

## Note Entry

Adding notes when using the notation view includes selecting notes from a palette and then adding them to the staff, using a step entry process, or recording the notes in real time using a controller. There are also some additional entry methods that are more advanced, such as digitization through scanning. To understand typical situations in which you would use each method, let's look at several practical examples.

a. Example 1

After a melody is composed and you want to add harmony or a bass part, you can draw in the additional parts manually. To add a whole note bass part just select the whole note duration from the notation palette and then click on the score where you want to add the note.

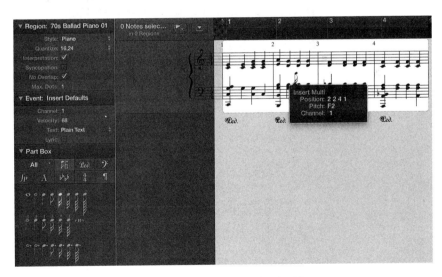

**Figure 5.15** Manually Inputting MIDI Notes in Logic's Notation View

b. Example 2

Adding notes one at a time using your track pad can become quite tedious and is not very efficient. A faster way to do this is to using a step entry process that utilizes a MIDI keyboard and your computer keyboard. You select the note value by pressing a key on the MIDI keyboard and then select a duration using preassigned key commands on your computer keyboard. Select the starting position on the score and after each note is added the position automatically moves to the position immediately following the end of the added note. Rests can also be added but do not require a note value. This entry method is used most often when copying notes from another format, such as a printed score that you want to digitize.

c. Example 3

Recording in real time while using the notation view provides visual feedback to help you perform in sync with the existing parts. It is sometimes easier to perform additional recordings while viewing the existing MIDI data in notation form. This is especially true when viewing multiple tracks simultaneously.

d. Example 4

Some notation applications allow you to scan printed scores and then convert them to MIDI data that is viewable in score format. You often have to clean up the data if they aren't converted 100% accurately and is covered in the editing portion of the section on notation.

It is not uncommon to use a combination of note entry options and there is no right way to use the notation editor feature set. You might complete a first pass by recording real time and then add additional notes using the manual options. Once you have notes entered there are many editing options available.

## Editing

The first consideration when editing in the notation editor is the view quantization that is separate from the actual note quantization. The reason for two different quantization settings is that a musical MIDI performance will include many

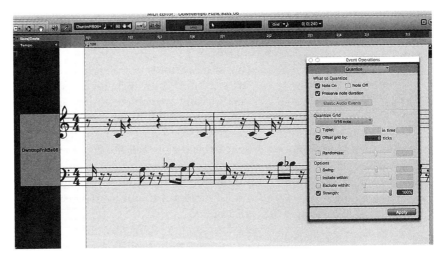

**Figure 5.16** Quantize Notation in Pro Tools

notes that are not on the grid but that doesn't work very well visually on a score. Eighth-notes played with a human touch might be a fraction of a second before or after the beat but when you print the part they will need to be placed visually exact. Just as with quantization in the MIDI editor, you should set the notation quantization to the smallest note duration you are working with. You may have the option to set the quantization strength and most of the time this should be set to 100%, which is less common for quantization in the MIDI editor.

Because the notation editor is designed to mimic music on the printed page there are limitations in the editing process. For example, there are additional steps to increase the length of notes and it typically isn't practical to edit any type of control data. Efficient editing often includes using multiple editing views and plays to their strengths. Let's look at several examples to demonstrate editing in the notation view.

a. Example 1

When adjusting the harmonic structure of chords, it is often helpful to see the chord in notation format because then you can see the accidentals and any changes you are making. When doing this in the piano roll it is still possible to see the differences, but it is harder to distinguish the notes in the chord since they all look like generic boxes.

b.  Example 2

Try moving notes from left to right. In the MIDI editor there are clear grid lines and you can snap to the grid or move the notes to any available position. In the notation view you are limited to positions that make musical sense within the quantization settings. The difference between editing this way in each view is that in the piano roll you can more easily adjust performance data to create a musical performance and in the notation view the notes always stay on the grid and it is very difficult to make small, detailed changes.

c.  Example 3

Learning how your notation editor deals with additional editing functions such as changing durations is important and will affect your efficiency in the process. In some sequencers it is easier to have a notation window open alongside a MIDI editor so that you can work in both simultaneously. Other sequencers provide powerful tools to edit everything you need in the notation editor. In some sequencers the notation functionality is very basic and you will have very little choice but to work in the MIDI editor. Changing note lengths in the notation editor is one example of a common editing task that varies from sequencer to sequencer. In Pro Tools, for instance, you can adjust the length using the trim tool but only in-line with the current grid settings. In Logic you cannot use any tools to change the length but have to adjust the note in the MIDI editor or numerically in the notation properties box. In this instance it is much easier to use Pro Tools, but Logic still has a notation function that is more powerful and flexible.

d.  Example 4

There are a number of additional notation options that can be added to your score but do not affect the MIDI data. Even in sequencers that do connect crescendos and accents to MIDI performance data, there are other things that do not affect MIDI data. Lyrics, titles, and some other markings are examples of things that can be visually added but which mean nothing to the sequencer. This is an unfortunate over-sight in most notation editors and something that is chang-ing. Cubase is the first DAW that incorporated a much tighter connection between the score and MIDI. Finale and

Sibelius are capable of such connections but also can be used to create nontraditional scores that are not connected to MIDI in any shape or form. There is at least one iOS app that has more advanced score options than Pro Tools and Logic when it comes to score markings being connected to MIDI performance. Symphony Pro translates accelerandos and crescendos into tempo and level adjustments. Even staccato and slurs translate into variances in the data.

## Advanced and Unique Tools

At this point we have covered hardware, MIDI basics, and the basics of editing. Before we get into the process of mixing and using audio effects, there is one last area of exploration when it comes to the capabilities of MIDI and this is a look at several slightly more advanced options. The categories for these are alternate storage/playback and transformation tools.

## Alternate Storage

Instead of storing MIDI in tracks in a linear fashion, some sequencers allow you to store MIDI in chunks that can be triggered at various times. Let's look at several examples:

Logic Pro Chord Memorizing—In Logic there is module called Chord Trigger, which allows you program chords that are

**Figure 5.17** Logic Chord Memorizer

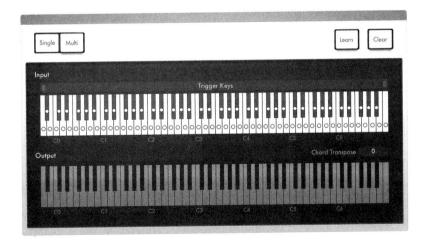

assigned to individual notes. When you play one of the assigned notes, Logic plays the preprogrammed chords. This is especially useful when performing live because you can link together harmonic structures that are triggered using simple key strokes.

FL Studio Playlist Clips—This is an example of a tool that functions in several roles. Clips in FL Studio are used in a traditional linear manner for sequencing but can also be triggered via controllers separate from playback. Just as with the Chord Trigger in Logic, each clip can be triggered by a single stroke of a key. There are options for when the clip is played after the key is pressed so that it can start immediately or in sync with the tempo during playback.

Sonar X2 Matrix—In Sonar you can drag MIDI and audio files into the Matrix, which creates a performance environment that does not rely on linear tracks and can trigger events across the Matrix at any time. In line with touch screen technology you can even trigger events using your fingers as you would with a hardware sampler.

Each of these examples works in different ways and has different strengths and weaknesses. The underlying principle is the create building blocks of MIDI that can be accessed at any time with any trigger. This offers flexibility for live performance which can also be used in the studio for a non-live production.

## Transformation Tools

Perhaps the most well-known transformation tool exists in the Environment Window in Logic Pro. While this feature is likely to be replaced in future versions of Logic due to Apple's tendency to simplify software, this feature will always be known for its confusing interface and raw power. Other sequencers offer similar options, often with much easier to use interfaces. Let's look at several things we can expect with transforming tools.

1.  Basic Transformation Options:
    Reverse MIDI—While it is possible to do this manually, using a function to reverse MIDI is much more efficient. It takes the selection and simply reverses the order.

**Figure 5.18** Transformation Tools inside Environment Window in Logic

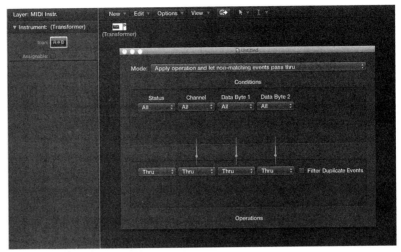

a. Basic Editing—All of the basic editing options such as note length and note value can be changed via transform. This permits you to make large and small changes using very precise data input and can be much more efficient than manual editing.

b. Transposition—This option allows you to change the pitch assignments by a specific amount and often allows key changes/harmony changes as well.

c. Humanize—This transformation adds imperfections into the MIDI data. While typically focusing on timing, it can often be used to add variance to any number of parameters. Think of this as the anti-quantization option.

d. Slow down/speed up—This is useful if you want to double or halve the speed. You change the tempo to any alternate but it is used most often in relation to the tempo.

e. Arpeggiation—This transformation adds additional notes based on a chord and/or other parameters as set by the transformation module. Typical options include range, speed, and note order.

f. Performance Changes—Adding a crescendo to the velocity data or a specific change to the pitch bend are two examples of using a transformer to change your performance. As with all of these transformation options, the key benefit is precise changes that can help sculpt your performance.

Transformations can take place as either real-time manipulations to entire tracks or to individual clips. Clips can all be transformed in a non-real-time process that changes the actual MIDI notes. The difference between real time and non-real time is often minor but there are some pitfalls to avoid.

1. If there are any elements of the transformation that are random then a non-real-time option is often more appropriate. If you want it to be played differently each time then keep it real time, but keep in mind that if you hear a version you really like, it will be lost forever if it isn't written into the data.

2. If you are using a real-time transformation you will often not see the change represented in the MIDI editor. Some sequencers allow you to switch a setting that allows the real-time change to be represented in the notes but it still can be a fairly complex task to follow which are the original notes and which is the result of the transformation.

3. If you have not settled on the final version of the transformation then it is advised to keep it real time and not add it into the actual data. It can be hard to get back to the original version and so, unless you keep the original in an alternate take or playlist, you should not change the original until you are sure it is exactly how you want it.

## Making MIDI Musical

You can edit your MIDI performances endlessly but unless you achieve your musical goals it doesn't do any good. There are a number of things you can do to achieve your goal of a musical performance, and that is the focus of this section.

## Imitation Is the Truest Form of Flattery

Stealing a song is against the law, but using its "feel" is not. The groove of your song should be the first place to start when working on creating a musical performance because it is easier to create the right feel initially than it is to create it later. Whether you are working with drum loops, sequenced parts, or audio recordings, there are tools to help craft the exact level of musicality that you want. The first method involves a close comparison with a nonsequenced version of the instrument with which you are working. The second tool is discussed above in the section on quantization. Groove quantization is a powerful way to infuse musicality into your sequence. The third tool uses tempo fluctuations at the project level. The last tool uses envelopes to create organic change.

## Comparisons

Nearly every part that you will program will have some real-world comparison. If you are programming strings then you can listen to an orchestra. If you are programming a bass part then there is an actual bass you could listen to. Even synthesizers have a non-synth equivalent if you consider the role it is playing. A synth lead could be compared to any number of solo instruments. The idea is that you find a comparison so that you can mimic the nonsequenced instrument.

Listen for the changes that happen to the sound as it starts, sustains, and then releases. The changing over time is a set of parameters that are referred to as its envelope. You can learn a lot about an instrument when listening to it being performed. Listen to it being performed in a style similar to your production. Are there breaks between notes or full sustain? How does the timbre change over time? What performance techniques are available to the instrument? Can it play multiple notes at a time, or one at a time? The more you listen and learn, the more easily you will be able to replicate the "musicality" of the instrument.

Write down five things that make the nonsequenced instrument uniquely musical. Is it its ability to change level over time? Is it the ability to start each note with a very subtle attack before growing to full volume? Create the list and then get to work adding the same items to your sequenced instrument. When listening with a critical ear you will discover a lot about the instrument. In many cases you will feel frustrated because the sampled, synthesized, or modeled instruments just don't stack up. Developing an ear for hearing the differences will help you get better at this process.

Another tool when making comparisons is the real-time analyzer, which allows you to see the harmonic content of your instrument. The musicality of your instrument is more than just the placement of the notes—it is also the way the instrument reacts to being performed and how the sound changes when sustained. The analyzer helps you see the harmonic changes over time and then you can add effects or automation to create the same results in a different instrument.

Perhaps the biggest limitation of samplers is that it is hard to include every single sound that the instrument can make in the patch. When choosing software to compose with, you should also try out the included sounds to see how realistic they are. The same applies to purchasing a third-party sample bank; try it out and decide if it is detailed enough for your purposes.

## Groove Quantize

Musical results can be obtained when visually lining up MIDI notes to an audio file with a good groove. While manual editing is effective, it can take long hours. Some sequencers such as FL Studio actually have a feature that allows you to drag an audio file onto the MIDI editor for help in aligning the MIDI. In other sequencers all you need to do is move an audio track next to the MIDI track and line things up. Zoom in so you are not just guessing with the placement and adjust until the desired results are achieved.

Using groove quantization is the same as manually moving the notes but instead lets the sequencer do the heavy lifting.

**Figure 5.19** Making a Groove Template in Logic

Every modern sequencer has some basic version of groove quantize and some even have more advanced tools. For instance, Logic Pro has only a simple groove quantization option which allows you to create a groove using an existing clip and then you can apply the groove to another clip. Cakewalk Sonar, on the other hand, has an entire dialog that allows you to set additional parameters so that you can sculpt the groove analysis and application process.

While groove quantization allows you to take the timing from one clip and put it on another clip, functions such as Create MIDI Track from Flex Pitch Data in Logic Pro or tools such as Melodyne allow you to store and reuse many other parameters such as pitch and level. You will have to use your judgment and ears to determine which parameters to apply to your MIDI data during the groove quantization process because "more" doesn't always equal better. A good rule of thumb is to use just as many parameters as you need to accomplish your goal and leave the rest behind.

Groove quantization can be used to change the timing of both audio and MIDI, using either audio or MIDI as the source. In every case the data are first converted to MIDI and stored as a groove quantization template. This template can then be used to adjust the timing of any clip. Not every sequencer

**Figure 5.20** Create MIDI Track from Flex Pitch Data

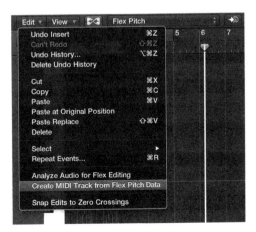

can easily quantize audio with a groove template, but with a little effort it is possible in most cases.

In some cases a two-step process is useful when quantizing using groove templates. The first step is to quantize to an exact grid and then apply the groove. This is especially useful when the original performance is not very accurate. While it is possible to groove quantize with acceptable results in a single step process, don't be afraid to tweak until it is exactly how you want it.

## Tempo Changes

Ever since the invention of the drum machine and sequencer, music has been able to be robotically accurate in its tempo. In a number of styles of music it is perfectly acceptable to have a precise and nonchanging tempo, but there are just as many in which having a fluctuating tempo is desired. It is typically best to set the project tempo before recording audio and MIDI, but minor tempo fluctuations are often added near the end. Changing the tempo in a project with recorded audio only works if the sequencer has the ability to change the tempo of the audio to match the conductor track. This involves time compression/expansion and will degrade the quality of the audio if used too much. In projects with just MIDI it is not an issue and you can alter the tempo as many times as you like.

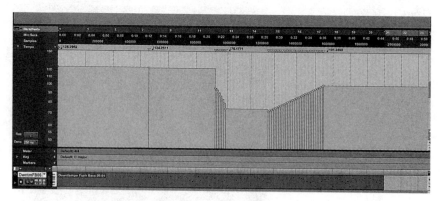

**Figure 5.21** Changing Tempo Information in Pro Tools

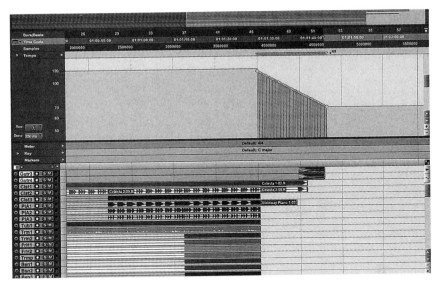

**Figure 5.22** Changing Tempo Information in Pro Tools to Create a Slowdown Effect at the End of a Song

The changes you make can mimic human performers in the style of music you are sequencing. Here are some examples of changes you might make:

1. Slowing down at the end of your song for emphasis.
2. Slowing down/speeding up during the chorus or bridge.
3. Orchestral/piano music can have a free form tempo with constant changes.

Adjusting the tempo in your project is often more complex than simply drawing a new tempo in the conductor track. In Logic Pro, for instance, changing the tempo also changes the placement of automation. You also have to prepare all of your audio tracks by activating the flex features. The point is that it isn't a simple click of a button and you have to be diligent in setting things up.

How do you know how much to change the tempo? That is a question that isn't easily answered because every project is different and every genre is different. The best advice is to immerse yourself in music that is similar and learn what is commonly done. Listen to your project and have others listen as well and get feedback on the tempo variations that you are trying. Most sequencers have the ability to use alternate tempo tracks and so you can try alternates. If your sequencer doesn't have that feature then just save your project as a different version and make the tempo adjustments in each different project. Experiment until you get it right.

## Envelopes

The sound of an instrument being played by a musician is often full of dynamics and tempo variations. The performance ebbs and flows with musical variation, and it's this quality that can help your MIDI sequences sound musical. Apart from aftertouch and other control information, MIDI can only turn a note on and off. Very few things indicate to a listener that an instrument is sampled or synthesized more than a sound without natural dynamics. If you are triggering a flute then it should include the typical level changes that exist when an actual flute is performed. A note might start at a certain level and then increase in loudness as the note sustains. Musical phrases increase in loudness but many samples and synths don't, unless the performer adjusts its envelope.

There are several ways to adjust the envelope of your sounds. The first is to adjust the envelope that is built into your sound source. The second is to use track automation to create the level variations. The third is to add audio/MIDI effects that can adjust the audio envelope. Each option can bring musical life to your project but each has its own strengths and weaknesses.

**Figure 5.23** A Sound Is Crafted by Its Envelope Containing an Attack, Decay, Sustain, and Release

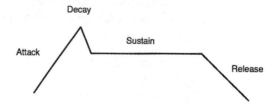

## Built-in Envelopes

Envelopes that built into your sound modules are the easiest way to create movement in your parts and they can often control multiple parameters. Just as an envelope might change the volume of your instrument, it can just as easily control the filter cut off frequency or LFO.

The envelope represents changes in level over time. The four most common envelope identifiers include the attack, decay, sustain, and release. Each phase represents a level and a time amount. When you adjust the attack it is changing the loudness of the first part of the sound and how long it takes to get there from silence.

It isn't necessary to exactly mimic acoustic or other preformed instruments in order to make your MIDI performances musical. The envelope can create motion in the instrument that is nontraditional or unexpected and still create a more musical outcome. Experiment and find the right mixture of change.

## Track Automation

Automation can be used to change the level of instruments in a very similar way to envelopes. You can turn the level up and down in any way that you want that emulates how a performer might change their levels when playing. Automation is covered in more depth in the chapter on mixing, but in this

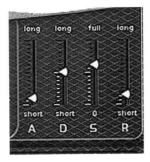

**Figure 5.24** Envelope Control inside of Logic Synthesizer

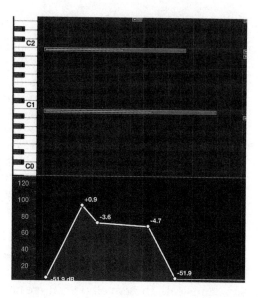

**Figure 5.25** Manually Drawing in an Envelope with Track Automation inside Logic

section we will look at some of the ways that automation can increase the musicality of your instruments.

1. A sequenced cello part that sustains on a single note may need to slowly decrescendo. The automation is able to slowly turn down the level of the cello.
2. You can use automation to add level variations to a bass part. If you set the automation to oscillate louder and softer in-time with the tempo then it could be just what the song needs.
3. If you have a sound that has no level variation, you can use automation to add a spike at the beginning but raising the initial level up a lot and then have it decay into a lower level.

The primary issue with using automation for this purpose is that the timbre of the instrument doesn't change when the level changes. This results in a sound that might sound louder but with a "soft" attack or a loud sound that is played softly. The timbre of a loud instrument is different than the timbre of a soft instrument, but automation doesn't differentiate between the two and can create situations where the timbre is not reproduced correctly. While this is a limitation, it doesn't exclude automation as a viable way to increase musicality of your project.

## Effects

One solution to the limitations of using automation is to use effects as a way to not only change the envelope of the sound but also change the timbre. Effects that are inserted have the ability to create an envelope, be controlled by automation, and affect the harmonic content. These three things, when combined together, provide the most realistic way of adding natural dynamics to your sounds.

Using an equalizer to brighten the sound of your instrument and then having it fade out and having the high frequencies fade too is one way of creating a natural dynamic change. Using a compressor to change the dynamic range is another option, especially when using a side chain to have the compressor pump the dynamics in tempo. Setting the key input

**Figure 5.26** Effects That Can Be Used to Manipulate How a Sound Is Crafted inside Logic

to a hi-hat of a compressor that is on a bass track will create a level change that mirrors the rhythm on the hi-hat.

The possible effect variations are near endless and are capable of both small and large changes to your sound. In the chapter on mixing, additional techniques are discussed that can be used in both the traditional production process and also to fine tune your MIDI performances in such a way that adds musicality or other performance enhancements.

# MIXING 6

Mixing is an important step in the production process that allows you to polish your audio into a final "mix." While most of your levels and sound placement happens at the data level in the sequencer, the mix phase adds another round of processing that includes the following elements: level adjustment, placement in the stereo field, dynamics processing, spectral processing, time-based effects, and automation.

## Level Adjustment

Level (or perceived loudness) is at the core of mixing. By controlling level, we control the loudness of each element of the mix. Although level is mainly controlled via channel strip faders on a mixing console or inside of a digital audio workstation, level can also be manipulated a number of different ways. Let's look at three categories of levels that we'll be working with, which include track levels, buses, and the master output.

MIDI fits into a fourth category because it can be adjusted along with audio tracks in your DAW's mixer, but it can also be adjusted by manipulating velocity data. It can often be difficult to figure out at which stage to adjust the levels because there are so many options but as we progress through this chapter it will become clearer.

### Track Levels

When discussing individual levels we are referring to each recorded MIDI and audio track. For instance, a rock song would

**Figure 6.1** Mixing

typically contain electric guitars, drums, bass guitar, and vocals. In order for everything to be heard and to sound like a coherent ensemble, it is often required to adjust each element's individual level. An example of why level adjustments are important is when mixing a drum kit. Drums are recorded using multiple microphones and when the recorded tracks are played back at their recorded levels; it often doesn't sound right until you adjust each level. Once the levels are set appropriately the kit will sound natural. The same is true when working with most instrument levels in order to achieve the desired sound.

## Buses

In addition to setting individual levels you can also adjust the levels of tracks that are grouped together. Let's continue with the drum example above as a way to understand the power and efficiency of adjusting group levels. Once we are satisfied with the overall individual levels of each drum in the kit, we then route these individual drums together so as to control the

**Figure 6.2** Adjusting Individual Levels inside of Logic Pro

overall level of the drum kit with a single control. This type of group level control gives you less faders to worry about while still being able to maintain an appropriate mix with each instrument. Like practically everything else in mixing, busing individual elements can be achieved in a variety of different ways.

On an external mixing console, you would select each fader you want to control as a group and manually bring them up or down together. Although this technique works, the more faders you try to move at a single time, the more difficult it becomes to move all the faders together and also to maintain their relationships together. When dealing with more than two faders at a time you can use your console's routing features to control the group as a whole. The most common way to do this is to use the console's routing features to group channels through "busing."

Busing is the process of interrupting the selected track's signal path before it reaches the master fader. On a mixing

**Figure 6.3** Standard Way in Which Channels Are Sent to the Master Fader

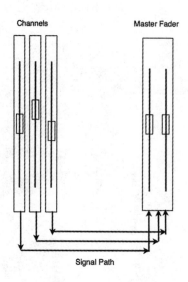

**Figure 6.4** Busing Interrupts the Path Channels Take to the Master Fader Allowing for Another Stage of Control

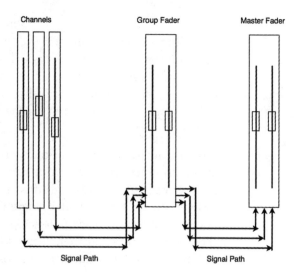

console all tracks are routed to the master fader. Busing takes the desired tracks and routes them to a different set of faders called bus faders. These bus faders are then routed to the master fader. This allows you to control the level of everything routed to the bus fader. You can route all of the drum microphones to one bus, all of the guitars to another, and the background vocals to yet another and then control each as a whole. By doing this, you can boost or cut the level of the drums without having to adjust each drum individually. Because the individual tracks are routed to the bus fader, you are still able to go to the individual faders and make additional adjustments, like turning up the snare drum, without affecting the entire group.

These same techniques are available when using your digital audio workstation. For instance, if you "shift-click" individual tracks in Pro Tools, you can create a selection and a group to sync the faders together. Just as when grabbing the selected faders on the console together, this "shift-click" method must be set up every time you want to control the group and is susceptible to accidents of changing the relationships of the individual levels if you are constantly bypassing the groups.

Another less common option is the VCA group control. Perhaps the best of both worlds when it comes to individual and group level adjustments, the VCA option sets one fader that when adjusted sends changes to individual fader levels. In the analog realm this is accomplished using a secondary voltage control that is sent to each individual fader. The benefit to using a VCA style group is that the individual tracks maintain a more pristine signal flow. An example of busing that demonstrates its inherent issues is when the individual tracks are turned down but then the bus is turned up. By turning down the individual track you reduce the dynamic range that cannot be reextended simply by turning up the destination bus. The VCA group reaches back and turns up or down the original levels for a much simpler process and still provides the efficiency of using a group.

## Overall Level

Overall level is something you should pay attention to at all times. All recording formats, be it magnetic tape or your hard drive, have an absolute level "ceiling" at which point louder sounds cannot exist. It is important to keep your overall level under control to avoid approaching the ceiling and creating distortion and clipping. The overall level of your mix is controlled by a master fader. Master faders are the same as a bused group fader but with everything routed to it.

## Placement in the Stereo Field

At the onset of recorded audio, engineers were stuck in mono. This means that they only had one channel to output their sound to. Before long, however, stereo became commonplace. Having two channels allowed the engineer more sonic space to place their recorded material, which, in turn, allowed more easily for all the recorded sounds to be heard. Although we have moved much beyond standard stereo recordings and entered the surround sound realm, stereo still stands as the main format in which records are made.

### *Panning*

When we talk about placing sounds in the stereo field, we are typically talking about the act of panning. Panning effectively moves the selected sound between the left and right speakers. Therefore, we would use the pan control to place a sound—say an electric guitar—anywhere between the two speakers we desired. This type of stereo control allows the engineer to not only make more sonic room for each instrument to fit together, but also allows the engineer to organize a sonic representation of how the ensemble appears visually. For example, when mixing a rock band, we could decide to pan the various instruments to their typical places on the stage: vocalist in the center, guitarist on one side, keyboard on the other, and so on and so on.

**Figure 6.5** Example of Possible Places Musicians Exist in the Stereo Field

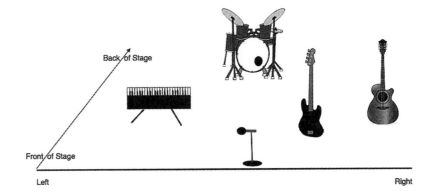

Panning however doesn't have to be limited to representing a live ensemble; panning can be used creatively by the engineer to organize the sounds in any way he or she sees fit. In order to better understand panning, we must first understand how it works. A pan control can effectively be thought of as a double-sided volume control. By turning the pan control to the left, the selected track's output diminishes in the right speaker while increasing in the left. Therefore, we get the sense that the sound is moving from one speaker to the other rather than just jumping from one to the other. In order to achieve this smooth motion between speakers, it was important for early inventors to use some sort of continuous controller so the mixing engineer would be able to execute these moves more easily. Therefore, the potentiometer, or "pot,"[1] was adopted as the main (although by no means exclusive) pan control. As with everything in mixing, panning exists in the hardware and software realms and acts the same in both. On both DAWs and hardware mixing consoles, the pan control will usually be located somewhere on each channel strip—typically near the level fader.

With the evolution of sound systems into the multichannel realm, with systems having as many as 8 or 10 speakers, panning has also had to evolve. Although panning is typically performed on the computer in these multichannel systems, hardware panning control still exists in the form of joysticks.

**Figure 6.6** The "Pan Pot" Controls where Sounds Are Placed in the Stereo Field

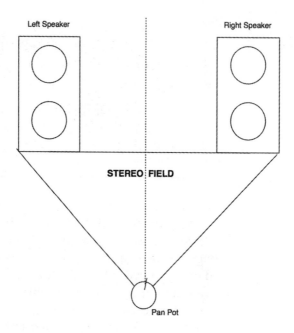

## Effects

The modern engineer has a wide variety of effects to choose from while mixing his or her track. In order to more easily tackle the subject, we can organize the vast amount of effects available into a few distinct groups: dynamic-based effects, spectral-based effects, and time-based effects.

### Dynamic-Based Effects

Dynamic-based effects do exactly what they sound like they do: they affect the dynamics of the track. Dynamic-based effects include compressors, limiters, expanders, and gates. It is important to dive further into each of these effects to understand how to incorporate them into a mix.

#### Compressors

Compressors effectively compress, or diminish, the dynamic range of an audio track. By lowering the overall peaks, or the

**Figure 6.7** The BF76
Compressor Plug-In

**Figure 6.8** The Waves
Renaissance Compressor

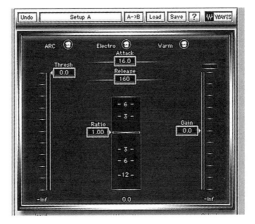

highest levels of amplitude in the track, the difference between the lowest and highest amplitudes of the track lessens by a desired degree, which gives the user greater control over the track as a hole. In order to better understand what a compressor actually does, let's take a look at the various controls typically found on a compressor.

### Threshold

The threshold is the level at which a compressor will start working. Once the user sets the threshold, anything that exceeds the threshold will be compressed while everything below the threshold will be left alone.

### Ratio

The ratio is what determines how much the compressor will actually reduce the level of the incoming signal, which passes the threshold. The user determines how many deci-Bells, or dB, a signal will be attenuated by based off of how many dBs it is over the threshold. For example, a compression ratio of 4:1 means that for every 4dB the signal is over the threshold, only 1dB will be outputted over the threshold. In other words, if a compressor is set to a 4:1 ratio and a signal comes in that is 4dB over the threshold, the signal coming out of the compressor will only be 1dB over the threshold (The signal has been attenuated by 3dB). This signal attenuation is known as Gain Reduction and a meter on the compressor will typically display the amount of gain reduction happening to the signal at any given time. Most compressors will allow users to select ratios from 1:1 up to 10:1 in single-digit steps (meaning you can select from 1:1, 2:1, 3:1, and so on and so on). However, some high-end compressors (especially in the digital realm), will allow users to select any number they wish and not limit them to whole numbers, meaning that a user could select a ratio of, say, 1.15:1. This type of extreme fine tuning of ratios is used heavily in mastering.

### Attack

The attack setting on a compressor tells the compressor just how fast to start compressing once a signal has passed the threshold. Typically, the attack settings of a compressor will be displayed in a unit of time usually allowing the user a range from 1ms to a few seconds (some compressors even allow the user to set the attack in microseconds). As with everything in mixing, it is important to listen to what you are compressing when determining what attack time is appropriate. For example, when compressing a transient sound like a snare drum, which has an extremely quick "snap" and then dies off suddenly, it might be beneficial to set a slower attack in order to maintain that initial "snap" whereas a quick attack time would compress that initial "snap." When compressing

**Figure 6.9** A Visual Example of Ratios

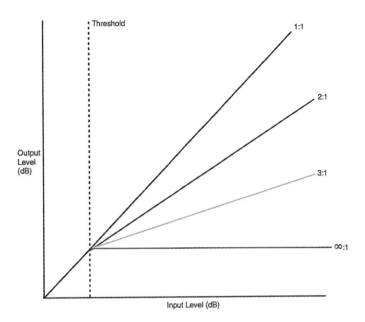

a bass, however, a faster attack time might prove more beneficial in order to control and lower the transients. Therefore, it is extremely important to listen to the signal in order to select appropriate attack settings.

*Release*

The release control on a compressor can be thought of as the opposite of the attack control. While the attack control tells a compressor how fast to start compressing, the release control tells the compressor how fast, or slow, to bring the compressor back to "normal." Just as with the attack control, the release control can be set between 1ms and a few seconds (again with microseconds not being uncommon to see). Like when setting the attack, it is important to listen to the particular sound you are compressing when setting the release. For example, when compressing a bass guitar, which you want to have very little dynamic range, you would set the release extremely slow in order for the compressor to be "working" as long as possible.

### Makeup Gain

As stated earlier in the ratio section, a compressor works by attenuating and reducing the gain of a signal. Therefore, most compressors will offer a way in which the user can boost the overall output of the compressor in order to compensate for the level that was reduced from compression.

### *Hard and Soft Knees*

All compressors, in some form or another, will feature controls for threshold, ratio, attack, release, and makeup gain. However, some compressors will also offer other controls for the user to manipulate. One control that might be found is the knee setting. The knee setting refers to the response curve of the compressor—in other words, how aggressively it reduces gain. Typically the user will be able to choose between a "soft knee" and a "hard knee." A soft knee will have a more gentle curve when attenuating the signal while a hard knee will have a more rigid curve. Although most compressors that offer knee control will only allow selection between hard and soft knees, there are a few compressors that allow continuous control over the knee setting.

### *Side Chain/Key Input*

Many compressors offer an alternate means of control via what is known as side chaining. In a typical scenario, the compressor is triggered by the signal of the track the compressor is inserted on. However, through side chaining, we can trigger the compressor via any other signal. For instance, by inserting a compressor on a music track and keying the compressor off of a vocal track, the compressor will be triggered by the voice: meaning, that every time the vocal is heard, the music track will be compressed. Radio and TV shows make great use of this technique that in the aforementioned scenario would lower the level of the music whenever someone was talking and would bring it back to normal when the talking stopped. In more recent years, this technique of side chain compression has also become a staple in

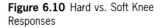

**Figure 6.10** Hard vs. Soft Knee Responses

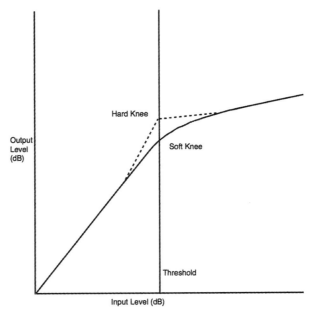

electronic music, producing the well-known "pumping synth" sound. In this scenario, the artist would add a kick drum playing quarter notes to the session and output it on an unused bus. Then, he would insert a compressor onto the desired synth track and select that bus as the keyed input. Then by setting the threshold and ratio to extreme degrees and adjusting the attack and release so that when combined they equate to an eighth note, according to the tempo of the track, a rhythmically pumped synth will result. The uses of side chaining are endless and can be used in both practical and creative ways.

### Stereo Linking

Although not found on software compressors, many hardware compressors offer the ability to "stereo link" them. Stereo Linking means that the user can connect two compressors and control them both with the controls of one of them. This is an extremely useful tool when stereo compression is

**191**

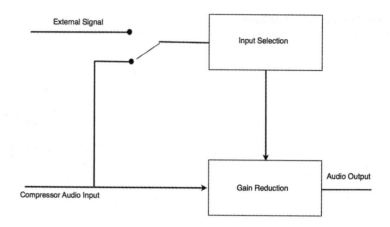

**Figure 6.11** Parallel Compression Allows External Sounds to Trigger Compression on a Designated Track

needed. When compressing a stereo MIDI or audio track with an external compressor, "Stereo Linking" is essential.

## Limiting

Limiting is compression with a higher ratio setting. Most engineers consider a compressor with a ratio of 10:1 or higher to be a limiter. Limiters are used frequently as a safety measure in both live sound and broadcast in order to protect the equipment from extreme peaks and to ensure the signal stays below a certain level. Limiting is also used extensively in mastering as a means to increase the overall level of a song without hitting the output ceiling.

## Expanders and Gates

For all intents and purposes, an expander is the opposite of a compressor. It works in the same manner as a compressor but rather than reducing dynamic range, it increases dynamic range. Typically, expanders will have the same controls as a compressor but will be used to increase dynamic range rather than diminish it. Gates, on the other hand, effectively cut out any signal below a certain point in which the user sets via the threshold control. Gates can be thought of as physical gates or doors that stay closed to unwanted things: in this

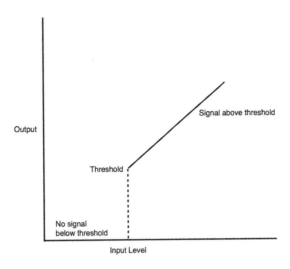

**Figure 6.12** Gates Only Allow Sound to Be Heard above a Designated Threshold

case, any signal below a certain level. In the same manner, gates open to desired things (signal above a certain level). Like most things in audio processing, gates can be used for a variety of different scenarios both practical and creative. In mixing, engineers will oftentimes place gates on individual drum mics in order to reduce bleed from other drums, which, in turn, effectively isolates the individual drum.

## Spectral-Based Effects

Oftentimes, while mixing a track, it is necessary to change the sound of a particular instrument either subtly, to bring it out in the mix, or drastically for creative reasons. As can be assumed, spectral effects change how the sound is heard in the sound spectrum. This family of effects includes equalizers, multiband compressors, and sonic enhancers, as well as a multitude of various "boutique effects."

### Equalizers

Equalizers, or EQs, work by cutting or boosting particular frequency ranges. This boosting and cutting is achieved by manipulating the signal's phase. Analog EQs contain capacitors and inductors in their circuitry, and these components are designed to shift the phase of the selected frequency band. When the phase-shifted signal is combined with the original signal, the frequency band is diminished or accentuated based on the degree of phase shifting. Digital and software-based EQs use digital means when changing the phase of a particular frequency band in order to achieve the same effect. Depending on the phase shift, the selected frequency band will either be boosted or cut. The depth of these phases shifts affect the "sound" of the EQ, which is why engineers favor certain EQs over others.

Although there are a variety of different types of EQs, most of them fall under the families of graphic EQs and parametric EQs. Before we dive into the difference between graphic and parametric EQs, it is important to examine the different parameters found on equalizers.

### Filter Types

Many EQs (especially in the software world) will offer selectable filter types for each band of frequencies being affected. The filter type will determine how the selected frequency band will be boosted or cut. The main filter types are known as pass filters, shelving filters, and notch filters.

### Pass Filter

A pass filter will effectively cut off all frequencies below or above the selected frequency. Pass filters are used in order to completely cut high end or low end on a signal. Pass filters can be divided into two groups: low pass and high pass. A low-pass (or high-cut) filter will eliminate all frequencies above a particular frequency. Therefore, this type of filter effectively lets LOW frequencies PASS through, thus the name low pass.

Likewise, a high pass (or low-cut) filter will cut all frequencies below a particular frequency allowing the HIGH frequencies to PASS through. It's important to note that the frequency at which the filter will cut above or below is not always selectable

**Figure 6.13** Low-Pass Filters
Roll Off High-Frequency Content

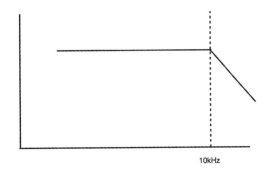

10kHz

**Figure 6.14** High-Pass Filters
Roll Off Low-Frequency Content

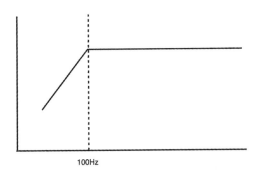

100Hz

by the user. Many hardware EQs, either sole units or found on a mixing console, will have set frequencies for their low- and high-pass filters. In the plug-in world, however, it is much more common to be able to adjust this frequency. This type of filter is extremely useful when cutting low-frequency "rumble" in say a vocal track or cutting high-end hiss.

### Shelving Filter

Like a pass filter, a shelving filter affects all frequencies above or below a specific point. With a shelving filter, however, the user is not only able to select the initial frequency but is also able to boost or cut all frequencies above or below it. Like pass filters, shelving filters are split into two distinct groups: high shelves and low shelves. The user also sets the amount

**195**

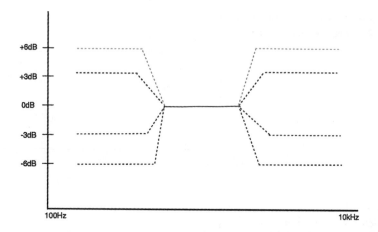

**Figure 6.15** A Visualization of Low- and High-Shelf Frequency Responses

by which the shelve boosts or cuts all the frequencies above and below the selected frequency. This type of filter is used extensively in mixing and mastering in order to add back some low end to a dull sounding signal, or vice versa, cutting some low end on a "boomy" signal. The same is true for high shelves; we can add air back to a signal that lacks it or lower some of the "biting" high-end factor.

### Notch Filter

Unlike Pass and Shelving filters, which affect all frequencies below or above a given frequency, notch filters affect the frequencies that surround a given frequency (which is called the center frequency). Notch filters can boost or cut this frequency range by a user-selectable amount.

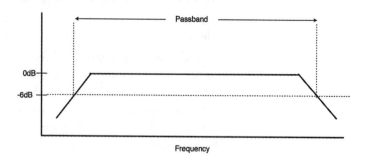

**Figure 6.16** Notch Filters Allow Users to Just Affect a Designated "Band" of Frequencies

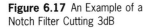

**Figure 6.17** An Example of a Notch Filter Cutting 3dB

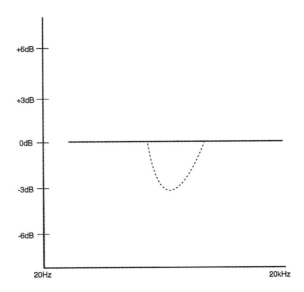

The range of frequencies around the center frequency that are affected by the notch filter are controlled by a parameter called the "Q." The Q controls just how wide or narrow the frequency range being affected is. The Q amount is displayed by a number that is inversely proportionate to the range of frequencies being affected: meaning, the higher the Q number, the narrower the frequency range, and vice versa.

Notch filters are used extensively while mixing in order to bring out or diminish certain attributes of a signal. For instance, a snare drum will typically have a ring to it whether it is desirable or not. A notch filter set to the frequency of the snare's ring can either accentuate this ring in the mix or diminish it. Notch filters are also used extensively when making room for sounds that share a similar frequency range—like a kick drum and a bass guitar.

## Graphic Equalizer

A graphic equalizer is a unit that features a number of notch filters, each with set Q's in which the signal passes through. The user can control the amplitude of these set frequencies

**197**

**Figure 6.18** Varying "Q"
Amounts on a Notch Filter Boost

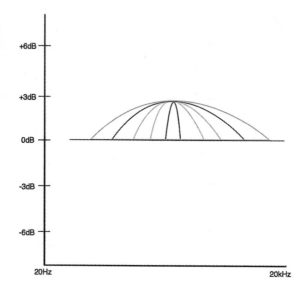

**Figure 6.19** Varying "Q"
Amounts on a Notch Filter Cut

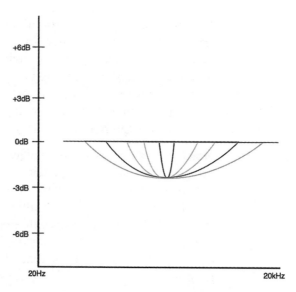

by either cutting or boosting them. The number of controllable frequency bands a particular graphic equalizer has will generally increase with cost. These notch filters are typically set at octave divisions apart from each other, meaning a ⅓ octave graphic equalizer, for example, would have center frequencies at ⅓ octave intervals. These equalizers are called graphic equalizers because, in hardware units, each center frequency has a slider that can be moved up or down that provides the user with a "graphic" representation of the EQ curve being applied to a signal. Graphic Equalizers allow the user to have extreme control over their signal. Graphic equalizers are often applied to group buses or the master bus in both studio and live sound settings, but like anything else in the audio realm, they can be applied however the user best sees fit.

## Parametric Equalizer

A parametric equalizer is a multiband variable equalizer. Like graphic equalizers, parametric equalizers cover the whole sound spectrum, but unlike graphic equalizers, the user determines their center frequencies and Q amounts. A parametric equalizer will typically feature a high-pass or low-cut filter, a few notch filters dedicated with controllable center frequency, Q amount, and cut and boost amounts, as well as a high shelving filter. This type of variability allows the user complete control over the sound. Unlike graphic equalizers, which have center frequencies all the way through the sound spectrum at dedicated intervals, parametric equalizers are more limited in the sense that more units are needed in order to cover the entire sound spectrum simultaneously. However, having complete control over not only the boost and cut amount to a given center frequency, but the filter type and the Q amount, makes up for the aforementioned "limitation."

Parametric equalizers are used heavily on individual sounds in order to sculpt them to the user's liking. In the plug-in realm, a combination of the two types of equalizers are often seen, allowing the user to not only have the extreme control of a parametric EQ, but also the benefits of having a graphic representation of the EQ curve in which the user may tweak as well.

## Multiband Compression

A multiband compressor allows the user to apply compression to individual frequency bands of a signal rather than to the signal as a whole. A multiband compressor first takes the signal and splits it into a number of different frequency bands using a type of crossover filter. The number of different frequency bands the multiband compressor splits the signal into will vary depending on the individual unit. The user can oftentimes adjust where these different frequency bands start and end.

After splitting the signal into frequency bands, the user has normal compression controls for each band. When working on a bass guitar tone, for instance, a multiband compressor might be beneficial when the engineer wants to diminish the overwhelming low frequency response of the bass without affecting it sonically with a normal EQ. By placing a multiband compressor on a bass guitar, the engineer is free to compress only the low frequency and get it under control while leaving all other aspects of the bass guitar alone—something that can't be done with just a compressor or an EQ. Multiband compressors are often found in mastering suites as well.

**Figure 6.20** The Waves Linear Multi-Band Compressor Plug-In

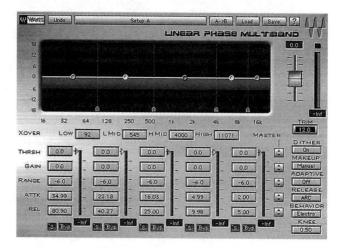

### Sonic Enhancers

A sonic enhancer like the Aphex Aural Exciter or the BBE Sonic Maximizer will add high harmonic content to a signal, making the signal appear "brighter" and "clearer" without actually boosting the high frequency content. These high frequency harmonics can be achieved by a complicated duplication circuit, which takes the existing high frequency harmonic content of the signal and adds it back to the original signal effectively doubling it, or through synthesizing high frequency harmonics and adding them to the original signal. Some units like the Aural Exciter also feature a similar feature for low end.

### Boutique Effects

A wealth of effects are available in both hardware and software varieties that dramatically change the sound of a signal. These types of effects are typically preset EQ curves designed to achieve a particular sound. An example of a "boutique effect" would be a Lo-Fi or telephone-type effect. This type of effect will most likely be an EQ in which everything below 300 Hz and above 3 kHz will be cut, resulting in a telephone-like sound.

**Figure 6.21** Sonic Enhancer Plug-In

**Figure 6.22** Avid "Sci-Fi"
Boutique Effect

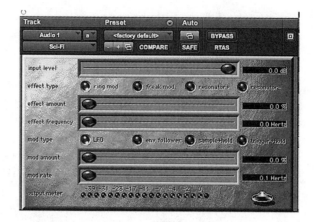

**Figure 6.23** Avid "Lo-Fi"
Boutique Effect

## Time-Based Effects

Time-based effects, as can be assumed, take place over time. Any effect that alters the signal's timing, even in the slightest degree, is categorized as a time-based effect. Therefore, this family of effects includes the obvious delay and echo effects but also contains flange, chorus, reverb, and pitch-shifting effects.

### Reverb

Audio engineers have long been interested in the effect naturally reverberant rooms have on a sound being recorded.

A highly reverberant room can add extreme depth to an instrument that it otherwise wouldn't have.

Therefore, engineers have long sought out means in which to add this depth to signals without physically recording in giant halls. Perhaps the first way engineers achieved this effect was through the use of echo chambers.

**Figure 6.24** The Waves Renaissance Reverb

**Figure 6.25** The Waves Tru-Verb Plug-In

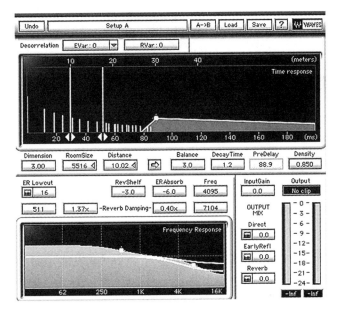

An echo chamber would typically be a medium-sized room with reflective walls and a speaker and microphone placed in it. The engineer would play the signal he wanted to add echo to through the speaker, allowing it to bounce off the reflective surfaces and then the microphone would pick up the resulting signal. Not long after, however, hardware units were designed to create this effect.

## Plate Reverb

Soon after the implementation of echo chambers, engineers began using plate reverbs. A plate reverb is a large piece of sheet metal with a transducer, akin to the driver of a loud speaker, attached to the plate along with a pickup, which captures the vibration of the plate. Most plate reverbs also have a dampening pad so that the engineer can adjust the overall reverb time. Most early plate reverbs had a mono transducer and pickup but some later models allowed for stereo content. Due to the plate reverb's immense size, many plate reverb units

**Figure 6.26** A Rendering of an "Echo Chamber"

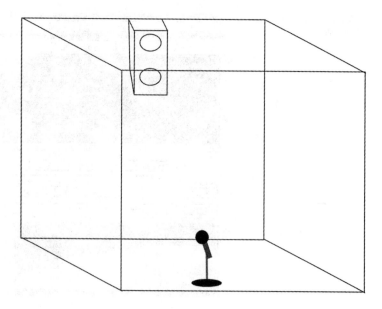

also featured remote control units so the engineer could control the plate while the plate itself was set in a separate room.

### Spring Reverb

A spring reverb is similar to a plate reverb but instead of a large metal plate, the transducer and pickup are placed on either ends of a spring. Due to their small size and low cost, when compared to a plate reverb, many semiprofessional studios adopted this technology. Spring Reverbs are mostly found inside of guitar amplifiers.

### Digital Reverbs

Since reverberation is, in essence, a large number of delays happening in quick succession of each other, digital devices soon came along, which through simple feedback circuits, the reverberation effect could be mimicked. Since all the delays are created digitally in these units, the user has an extreme amount of control over all aspects of the effect. Some parameters that may be found on a modern digital reverb are as follows.

### Reverb Type

Most modern reverbs have an extreme amount of onboard modeling so that they can mimic anything from a grand orchestral hall or cathedral, all the way to the cheapest spring reverb. Therefore, on most reverb units, the user is able to choose what type of reverb he wants to apply to his sound.

### Pre-Delay

The pre-delay of a reverb is the amount of time between the initial, dry, sound and the reverberated delays. This control allows users to fine tune just how large or small the reverb is perceived as. In a large cathedral, for example, there would be a significant amount of time between someone clapping her hands and the resulting echo whereas if one were to clap her hands in a bathroom; this time would be much shorter. Therefore, modern reverb units give the user this control.

### Decay Time

The decay time of a reverb is the amount of time it takes for the reverb tail to decrease to 0dB. By controlling this amount, the user can shorten or lengthen the reverb tail in order for it to fit into a particular mix.

### Diffusion

Although one of the subtlest controls on a reverb, the diffusion parameter determines how "smooth" the reverb is perceived as. In an actual space, there are many aspects besides the physical walls, like angles, people, soft vs. hard surfaces, etc., that affect how the reverb tail dies out. The diffusion control mimics how the reverb would decay in a real space.

### Early Reflections

In a physical room, some reflections can be detected before the whole room is excited and causes reverberation. These reflections are aptly named early reflections. Although not all reverbs will have this control, it is an important one to understand because it allows the user even greater control over the sound.

**Figure 6.27** The Different Aspects of Reverb

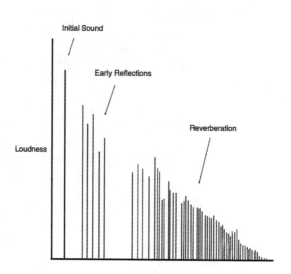

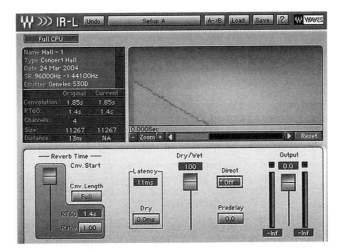

**Figure 6.28** The Waves Impulse Response Reverb

## Mix

The mix control lets the user determine how much of the initial "dry" signal is heard in relation to the effected "wet" signal. It is a fairly common practice to bus signals to a reverb in the same way we discussed in the level section of this chapter. When sending track to a reverb through a bus, one would typically leave the mix control at 100%, meaning only the "wet" signal is heard. Then the user would control how much of the dry signal is heard by the amount he sends to the reverb. It is only when inserting a reverb onto a track that this control is used heavily.

## Delay

A delay is an effect that stores audio and then plays it back later in time. Delays can be used to create extremely fast repetitive sounds akin to reverb or more drawn out, longer-spaced delays like and echo, as well as everything in between. Early delay units stored audio on tape, and the user could speed up or slow down the tape in order to speed up or slow down the rate of delays. Modern, digital, delays store audio in RAM either onboard the individual unit, or on the user's computer.

Delays are used to create a number of other effects besides the common echo-like chorus and flange.

### Chorus

A chorus is a delay unit that plays back the delayed sound, after slightly pitch shifting it in quick succession with the initial sound. The delayed sounds happen so close in time to the initial sound that it is not heard as two discreet sounds, but rather as one whole one.

### Flanger

A flanger is again a type of delay. Like with a chorus, the flanger effect repeats the delayed sound extremely close in time to the initial sound. The delay time, however, changes slightly causing the overall sound to appear to be changing in time.

### Pitch Shifting

Although it might not seem to be a time-based effect, pitch shifting, in fact, is just that. In the analog tape domain, pitch shifting was achieved by speeding up or slowing down the tape in order to raise or lower its pitch, respectively. In the digital domain, pitch shift is achieved by writing audio to a memory and then resampling it to either a higher or lower sample rate. The newly sampled audio is then returned to the original sample rate resulting in a signal that is either higher or lower in pitch than the original. Unlike MIDI information that can be transposed higher or lower in pitch, audio must be resampled through pitch shifting in order to raise or lower it. Pitch shifting can be used for a number of different applications, but most commonly, it is used to fix vocal tracks with minor imperfections.

## Automation

When performing a mix on a project, it is extremely rare that once the faders are set to appropriate levels, they

**Figure 6.29** Waves Pitch Correction Plug-In

remain there for the entire duration of the song. In most cases, a vocal track, for instance, will have to change level throughout the mix in order to maintain its place within the mix. In years past, engineers were responsible for moving faders up and down to accomplish this when recording their mix to tape. In modern days, however, the user can control these level changes with a computer. In fact, prior to digital audio workstations coming about, studios would sometimes have motorized faders on their console that would be controlled with a dedicated computer. This type of motorized fader, although mostly replaced by digital audio workstations, is still seen in some studios. The modern DAW achieves these level changes through what we call automation.

### Automation Modes

Most DAWs will have various modes of automation in order to make it easier on the user while writing automation. These modes will perform complex functions for the user in order to allow them to do things they would not ordinarily be able to do on a traditional mixing console. It is important to read the automation section of your DAW's manual in order to learn what each of these modes do as all DAWs automation features are unique.

Automation is not limited to just fader level movement; most things like pan positions, mutes and solos, and even controls inside of plug-ins can be automated. This allows the user to have a complex mix in which tracks can move with the mix rather than remain stagnant, ultimately yielding a much more organic end product.

Although mixing is a skill that takes practice, utilizing the different aspects listed in this chapter will bring the user closer to his desired end mix.

Understanding the individual parts of mixing is one thing, but crafting a mix with all of the included elements is something completely different. The following example is designed to show you a more cohesive look at the mixing process when working with MIDI equipment.

## Example—Sculpting Sound Sources

When using MIDI you have an incredible amount of control over the sounds you are triggering. If you work within the

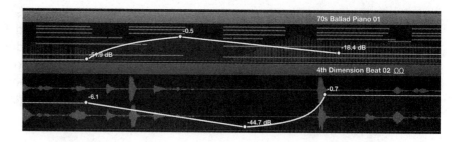

**Figure 6.30** An Example of Automation

MIDI parameters, then it is possible to create a song without mixing in the traditional sense. Instead the mix happens with the individual instruments using controls such as velocity and level/pan control on the instrument itself. Here is a list of instruments from our hypothetical mix:

1. Drums
2. Bass
3. Keys
4. Horns

1.  Sampled drums often sound really good without any mixing because they are processed during the instrument creation process. Manufacturers think that users won't like their instruments unless they already sound finished, and yet many engineers purposely seek out sampled instruments that sound more natural so they can process them to their own taste. In this situation find a drum kit that you like and make sure the velocities are all set appropriately. If your drum module has a reverb effect then try to find one that works in the genre and with the drum sound.
2.  Getting the bass sound right is more about picking a patch that works than processing in this scenario. Instead of using a compressor or limiter you can set the velocities to be consistent.
3.  Getting the keyboard part to fit in the mix is harder without processing but can be accomplished through panning out of the center to make room for the other instruments and being careful with note lengths; and you must sustain pedal usage to keep the sound clear. It is almost always better to adjust levels of keyboard instruments using the velocity control because it changes the sound of the instrument instead of just the volume.
4.  Horns are tricky because "fake" horns never quite sound as good as a real horn section. It is possible to make a close imitation with the right patch and careful programming of velocities, modulation, and pitch bending. Horn players rarely play exactly in tune all of the time and instead they are constantly bending notes. It is possible to mimic a realistic performance by using the pitch wheel and sometimes the mod wheel to adjust the timbre of the instrument in various ranges and loudness.

All of the necessary controls are available on the instruments using MIDI to make a great sounding track. Traditional mixing still plays an important role when it comes to song production because of the complexity of instruments involved and the inclusion of non-MIDI tracks.

## Note

1. A potentiometer is a variable resistor with a finite path. Typically, these potentiometers have a pole extended from them with a knob attached in which the user can rotate to sweep the various resistance ranges. An example of a potentiometer would be the volume control on a stereo as well as the volume or tone knobs on an electric guitar.

# USING MIDI LIVE     7

MIDI has become a staple in live performance. The technology has not only made it easier on artists, allowing them to have the sounds of 100 instruments while only bringing 1, but has also changed the way performers play live. The advent of MIDI on stage has also transformed the concert-going experience and has allowed for extreme creativity along the way.

## Traditional Setups

In the early days of MIDI, artists were skeptical of performing with the new technology. With its inconsistencies and frequent fail rates, artists were unwilling to trust the success or failure of a show on MIDI. The benefits of the technology, however, soon overcame the artist's original skepticism.

Keyboardists were among the first to begin adopting the technology into their live setups. Using MIDI on stage allowed

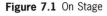 **Figure 7.1** On Stage

**Figure 7.2** Traditional
MIDI Setup

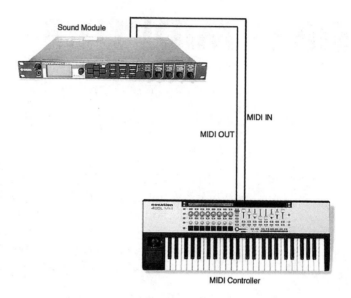

keyboardists to play pianos, electric keyboards, organs,
marimbas, synthesizers, and a wealth of other instruments
without actually having to bring each of these instruments to
every show. These performers would simply have a flight
case with a variety of MIDI sound modules and a keyboard
controller on stage, which allowed for extreme portability.
This was a giant leap forward for performers because, for the
first time, musicians did not have to choose between portability and the sounds they wanted. This allowed the musicians to no longer be limited to the sounds of the instruments
they brought to a show. This type of sound module/keyboard
controller setup is still extremely prevalent in modern live
performances and remains one of the most common MIDI
setups for live applications. However, on the modern stage,
the sound modules will oftentimes be replaced by a laptop.

Besides having access to a variety of different instruments,
MIDI allows keyboardists to map different sounds to different ranges on their controllers, which allows the keyboardist
to execute performances that would be near impossible if he
were physically switching to different keyboards for each
part.

The keyboardist can also map out effects like filter sweeps and modulation amounts to different knobs on his MIDI controller for easy access. Mapping out of effects and sounds is done inside the included MIDI controller software along with the software the performer is running for his sounds.

Due to the overwhelming variety of MIDI controllers on the market, practically any musician can benefit from using MIDI on stage. Like with keyboardists, drummers are able to use MIDI drum sets, which not only allow for extreme portability, but also allow for a wide variety of sounds other than traditional drum set sounds. Although complete stand-alone MIDI drum sets are not as common as they once were on stage, a combination of an acoustic drum set and MIDI pads is becoming extremely common among drummers. These

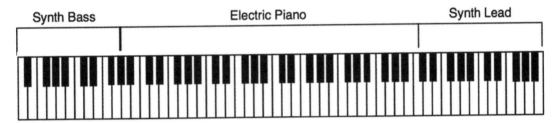

**Figure 7.3** Example of Different Instrument Keyboard Mappings

**Figure 7.4** MIDI Drum Pads

MIDI pads are either connected to a stand-alone sound module in order for set sounds to be triggered when hit, or they are connected to a laptop where loops and sound effects can be triggered. The same functionality is available for wind/brass players and guitarists as there are controllers modeled after these instruments.

## MIDI Control

Many guitarists have realized the benefit of using MIDI onstage. Aside from turning their guitars into virtually any instrument, MIDI allows for extreme control over effects and patches in a live guitar setup. By using a MIDI foot controller and interconnecting it via MIDI with each effect and amp-modeling unit, the guitarist can easily make drastic, preprogrammed changes to his guitar tone that would not otherwise be possible through traditional stomp boxes and channel selector foot switches.

When using MIDI to control a guitar setup, the guitarist is dealing with two types of MIDI instructions: "Program Change Instructions" and "Continuous Controller Messages." Program Change Instructions tell the individual units when to change patches. When used in conjunction with multiple effects units and amp-modeling units, the guitarist can create extremely complex patch changes by only stepping on one pedal. Therefore, the guitarist could switch between a distorted, high-gain, lead channel with delay to an ultra-clean channel with chorus, reverb, and compression with just one preprogrammed foot stomp. Continuous Controller Messages send a continuous value between 0 and 127 to the effects and amp-modeling units so the guitarist can control various parameters in real time. Therefore, the guitarist can do simple maneuvers like volume and wah wah swells or can even program in advanced control like changing the channel's gain setting while increasing the mix control on a delay unit with one movement of the foot controller.

**Figure 7.5** MIDI Foot Controller

**Figure 7.6** Example of MIDI Guitar Rack Control

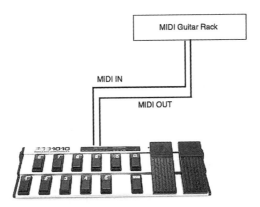

In a traditional guitar setup like the one listed above, the guitarist is limited to digital amp simulation units that would accept MIDI messages for their guitar tones. Although amp simulation has come a long way, many guitarists still prefer analog amp tones to their digital counterparts. This desire to use actual amps led many amp manufacturers to create digital controls for analog amps that include MIDI connections so the guitarist has the best of both worlds.

Any musician can use this type of MIDI control on stage. Keyboardists can change sounds and have real-time control over parameters along with bassists who can change amp tones and manipulate effects as well as vocalists who can have real-time manipulation over different vocal effects. The possibilities are endless for using MIDI control in a live setting.

## DJs and Electronic Artists

MIDI is perhaps seen most frequently when used in electronic music. The ability to control multiple devices simultaneously while having access to real-time manipulation of preprogrammed sequences lends itself perfectly to electronic music. In modern times, the majority of electronic music performances involve a single musician with a laptop and a few controllers.

Typically, the laptop will be running the DAW or sequencer of the musician's choice and the controllers will be set up to control the DAW or sequencer as well as any hardware synthesizers.

**Figure 7.7** Modern Electronic Music MIDI Controller

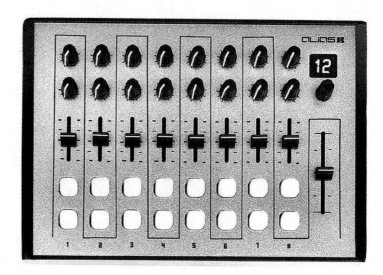

The gap that once existed between electronic musicians and DJs is quickly narrowing. Traditionally, the DJ was the sole performer who incorporated preprogrammed loops and affected them in real time while the electronic musician utilized live performance on electronic instruments. In today's music industry, however, the line that separates DJs from electronic musicians is not as clear. It is becoming more common to refer to an artist as an electronic musician while he's in his studio, and then refer to him as a DJ while performing live.

MIDI is utilized heavily in both live and studio settings by the modern electronic artist. These artists will use MIDI to control external synthesizers and sound modules as addressed earlier but will also heavily use their DAW or sequencer of choice as a pseudo-instrument via MIDI control and programming.

When creating material for a live performance, electronic artists will typically begin by creating a composition. Once the composition is written, the artist will then make sure she has independent control over all of the elements in the song such as bass, rhythm sections, lead melodies, vocals, etc. It is extremely common that the artist will map each of these elements to her MIDI controller so that she can "turn on" each element as she desires in real time. It is important to note that these artists will commonly have each element of the entire song playing continuously at all times. Then, while performing, the artist is free to enable, or un-mute, whatever instrument or element she pleases at any point in the performance in order to create a unique live composition. Next, the artist will begin placing effects over each of these tracks in which she can manipulate in real time. Some typical effects would include filters, delays, reverbs, bit crushers (or other forms of distortion), and modulation, just to name a few. The artist will also make sure to map each desired parameter of these effects to her MIDI controller. Finally, the artist will place master effects onto the song that would include tempo manipulation, pitch shifting, and filters, just to name a few. Again, the artist will make sure she maps out the desired parameters of these effects that she wants to control onto her MIDI controller.

**Figure 7.8** Example of Possible MIDI Controller Mapping

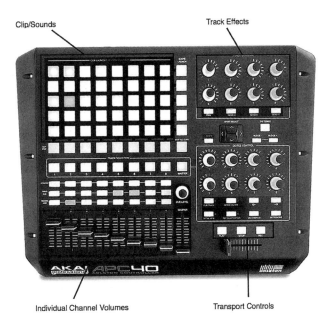

Clip/Sounds

Track Effects

Individual Channel Volumes

Transport Controls

By giving themselves access to a vast array of clips and effects, artists can create extremely unique performances at every show. The ability to map effects and clips to a MIDI controller as well as the artist-inspired evolution of DAWs and sequencers have been instrumental to making electronic music performances become not only less stagnant, but extremely spontaneous and intimate.

## DAWs and Sequencers

DAWs and sequencers exist at the heart of live MIDI performance. Through them, the artist has control over all of his prerecorded and programmed clips, as well as all of their effects, synthesizers, and drum machines. The artist will use his DAW or sequencer of choice in order to map out and place desired controls on his MIDI controller. Currently, there are many choices in software for the live performer; each program is unique and has its pros and cons. In the end, it is up to the user to determine which software is best suited for his individual needs.

### MainStage

MainStage is a live performance software, developed by Apple. The original software came free when users purchased Logic Pro. MainStage is designed to organize all of the preinstalled instruments on the user's computer into one easy-to-access window for live performance. Although the original MainStage allowed for some control over effects and backing tacks, the software was really intended to be used as a software-based sound module. However, after the extreme popularity of other live MIDI software became apparent, Apple went back to the drawing board to design MainStage 2.

MainStage 2 features the same capabilities of MainStage 1, but with so much more. The software is geared toward live performers who perform alone so there are some unique features in order to create a "one-man-band." First, the software is completely compatible with the majority of MIDI

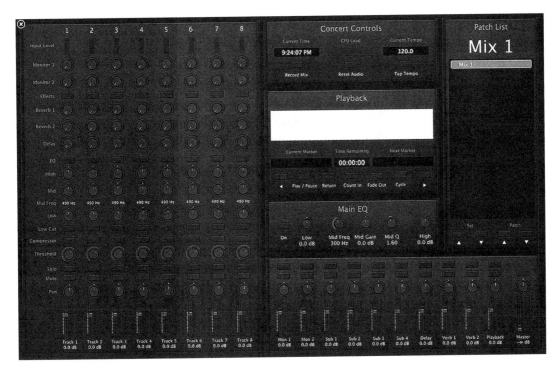

**Figure 7.9** MainStage 2 Interface

**Figure 7.10** The MainStage 2
EQ Is the Same as the Logic EQ

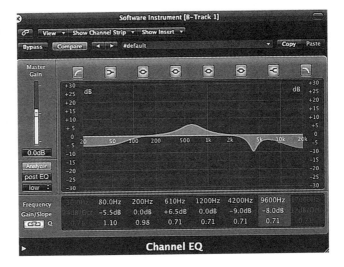

**Figure 7.11** Other MainStage
Plug-Ins Such as This Bit Crusher
Are the Same as in Logic

controllers on the market. Also, MainStage 2 allows the user
to map any control available to the software onto her MIDI
controller of choice. One nice feature about MainStage 2's
mapping capabilities is that once the user maps a parameter
to her MIDI controller, it stays that way until the user changes
it—eliminating the need to re-map parameters for separate
patches and songs.

Because MainStage 2 is geared toward one-man-bands, Apple
has incorporated some unique features into the software. The
user can load preprogrammed MIDI files and audio files into
the software to be used as backing tracks. Once these files are
loaded, the user designates where different sections, like the
chorus or bridge, for example, occur in time and set them to
the grid inside the program. Then the user can map each
section to a foot controller so that she can switch to any
section in the song, via the foot controller, at any time she
wishes. This allows the user to perform in a much more
spontaneous way than she would be able to by simply playing
along with a preset backing track.

Continuing with the one-man-band scenario, MainStage 2
gives users a vast array of "looping" controls in order to create
new compositions live. The user can create these loops completely electronically with MIDI drum pads and keyboards or

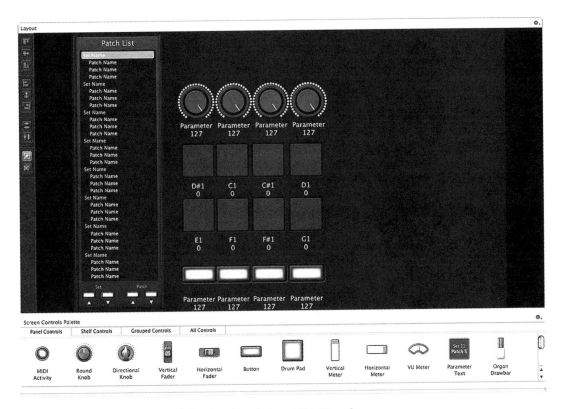

**Figure 7.12** Users Can Create Their Own Interfaces inside of MainStage 2

he can plug in an instrument like a guitar and create audio loops. The artist can also manipulate his loop compositions by adding or removing parts and restarting parts all via a user-mapped-out MIDI controller.

MainStage 2 is also tailored to the electronic artist. The artist is free to import MIDI files and then map each of them to his desired MIDI controller in order to enable or disable these loops at any time. The software also comes with a wealth of onboard effects that the artist can then place on individual tracks or on the song as a whole. The artist is then free to map these effects to any part of her MIDI controller of choice.

**Figure 7.13** Typical 'One-Man-Band' Interface in MainStage 2

**Figure 7.14** MainStage2 Drum Pads Interface

## Sonar (Live Matrix)

Sonar is a digital audio workstation created by CakeWalk. Although the program has always been a traditional recording software, pressure to compete in the ever-growing live MIDI market resulted in the creation of what is known as the "Matrix" view. The Matrix view is compiled of a variety of

**Figure 7.15** The Live Matrix
inside of Cakewalk's Sonar

cells arranged as columns and rows. Each cell has a single audio file and effects like a step sequencer and MIDI groove clips. The user then can trigger these sounds via the laptop keyboard or by mapping each sound to a MIDI controller. The user can also choose for the clips to start playing immediately, or in sync with the next beat. This feature is extremely helpful to live musicians because it allows them to completely play in time even if they trigger the sound a second early.

Although the program is designed for users to affect and control preprogrammed clips in live performance, Sonar's Matrix view also allows for live composition. By enabling something called "Capture Matrix Performance," the program records the loops the performer clicks. Therefore, the user can start by clicking a drum loop and once satisfied can add a bass loop to it by just clicking one of the bass loops. All the loops the user chooses will remain playing until the user unclicks them. Again, the user can select to have the loops start playing immediately when clicked, or she can set it so that the loops begin playing on the next beat. During the whole performance, Sonar is recording each loop and creating separate tracks for them to be recorded on. When the user clicks "stop" on the transport, all of the recorded loops will become audio files and then the user has a complete recording of the performance she just made. This can be an extremely beneficial means of composing songs on the fly or even a way of recording a live performance to release to fans at a later date.

Sonar's Matrix view also allows for traditional manipulation of clips on the fly. Like with most live performance MIDI programs, users can apply a wealth of onboard effects to each of their individual tracks as well as their overall song. Then through Sonar, the user is free to map any parameter of these effects to his MIDI controller. Due to the new Matrix view, Sonar is becoming an extremely popular live performance MIDI program.

## FL Studio

FL Studio is a digital audio workstation created by the company Image-Line. It was released in 1997 under its original name of FruityLoops. FL Studio is now on its 11th version, which was released in April of 2013.

Like most DAWs, FL Studio allows users to organize MIDI loops, record MIDI data, record audio, and manipulate everything via plug-ins. However, it wasn't until version 11 that

**Figure 7.16** FL Studio Interface

**Figure 7.17** The Effector Plug-In inside of FL Studio

FL Studio offered users a designated "Performance Mode." Like the other programs mentioned in this chapter, FL Studio's Performance Mode allows users to organize preprogrammed MIDI and audio loops into a play-list view and map them to a MIDI controller. Once mapped to his or her MIDI controller of choice, the user is then free to start affecting the various clips with powerful built-in effects.

One of the new effects that comes with FL Studio 11 is called "Effector." Effector is a multi-effects plug-in that allows for real-time manipulation of audio and MIDI clips. Effector contains 12 separate effects that include a distortion, a bit crusher, a high- and low-pass filter, a flanger, a phaser, a delay, a reverb, a stereo panning and binaural effect, a gate, and a granulizer, as well as vocal formant and ring modulation effects. One of the biggest benefits of Effector is that it's able to interface with touch pad controllers, allowing users extreme control with a visual representation overall of the onboard effects.

Another benefit to FL Studio is the ability to create visuals to complement the artists' music. Using the onboard "ZGameEditor Visualizer," users can create 2D and 3D video game-style visualization objects. ZGE Visualizer creates

**Figure 7.18** Z-Game Editor
Visualizer inside of FL Studio

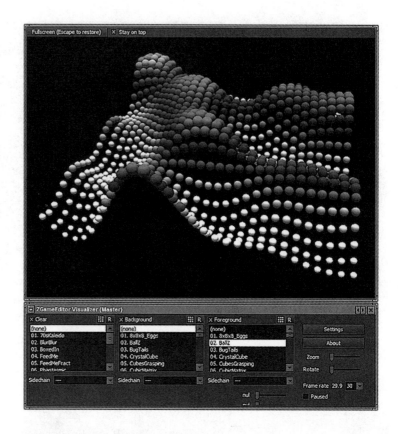

**Figure 7.19** FL Studio EQ

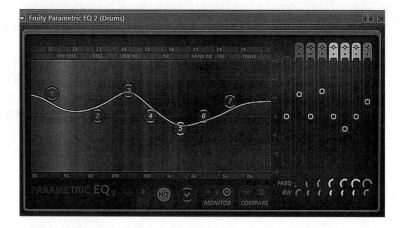

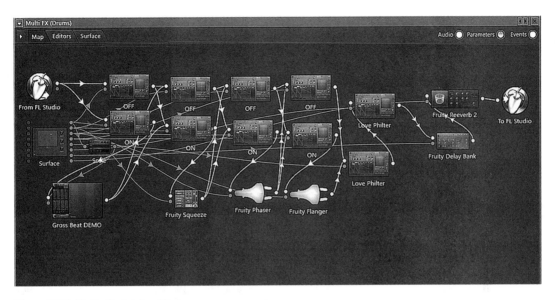

**Figure 7.20** FL Studio Patcher Window

real-time or rendered video effects that the user can automate to choose to have automatically synced with his FL Studio project. The capability to create visualizations that correspond with the user's music is a huge benefit in the electronic and multimedia art world where graphics are a huge part of the performance. Users can also render out these videos in order to upload them to YouTube, or any other video site, in order to promote their music.

FL studio has always been a popular sequencer and DAW but now with the advent of the new "Performance Mode," FL Studio is becoming one of the more popular live MIDI programs on the market.

### *Ableton Live*

Perhaps the software that started the entire live MIDI program revolution was Ableton Live. Ableton changed the way people thought about live MIDI performance and has remained the

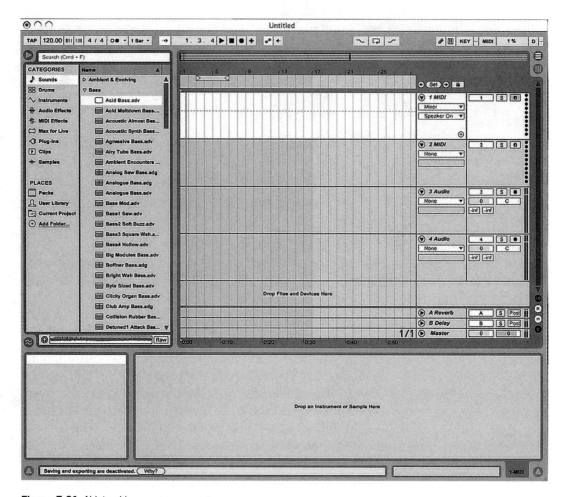

**Figure 7.21** Ableton Live

most popular live MIDI program since its inception. By introducing the ability to start and stop clips in perfect synchronization with the rest of the song, Ableton went on to change live electronic performance and still does so today.

Ableton Live is a sequencer and digital audio workstation that specializes in giving the user extreme control over all aspects of the software. When using Ableton, users are free to map virtually any knob on a controller or even a computer

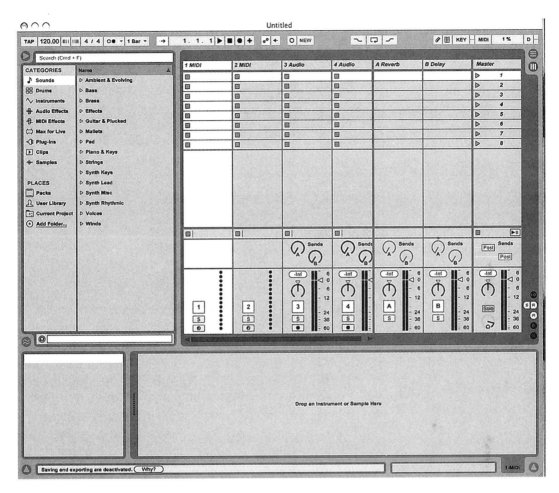

**Figure 7.22** Ableton Live

keyboard to any parameter inside of the software, allowing for extreme customization of workflow. Ableton has become the go-to software for musicians who incorporate computers into their live shows. One of the biggest benefits to this software is its real-time functionality. Any clip can be muted, activated, pitch shifted, effected, warped, and anything else the user desires in real time without affecting the system's playback.

**Figure 7.23** Filter Delay Plug-In inside of Ableton Live

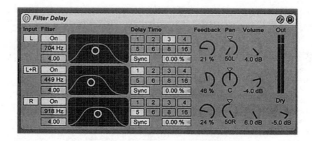

**Figure 7.24** Auto-Filter inside of Ableton Live

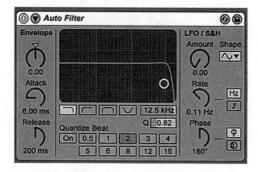

This type of real-time control is crucial when performing live in order for the audio outputted to be uninterrupted when changing settings. Everything that the user affects in Ableton also stays tightly locked to the grid. This means that when a clip is brought in or taken out, it is done so on exact beats regardless of whether the user triggers the clip exactly on a beat. Ableton was the first software to incorporate this type of technology into live MIDI performance, and it has been so popular that virtually every live MIDI program has incorporated it since.

By introducing MIDI controllers to the software, the software becomes "playable" to the performer. Many controller companies have paired with Ableton to come out with controllers specifically designed for the software. One of the most famous examples of this is "Push," a MIDI controller designed specifically for Ableton. Push features a large amount of touch pads as well as rotary knobs and a center cursor. The user is free to map any parameter or clip she

**Figure 7.25** Ableton Live EQ

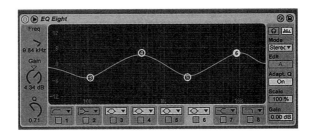

wishes onto the various touch controls on the Push. Like Push, the various types of Ableton designed controllers will typically have a large number of pads and some sliders and faders in lieu of traditional keyboard keys. Users are then free to assign different audio or MIDI clips to each of these pads and a wealth of effects parameters to the knobs and sliders. This allows the user to activate or mute certain clips in real time while adjusting overall or individual effects while the software plays back the project as a whole. The user can either save these MIDI assignments in order to recall them with each project or can create completely new assignments for each individual project. Although many sequencers have started to incorporate this type of functionality into their programs, Ableton is still the dominant software on the market.

## Max/MSP

Although not necessarily a DAW or sequencer, Max/MSP is a visual programming software designed for music and multimedia applications. Introduced initially as "Pure Data" by Miller Puckette, the software became an open-source phenomenon allowing for extreme innovation and creativity due to its extremely modular setup and intuitive interface. Musicians, composers, and installation/media artists were quick to adopt this new technology because it allowed them to program whatever they needed or desired for their individual projects.

The Max/MSP software interface is a blank window in which users create "objects" that communicate with any device both inside and outside of the computer. The software comes with over 700 predefined objects but allows the user to create his own as well as share objects with other users. Objects range anywhere from buttons to meters, to sliders, to advanced things like oscillators and movie boxes and messages. The user then interconnects these objects with other objects in order to create the desired product. Max/MSP is 100% user driven so there are virtually no boundaries when creating. Max can be used for almost any application. Users can use Max to create a custom software synthesizer or can create complex multimedia interactions between video and audio. Max uses the MIDI protocol so MIDI controllers can be programmed to affect any parameter inside the Max/MSP software as well. This type of MIDI functionality allows users to control anything from video to audio or even audience interactive content

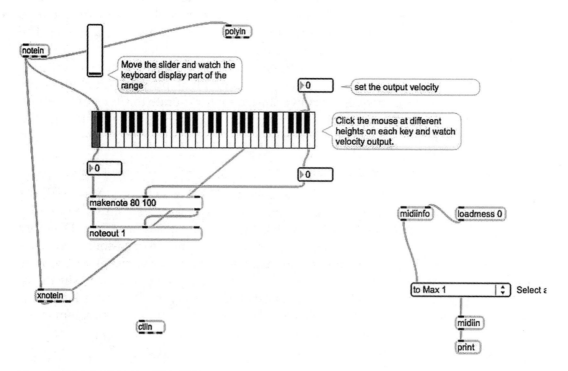

**Figure 7.26** A Patch inside of Max/MSP

all from standard MIDI commands, meaning the music and display can be completely intertwined.

Ableton works directly with Max/MSP through something called "Max For Live." Users can create various effects, meters, synthesizers, and controller interfaces inside of Max/MSP

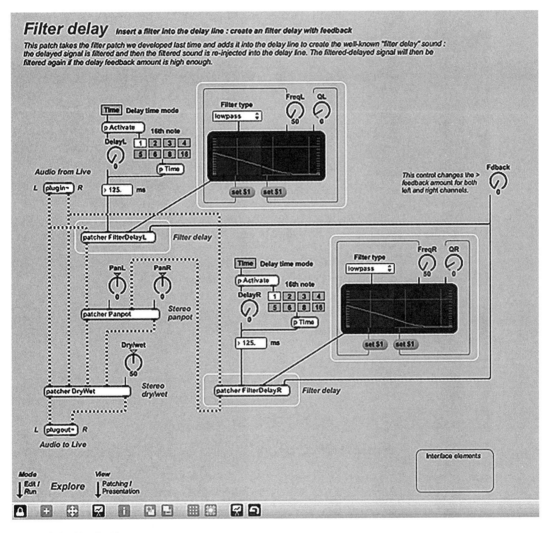

**Figure 7.27** Max for Live

that will show up in Ableton Live using Max For Live. Once inside of Ableton, the user can open up an edit window for each of his Max For Live devices and customize and change anything he wishes. This edit window interface looks just like a Max/MSP project window so people comfortable with using Max/MSP will be comfortable editing with Max For Live. Users can then share their Max For Live creations with other users. Both Ableton and Max/MSP pride themselves on catering to the open-source community, which is why so many musicians and artists have fled to these programs.

Using Max/MSP or software like it, performers can incorporate visuals and lights into their shows that directly correlate with the music being played. This type of multimedia incorporation can be as little as creating a Max patch that turns a strobe light on at each kick drum hit; or it can be an extremely complex, choreographed sequence in which anything the performer desires can be achieved. The electronic super group Daft Punk incorporates this type of integration into their show so they are not only controlling the music, but the entire show—lights and all—at any given time.

Multimedia integration during live performances has completely changed the dynamic of a show and transformed it into more of an interactive art installation. Perhaps due to the oftentimes monotonous stage presence of a single musician at a turntable, the integration of various medias was an evolution that needed to happen to electronic music. Nonetheless, multimedia integration is becoming apparent in many different genres of music besides electronic and dance music. Many bands have begun to incorporate multimedia presentations into their live performances.

## MIDI Mapping

An important aspect to performing live with MIDI is the ability to map various parameters to a MIDI controller. Typically, any user adjustable parameter inside a DAW or sequencer can be mapped to a controller meaning; the user can hit a pad, turn a knob, or press a key on his controller in order to perform certain functions rather than having to use the mouse and computer keyboard. The first step in mapping out MIDI controls is to ensure you have the proper drivers installed on your computer for the specific MIDI controller in question. Next, it may be helpful to ensure you have the most current driver as they tend to be updated frequently. All MIDI mapping will take place inside of the specific DAW or sequencer you are using. Every program will be slightly different when dealing with MIDI mapping but the theory is the same throughout. Basically, you are telling the software to allow external control over individual parameters. Most DAWs and sequencers will feature an "auto-map" type function that will automatically map certain common parameters to recognized MIDI controllers (recognized meaning the user has the driver for that controller installed on the same computer as the DAW or sequencer). However, these auto-map functions can be extremely limiting as it selects which controls on the device will perform various commands, which sometimes contradicts the desired workflow of the user. These auto-map functions will also decide the values (between 0 and 127) that each control can adjust between. Therefore, it is important to know the basics of mapping MIDI in order to create a personalized and complementing workflow. I'll address the basics of mapping MIDI information to external controllers in the four DAWs listed above: MainStage, Sonar, FL Studio, and Ableton Live.

## MIDI Mapping (Main Stage)

Once the appropriate drivers are installed on your computer and the MainStage software is open, the user is free to map MIDI controls to the program. MIDI mapping is done through "learning" or "assigning." In "learn" mode, MainStage maps default controls such as key depression, pitch bend, and modulation, to their appropriate controls in the program when the user first uses any of these controls. To map faders, knobs, and buttons, MainStage uses "assign" mode. To make assignments, first the user must open the "assignments and mappings" table. The left column of the assignments and mappings table lists the available assignments in the patch, the middle column lists any screen control to which hardware control is assigned, and the right column shows the mapping for each control. Users can then modify, delete, or add mappings all in the assignments and mapping table.

### MIDI Mapping (Sonar)

When using the "Matrix" view in CakeWalk's Sonar, MIDI mapping is fairly simple and intuitive. First the user must ensure the proper drivers are installed on his computer for his particular MIDI controller and then he must open up Sonar. Like most DAWs and sequencers, Sonar will automatically recognize MIDI controllers and assign the keys, pitch bend, and modulation wheel to their appropriate controls without the user having to assign anything. To assign specific knobs, keys, or pads to clips inside of the Matrix view, the user must right click the desired cell he wants to map and then click "MIDI Learn." Because the Sonar Matrix view is extremely similar in layout to Ableton Live, many controllers designed specifically for Ableton that feature "automap" functionality, like the Novation Launchpad, can be utilized to work with Sonar's Matrix view by simply enabling the "automap" function on the controller.

### MIDI Mapping (FL Studio)

Like most DAWs and Sequencers, FL Studio allows users to map various controls on their MIDI controller to control virtually any aspect of the program. In "Performance Mode," users are free to map various performance-related controls to their MIDI controller of choice. FL Studio's Performance Mode features an "auto-detect" function in which it recognizes popular MIDI controllers and default maps performance controls to said controllers. Typically, this auto-detect function is more than suitable for performers, however, users can completely customize their mappings. To begin mapping controls to a particular MIDI controller, users must select their controller and then open up the "MIDI options" page by clicking F10. Then, users are free to map the various performance controls to their desired positions on their controller. Although any type of traditional MIDI controller can be used in performance mode, FL Studio suggests that "performance pad" type controllers are best suited for performance mode.

## MIDI Mapping (Ableton Live)

Perhaps the easiest and most intuitive program to map MIDI is Ableton Live. Because Ableton specializes in complete user-customized control, the programmers have made it

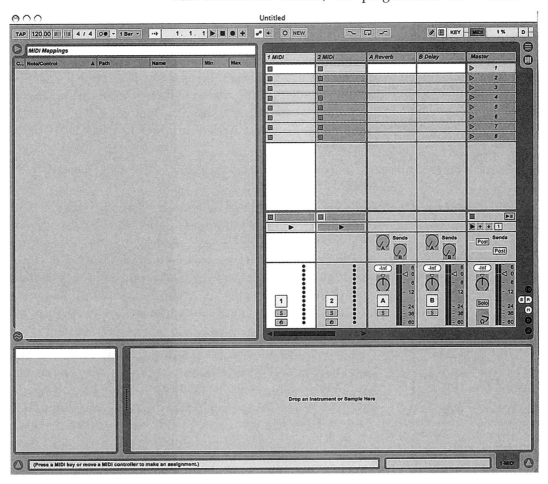

**Figure 7.28** MIDI Map View inside of Ableton Live

extremely easy to map MIDI to any control inside of the software. Again, the user must ensure that the appropriate drivers for his MIDI controller are both installed and up to date on his computer. Once the controller is connected and the Ableton software is running, the user will select the MIDI icon in the top right corner of Ableton. By selecting the MIDI icon, any assignable control in the software will become highlighted. Ableton's control chain list will also become visible on the left side of the screen. The user then clicks one of the highlighted controls he wishes to assign. Once the control on the software is clicked, all the user has to do is turn the control he wants to assign it to on his MIDI controller and Ableton will create the assignment. The user can also ensure the MIDI assignment was successful by looking in the control chain to the left of the screen as the new assignment should appear in the chain. The user can then save his particular MIDI mapping as a template in order to recall it at a later date if he so wishes.

## OSC

Although MIDI has been the industry standard since 1983, it certainly has not been immune to criticism. Various sects of people believe that MIDI is somewhat limiting in its nature as well as being viewed as a dead-end technology. Therefore, much time and effort has been placed into coming up with a new protocol to become the industry standard. The main forerunner in this search is something known as Open Sound Control, or OSC.

First developed by Adrian Freed and Matt Wright at the University of California Berkley's Center for New Music and Audio Technology, or CNMAT, OSC was not originally intended as an attempt to combat the perceived limitations of the MIDI protocol. Instead, OSC was originally developed in order to share music performance data, which include gestures, parameters, and note sequences, between computers, musical instruments, and various multimedia devices. However, it was not long until OSC began to be viewed as a possible replacement for the 30-year-old MIDI technology due to its immense possibilities and promise.

Like MIDI, OSC is a protocol, which sends messages between devices, in order for them to communicate together. Although OSC is not limited to a certain standard for transmission, most devices that feature the technology have traditionally transmitted OSC data through an Ethernet connection. By transferring these messages over Ethernet, OSC can be substantially faster than traditional 5-pin MIDI DIN connectors. OSC has a potential transfer rate in the range of 10+ megabits/second whereas MIDI only has a 31.25 kilobit/second transfer rate. With the emergence of mobile devices and tablets into the multimedia realm, OSC is more frequently being transferred over a WiFi or Bluetooth connection.

One of the biggest complaints that has surfaced about MIDI over the years is its unreliable clock. Unlike MIDI, OSC does not have any mechanism for clock synchronization but instead relies on the interfacing devices to provide a means of absolute time. Rather than having a means of clock synchronization, OSC messages contain high-resolution time tags allowing for rapid resynchronization to eliminate the possibility of jitter (unwanted artifacts resulting from an unreliable clock source). The messages that OSC send can also be bundled together requiring the host software to receive them simultaneously allowing for even further synchronization.

Another one of the big advents of OSC is its unique naming scheme, which gives messages an HTML, URL-type address rather than the complicated mess of numbers that make up traditional MIDI messages. This URL-style naming scheme creates a hierarchal set of objects, which include synthesis voices, output channels, filters, and a memory manager making it easy to identify what each message is. The OSC naming scheme also allows for logical interfacing between programs.

Finally, OSC is extremely customizable. Due to the lack of consistent definitions of OSC messages, users are free to define them in regard to their own needs, allowing for an extremely personal workflow. MIDI on the other hand, is stuck with set definitions such as note-on, note-off, etc. By not limiting the user to set definitions of messages, controllers and software that utilize OSC data, can be adapted to the user's needs rather than the user having to adapt his needs to the controller and software. When using OSC, the user must typically set definitions for the OSC messages being transmitted inside of both the software and controller. Some devices and software, however, have preset definitions for OSC messages but they are not standardized—meaning various OSC messages can have completely different definitions in different software.

## OSC Devices

The most popular device to feature OSC was the Lemur by the French company Jazz Mutant. The Lemur was an extremely advanced touch surface controller, which could be programmed by the user in order to control any software or device of their choosing. The user was also free to create a graphic interface made up of touch faders and touch knobs, which would then be programmed to control any parameter available on his software and devices. The Jazz Mutant Lemur was extremely innovative being the first practical, completely customizable touch surface controller. The Lemur gained extreme popularity with DJs and electronic musicians alike, and it truly seemed like it was the future as far as controllers were concerned. However, the Jazz Mutant Lemur's rise to success was short lived due to the release of the Apple iPad. The iPad could potentially do all the things that made the Lemur so successful, along with much more. Another important factor, which led to the eventual discontinuation of the Lemur, was the fact that the Apple iPad was so much more affordable than the Lemur. In retrospect, although the iPad can do everything the Lemur can, the Lemur does these things more reliably due simply to the fact it was a dedicated device created by extremely intelligent engineers in the audio and multimedia fields.

Although the Lemur has since been discontinued, it has resurfaced in the form of an "app" available to the iPad. In fact, the majority of successful OSC controllers are in the form of apps. The most notable OSC controller is the app "TouchOSC" available for both Apple and Android platforms. TouchOSC, like the Lemur, is a completely customizable graphic interface in which the user controls various parameters of his choosing. Due to the fact in that it deals with OSC data, the user has extreme control over not only what the app controls, but how it controls it.

TouchOSC comes with free editing software, available to Mac, Linux, and Windows, in which the user creates and edits his layouts. The user must first set the size of his layout, which will depend on the device it will be displayed on. The user then decides if he wants this particular layout to be displayed vertically or horizontally on his device. Next, the user defines OSC messages. The app comes with preset OSC message definitions, but the user will typically have to manually define certain messages in order for the app to properly communicate with their host software. The defining of messages is where the OSC protocol really shines, as the user is not limited to values between 0 and 127 and 16 channels like with the MIDI protocol. Next, the user adds various controls to his layout with which he will eventually control his host software. Some examples of controls available to users are push buttons, toggle buttons, XY pads, faders, rotary knobs, multi-toggles, and timers, among many others. Once these controls are placed on the layout, the user then resizes them to represent his individual needs. Once the user is satisfied with his layout, he must set the properties of each control, determining the value range it will encompass as well as setting the definition of the OSC messages it will transmit. Again, the app offers default presets for OSC message definitions but the user will typically have to edit these definitions in order to best suit his needs. Once the layout has been finished, the user must sync it to his device in order for it to show up when using the app. This syncing is typically done via USB in a program such as iTunes.

Because Max/MSP accepts the OSC protocol, TouchOSC can be used to control Max/MSP as well. This ability to interface TouchOSC with Max/MSP opens the door for extreme possibilities, especially when interfacing with Max For Live. The possibilities are endless on what the user can control when interfacing TouchOSC with advanced coding software like Max/MSP and using both to manipulate host software like Ableton Live.

TouchOSC, however, is not limited only to the OSC protocol. TouchOSC also allows users to utilize the MIDI protocol if they prefer it. The layout editing and configuring is performed much the same as it would be when using OSC, but of course, the user is limited in values between 0 and 127 as well as the 16-channel limit. However, due to the fact that not all software supports the OSC protocol, MIDI may be the user's only option when using the app to control his chosen host. One major benefit of using MIDI with TouchOSC, however, is the ability to interface the app with traditional MIDI controllers and sequencers. The user can effectively turn TouchOSC into a graphic control surface in which he can interface with his older hardware controllers in order to expand on the physical controls he has access to in a performance.

### OSC vs. MIDI

Although the technical differences between the OSC and MIDI protocols have been given above, it is important to examine the practical differences between the two technologies. Although OSC is not stuck with having set definitions, making it that much more customizable and innovative, it is this precise lack of definitions that makes it challenging to implement. When using MIDI, any MIDI message, be it note-on or note-off or anything else, will have the same definition regardless of which software or controller it is being used with. This form of standardization is extremely beneficial not only because it allows for universal continuity, but also because it allows for greater product innovation. Due to

OSC not having set definitions for its messages and being completely user customizable, companies are hesitant to create controllers and software built around the protocol because they can't guarantee it will interface properly with other OSC controllers and software. Therefore, companies are more willing to create products built around the MIDI protocol where they can be sure these products will properly integrate with other MIDI products. Another reason companies are hesitant to create OSC products is because typically, a certain amount of knowledge and experience is required to work with OSC, eliminating the chance of "plug-and-play" type devices that can be achieved while using MIDI. OSC, on the other hand, gives users universal complete control over their software and devices and does so extremely reliably (when used over Ethernet). Currently however, only select devices and software incorporate the OSC protocol, whereas the MIDI protocol is universally adopted and available in virtually any device and software imaginable.

Both the OSC and MIDI protocols have their place among musicians and multimedia artists. Where MIDI lacks, OSC shines through, and vice versa. Both technologies offer unique and desirable functions. When used together, MIDI and OSC create an extremely powerful control environment. In the end, it is up to the user to determine which technology is better suited for his particular needs.

## Controllerism

With the advent of software like Ableton Live and its ability to completely interface with MIDI controllers in virtually any user-specified fashion, a new community has begun to emerge known as "Controllerists." Controllerism is the art of performing live solely on some type of MIDI or OSC controller. The performer will have many preprogrammed functions interfacing his software and controller in order to execute an interesting and riveting live performance. Controllerists typically perform alone, but groups of Controllerists are starting to emerge. Many Controllerists will also build their own innovative DIY MIDI and OSC controllers for live performance. Like Circuit Benders, these Controllerists will take apart various MIDI controllers and customize them to their individual needs.

The man that coined the term "Controllerism" is known as Matt Moldover, a self-proclaimed Controllerist who got his start from viral Internet videos showing off his innovative controller designs along with his extreme ability on the devices. Moldover has become extremely popular and performs the world over on his custom controllers.

Electronic music has long been associated with a single artist who writes and performs music alone. Therefore, the organic band dynamic has disappeared from many electronic compositions and performances. A paradigm shift is beginning to emerge in contemporary electronic music allowing for multiperson collaboration. Many DIY Controllerists have begun creating controllers in which multiple performers, or even audience members, are free to create music together. These devices have been termed "Jam Boxes" and exist on a fine line between installation art and live performance. When using these Jam Boxes, separate people on different areas of the device control all different aspects of the song like bass, drums, samples, and master effects, to name a few. The device is typically connected to one universal computer running the host software like Ableton Live or software like it. This has become an extremely innovative and popular way of incorporating different artists and audience members into a performance.

One of the first Jam Boxes created for the purpose of multi-artist involvement was a synthesizer known as the "Reactable." The Reactable is a large table with a giant interactive top. The artists place objects, known as "Tangibles," onto the interactive top, which reacts by outputting certain sounds and prompting more features to appear on the display. In essence, the Reactable acts as a modular synthesizer wherein each Tangible placed on the tabletop opens up a wealth of new paths and opportunities to affect the sound. The Reactable's sound engine is powered by the program "Pure Data," the open-source version of Max/MSP, and is run on a personal computer. There is a video camera underneath the table that records the user's movements and interactions with the device. There is also a projector underneath the table that projects the prompts and interactive display onto the table-top. Both the video camera and projector are connected to the computer and communicate with Pure Data. The Tangibles that the artists place on the tabletop have fiducials, or black and white images made up of various patterns of circles and dots, on their underside that allow the software to know which Tangibles are in use. Some Tangibles are flat with only one corresponding fiducial while some Tangibles are cubed with a corresponding fiducial on each side allowing for multiple functions of the same Tangible.

The Reactable has gained a lot of popularity in the multimedia art realm, allowing for patrons of the art show to join with other patrons in order to play this interactive instrument. Some artists such as Bjork have incorporated the Reactable

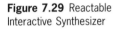

**Figure 7.29** Reactable Interactive Synthesizer

into their live show as a means to create an interactive spectacle. The introduction of the Reactable has made many musicians and companies rethink the way electronic instruments are created as well as the various interactive features they can offer musicians. Due to the success and innovative aspects of the Reactable, many companies and Controllerists have begun creating their own user interactive Jam Boxes.

Reactable now offers a mobile app that acts similar to their hardware Reactable. The app is designed after the original Pure Data software and allows users to insert virtual Tangibles onto the display. Although the app is somewhat limiting as far as its ability to interface with other devices and software, it acts as an interactive musical instrument for musicians and artists to enjoy.

## Expressive Control

Because electronic music performers have typically been sole performers, artists have begun experimenting with visually stunning expressive control in order to create a more impressive live show. One example of expressive control artists have begun using is body movements. Using Max/MSP, Max For Live, and a body recognition device like "Xbox Kinect," artists have created scenarios in which preconceived body motions transfer messages to their host software, which transforms these body motions into functions within the program. Using this method, artists have the ability to control any parameter of their host software with a simple gesture. In this way, artists transform their bodies into MIDI controllers, allowing for extremely innovative live performances. This type of body movement control is also seen at multimedia art installations. Some performers and artists have even begun experimenting with audience involvement and participation when dealing with body movement control.

Another example of extreme expressive control is the artist Imogen Heap's glove controllers. Although not specifically MIDI related, Imogen Heap's gloves demonstrate the immense possibilities of expressive control. Imogen Heap teamed up with a vast array of programmers and electrical engineers to create a wearable controller in which, through articulated gestures, she would be able to control various aspects of her music. Imogen Heap is able to perform filter sweeps and volume changes through hand twirls and wrist turns as well as a vast array of other parameter changes through hand gestures. Imogen Heap also wanted to be able to show the audience what was going on while she performed with the gloves so she had her programmers create program switches that would be obvious to the audience: for example, the act of physically picking up drum sticks would switch the glove controllers to drum mode.

Expressive control is an up-and-coming art form and is transforming live performance into a more visually appealing experience. The customizable nature of MIDI allows artists extreme control over their performances while exhibiting extraordinary creativity. Although the technology of MIDI is 30 years old, it still plays an undeniable role in shaping live performances and allows for extreme creativity and innovation on the part of the artist.

MIDI is an extremely powerful and versatile tool when used for live performance. MIDI can be used in all genres of music and can benefit any musician on stage no matter the material of music he or she plays. MIDI can be utilized as an instrument when used in conjunction with sound modules and a controller, but it can also provide extreme control over equipment on stage that a performer cannot physically control otherwise when playing live. When used in conjunction with a sequencer or DAW, MIDI allows artists to trigger prerecorded samples and clips as well as affect the music overall. When performing alone, MIDI allows the artist to become a one-man-band with all the spontaneity and intricacies expected from a full group. When paired with a user-mapped controller, MIDI allows the artist to control huge amounts of parameters with one small device. When paired with programming software like Max/MSP, MIDI can be used to control virtually anything in the multimedia realm allowing for live performances, the likes of which had never been seen prior to MIDI's introduction. When situations arose in which performances were beginning to become stagnant and unimpressive, artists were able to use MIDI in order to create an entirely new and innovative means of controlling their equipment through body gestures and preprogrammed movements. And finally, MIDI has come full circle in its live performance implementations from first allowing musicians to move away from other musicians and perform alone to encouraging group performance in the fast emerging multiperson interactive world.

MIDI has undeniably changed the way musicians perform as well as the way they look at what a performance can be. MIDI has become a staple in live performance that is here to stay. When used in conjunction with other similar technologies, such as OSC, the opportunities are endless. In the last 30 years, MIDI has undoubtedly left its mark on live performance and will continue to do so in the future. With the evolution and innovation of MIDI happening right now in the live performance realm, the future of live MIDI is extremely promising. MIDI has become synonymous with live performance and will most likely become even more so in the near future.

# MUSIC THEORY PRIMER

# 8

*by Paul Musso, Professor of Music at the University of Colorado Denver*

This chapter is included because understanding music theory and the terminology involved with our musical language is incredibly helpful for engineers, producers, and musicians who are using MIDI in the production process.

## The Elements of Music

The three elements that encompass music are rhythm, melody, and harmony.

### Rhythm

Rhythm is defined as motion in music or "movement marked by the regulated succession of strong or weak elements" (*Oxford English Dictionary*). Rhythm is comprised of organized patterns. Within the patterns are varying durations. When a singer or instrumentalist produces a note, it is usually held for a specific duration. This makes the motion or movement possible.

The example below is a simple series of notes.

When specific durations are added to each note it becomes the familiar children's song "Mary Had a Little Lamb." The rhythmic motion is visually obvious in example two, even to the musically untrained eye. Example two is also more interesting than the first example because of the variety in note durations.

The three basic elements of rhythm are the following:

Beat
Tempo
Meter

The term "beat" means continuous pulse. Modern definitions of the term "beat" have come to mean entire complex rhythmic patterns—what some musicians would call "grove." Beat is simply the pulse of the music.

Tempo is the pulse or speed of the beat. The metronome, a device that mechanically provides beats per measure, measures tempo. Metronome indictors are traditionally Italian words that mean slow, medium, and fast pace. Here is a list of common metronome markings and the beats per measure (BPM) for each:

| Largo | Very slow | 40–60 bpm |
|---|---|---|
| Larghetto | Rather broadly | 60–66 bpm |
| Adagio | Slow and stately | 66–76 bpm |
| Andante | Walking pace | 76–108 bpm |
| Moderato | Moderately | 108–120 bpm |
| Allegro | Fast and bright | 120–168 bpm |
| Presto | Very fast | 168–200 bpm |
| Prestissimo | Extremely fast | 200 + bpm |

Modern tempo indicators are easy to discern because they literally describe the music: Medium Swing, Fast Bossa Nova, and Slow Rock . . . Most pieces of music will either contain one of the Italian tempo indicators above, a description or a simple quarter note equals indicator ($\quarternote$ = 100). Tempo is extremely important in today's music, especially electronic music. Specific styles of electronic music have strict tempo parameters. Hip Hop is around 85–100 BPM, Trance is 135–150 BPM, and Drum Bass is 150–170 BPM.

Meter is the grouping of the beat. The beat can be grouped in any number. Four, three, and two are the most used groupings of the beat or the most common meters. When the beat is grouped, the first number of the beat is accented so that there is a clear delineation.

Meter occurring in four would be counted like this: **1** 2 3 4 **1** 2 3 4. Notice the bold 1. This would indicate a louder, accented beat. Meter does not occur without accents.

### *Melody*

Melody is pitch arranged in time, or a series of tones that create a musical statement. The literary equivalent of a melody is a sentence. Many melodies seem to have form or shape like a sentence with a beginning, middle, and end. When the lyrics are added to "Mary Had a Little Lamb," it becomes clear to see how this is a melody.

Pitch is the frequency of a note (high or low) and is measured mathematically in hertz (Hz) or cycles per second. The more cycles per second, the higher the note. A 440 is a commonly used pitch. This means the note A above middle C is vibrating 440 times per second. Written notes represent pitches—the higher the note on the staff the higher the pitch.

### *Harmony*

Harmony is the combination of tones that accompany a melody. Harmony occurs below the melody most of the time. The listener perceives the highest note as the melody and the harmony supports the higher note. Notice how example four contains two notes. The top note is the melody to "Mary Had a Little Lamb"; the notes below the top notes are considered harmony.

Harmony can be as simple as one note below the melody (ex. 4) or it can be several notes below the melody, like the example below.

## Musical Texture

Most music can be classified into three kinds of texture: monophonic, polyphonic, and homophonic.

Monophonic texture is one single melody without chordal accompaniment or additional pitches. Example three is an excellent example of monophonic texture.

Polyphonic texture is classified as two or more notes being played simultaneously. The voices, or different notes, function as independent lines in polyphonic texture. Examples four and five are both polyphonic. Example four contains two separate voices, and example five incorporates three different voices.

Homophonic texture is classified as a melody with accompaniment. The accompanying instrument is usually a piano or guitar but could be an entire rhythm section (piano, bass, drums, guitar). Most popular music is homophonic. Singer/songwriter styles feature homophonic texture almost exclusively. Imagine a guitarist singing and strumming the guitar or singing and playing piano accompaniment—this is the simplest form of homophonic texture.

## Music Notation

The system of notating music evolved over 1,500 years and became our current system in the 16th century. The current system of notation involves using devices like a staff, clefs, ledger lines, and note values to accurately convey music on paper.

A staff consists of five lines used to place pitches.

Here is the five-line staff used in music notation since the 16th century.

When notes are placed on this staff we can determine if they are higher or lower, but we cannot determine the actual pitches.

A clef is needed to indicate the actual pitches of these notes. There are several clefs that are used in music, but the most common two are the treble and bass clef.

The treble clef is also called the G Clef because the bottom curl indicates the note G on the second line from the bottom. All other pitches can be calculated at this point.

The bass clef is also called the F Clef because the two dots surround the note F, which is the second line from the top.

The names of the notes on the spaces of the treble clef are F A C E.

The names of the notes on the lines of the treble clef are E G B D F. It is most effective to utilize a mnemonic device to remember the names of these notes. Most people learned the mnemonic "Every Good Boy Does Fine" to remember the note names of the line notes. "Elvis' Guitar Broke Down Friday" also works.

Here is a short list of the instruments that read music from the treble clef: saxophone, flute, oboe, clarinet, trumpet, violin, and guitar. All of these instruments produce sound in the mid to upper range.

The names of the notes that occur on the lines of the bass clef are G B D F A. A common mnemonic for these notes is Good Boys Do Fine Always.

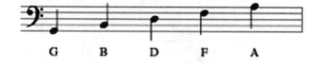

The names of the notes that fall into the spaces on the bass clef are A C E G. Two common mnemonics used to remember the spaces in bass clef are All Cows Eat Grass and All Cars Eat Gas.

Here is a short list of instruments that read music in bass clef: trombone, tuba, cello, double bass (upright bass), and bass guitar. All of these instruments produce sound in the lower range.

## Ledger Lines

Ledger lines are lines above and below the staff used for notes higher and lower than the staff. The staff would contain over 15 lines and would be extremely complicated to read without ledger lines. All ledger lines are spaced equidistant from each other and are consistent with the measurement of the lines within the staff.

The following graphic demonstrates the notes on ledger lines above and below the treble clef. The high G and lower D are notes on the perimeter of the staff and are not included in the mnemonic. The highest note on a line is an F in the treble clef. The G is a step higher and the notes move alphabetically to F. The same is true with the descending notes. The D is one step below the bottom line E and then descends alphabetically to F.

This graphic demonstrates the notes on ledger lines above and below the bass clef staff.

## The Musical Alphabet

The musical alphabet consists of seven letters. The alphabet starts on A and ends on G: A B C D E F G. It then starts over with A: A B C D E F G A B C D . . .

When a letter appears again after all seven letters it is considered to be the distance of an octave. The same letters (note names) in different octaves have a similar sound.

The reason for this is that the frequency of the note doubles if the octave is higher or is cut in half if the octave is lower. For instance, the A note on the second space of the treble clef is 440 hertz. When this A is played in the higher octave, it vibrates at 880 Hz. When it is played an octave lower it vibrates at 220 Hz.

## The Grand Staff

The piano reads a unique staff that incorporates both the treble and bass clefs; it is called the grand staff or great staff. Middle C is the note that separates both clefs. In the graphic below, middle C is written in both clefs. Both notes are middle C.

If ascending consecutive notes were written from bass clef to treble clef, middle C would actually appear in the center of both clefs. Notice how the D note following middle C appears in the treble clef.

## The Piano Keyboard

The layout of the piano keyboard is one of the most important visual tools for understanding theoretical music concepts. Notice how the white keys represent the letters from the musical alphabet. All of the notes on the white keys are called natural notes. The black keys are called sharp or flat notes. The keyboard also represents all twelve notes possible in Western music (C C# D D# E F F# G G# A A# B). The distance from C to C# is the shortest distance between two notes in Western music and is call a half step. The distance from C to D is called a whole step. A whole step is comprised of two half steps: C to C# and C# to D.

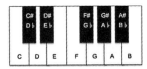

The piano keyboard pattern repeats after each octave. Notice how the C note follows the B note and the octave begins again. The two-octave graphic also illustrates the location of all half steps. A very important feature is the distance from

E to F and B to C where no black keys are present. This is one of the most critically important concepts in music theory. E, F, B, and C are all natural notes but there are no black keys between E–F and B–C.

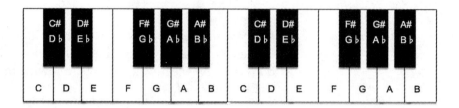

## Sharps and Flats

When a natural note is raised by a half step it becomes a sharp note. When the note C is raised by a half step it becomes C#. This is true with the notes D F G and A. When raised by a half step, D becomes D#, F becomes F#, G becomes G#, and A becomes A#. When the notes E and B are raised by a half step they become F and C respectively.

When a natural note is lowered by a half step it becomes a flat note. If D is lowered by a half step it becomes a D♭. The same is true for E G A and B; however, when F is lowered by a half step it becomes E. C lowered by a half step becomes B.

The first black key is labeled with two note names: C# and D♭. This is known as an enharmonic equivalent. A single pitch like E♭ can also be called D#. Both sharps and flat names are needed for pitches when considering keys and scales—more to come on that subject. E sharp and F♭ are legitimate note names as are C♭ and B#.

## The Five Accidentals

The five accidentals used in music notation are sharp, flat, natural, double sharp, and double flat.

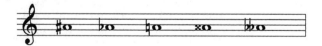

The five accidentals used in music notation are: sharp, flat, natural, double sharp, and double flat. A sharp raises the note by a half step, a flat lowers the note by a half step, the natural returns the note to its natural pitch, the double sharp raises the note by a whole step, and the double flat lowers the note by a whole step. All accidentals are used in music notation. Double sharps and double flats are use less often than sharps, flats, and naturals. Here is a list of the double sharp and double flat enharmonic equivalents used for natural pitches.

| Pitch | Enharmonic Equivalent |
|-------|----------------------|
| C | D double flat |
| D | E double flat |
| F | G double flat |
| G | A double flat |
| A | B double flat |
| D | C double sharp |
| E | D double sharp |
| G | F double sharp |
| A | G double sharp |
| B | A double sharp |

Accidentals dictate the measure. This means the accidental will change all notes in the measure on the specific pitch with the accidental attached. For instance, in the example below, the F# remains F# until the F natural is introduced. The F natural negates the F#. The third note F# is then an accidental again and dictates that the following F become sharp. The F in the next measure, after the line, is then an F because the accidental (F#) only pertained to the previous measure.

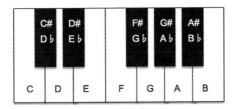

Precautionary accidentals are used to remind the musician that a note is a sharp, flat, or natural. Precautionary accidentals are written by adding parenthesis to an accidental. They are used when the measure contains several accidentals to avoid confusion for the reader. The C natural and G sharp at the end of the measure below may use precautionary accidentals to make the pitches clear to the musician.

## Note Values

Rhythmic notation has a specific protocol and has evolved over the centuries, like melodic notation. The foundation of rhythmic note values starts with the whole note, pictured in the top measure in the graphic below. Most of the other note values can be calculated from the whole note by dividing it in half, quarter, eighth, sixteenth . . . The whole note most commonly receives the value of four beats. This assumes ⁴⁄₄ time, which will be addressed later. If we assume the whole note receives four beats, the half note (next division down) would receive two beats. The quarter note would receive one beat. The eight note would receive a half of a beat. The sixteenth note would receive a quarter of a beat.

The chart below illustrates the note values from whole note to sixteenth notes. Notice how the half note is open in the middle with a stem, like a whole note with a stem. The quarter note is a filled in note head with a stem. The sixteenth note contains a filled in note head with a flag at the top (the flags are all connected in the graphic below). The sixteenth note is similar to the eighth note but with two flags. The thirty-second note contains three flags.

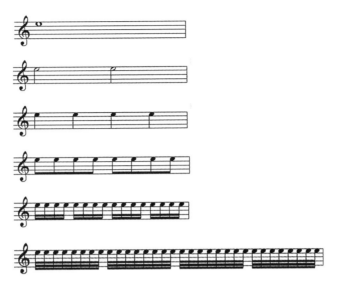

Note values all have a rest counterpart, indicating silence. Here is the note value graphic with rests instead of notes:

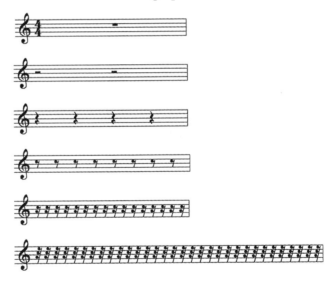

## Time Signatures

Earlier in the chapter, meter was introduced as grouping of the beat. Meter is indicated by a time signature. The time signature indicates how many beats per measure. There is no limit to the number of beats per measure; however, the most common meters are four, three, and two. Time signatures are comprised of two numbers stacked on top of each other. The top number of the time signature indicates the meter. In the example below, ²⁄₄ meter indicates two beats per measure, ³⁄₄ meter indicates three beats per measure, and ⁴⁄₄ meter indicates four beats per measure.

A measure is the distance between bar lines.

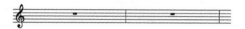

The bottom number of the time signature determines what kind of note receives one beat. The bottom number can only be a number specific to a note value. If the bottom number is four, the quarter note receives one beat. If the bottom number is two, the half note receives one beat. When the bottom note is eight, the eighth note receives one beat. Here is a list of the possible bottom numbers for time signatures:

The ⁴⁄₄ time is the most commonly used time signature (four beats per measure, quarter notes receives one beat). It is so common that the letter "C" is used to symbolize it (C for common).

The ²⁄₂ time signature is called "cut time," which represents ⁴⁄₄ cut in half. There are two beats per measure and the half note receives one beat. This time signature is generally used for faster marchlike tempos.

## Notation Protocol

Here are the three parts of a note containing a flag:

There are specific notation rules that pertain to the placement of stems and flags.

If the note head is lower than the middle line (B in treble clef), the stem belongs on the right of the note head. If the note head is higher than the middle line, the stem belongs on the left of the note head. The flag placement is always to the right regardless of the stem placement.

When more than one consecutive eighth note is present, the flags are beamed to create visual order and simplicity. Notice how much easier it is to read the four eighth notes on the right when a beam is applied two at a time.

The notes above could have been connected with one single beam as well, like the following graphic.

## Counting Beats

The process of counting beats depends on the time signature because the time signature determines the meter and the type of note that receives one beat. In ⁴⁄₄ time quarter notes receive one beat and half notes receive two beats. The half notes in measure two are played on beats one and three while holding beats two and four.

When eighth notes are counted in ¼ time an "and" is added to each of the four numbers. The best way to conceptualize eighth note counting is to think of the "and" belonging to the previous number. Musicians refer to the "+" eighth notes as the and of one, the and of two, the and of three, and the and of four.

## Ties

A tie is used to hold the duration of the note longer than the original note value and to hold the duration of the note over a bar line. In the example below the tie on beat four of the first measure is held into the first beat of the following measure. The first beat of the second measure is held and counted but not played. I used parenthesis to indicate the places where the notes are being held and the notes played.

## Dotted Notes

When a dot is added to a note it add half of the value to the original value of the note. In the example below, the first note has a tie added to it, giving it three beats. The dot in in the following measure achieves the same result. The dot transforms the half note into a note that now receives three beats instead of two.

When a dot is added to a quarter note, it adds a half of a beat to the quarter note resulting in a note lasting 1 ½ beats.

Here is a table that demonstrates what a dot does to various note values:

|  | Total Number of beats |
| --- | --- |
| Dotted Whole Note | 6 beats |
| Dotted Half Note | 3 beats |
| Dotted Quarter Note | 1 ½ beats |
| Dotted Eighth Note | ¾ beat |
| Dotted Sixteenth Note | ⅜ beat |

## Sixteenth Notes

Sixteenth notes are counted by using the phrase "one e + a." Doing this keeps the numbers (1234) and the "+" in line with the eight note counting protocol placement. Notice how the "+" indicators from the bottom eighth notes are all in line with the top sixteenth notes. Musicians refer to parts of the beat by using this terminology. It is common to hear musicians refer to the "e" of two or the "a" of three.

When musicians count time in music, they often subdivide the beat. Subdividing is a system that incorporates silently counting the highest division of the beat. If the highest division of the beat is an eighth note, a musician will count 1 + 2 + 3 + 4 + in her head while reading music. This prepares the brain for the eighth notes when they are encountered and also ensures that the musician does note skip beats when counting half notes and whole notes. Sometimes counting rests or held notes can be as challenging as counting complex rhythms. When the highest division of the beat in a song is the sixteenth note, the musician subdivides with sixteenth notes, counting 1 e + a 2 e + a . . . continuously while reading and playing.

## Compound and Simple Meter

Simple meters are time signatures that group eight notes in two. Simple meter includes the following common time signatures. The implication of simple meter is that the accents occur at the beginning of every pair, or on the number (1234), not the "+."

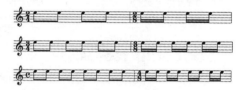

Compound meter time signatures group the eight notes in three and the accent occurs at the beginning of each grouping of three. Here are some common time signatures that utilize compound time.

## Duple, Triple, and Quadruple Time

Duple time signatures contain two total groupings of beamed notes (simple or compound) per measure. The following example illustrates two options for duple time. The first in ²⁄₄ time is duple simple because it groups the eighth notes in two and duple because there are two total groupings. The second time signature in ⁶⁄₈ is duple compound. It is duple because there are two total groupings and compound because the eighth notes are grouped in two.

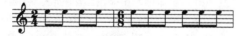

Triple time signatures contain three total groupings of beamed notes (simple or compound) per measure. The following example illustrates two options of triple time. The first in ¾ time is simple because the eighth notes are grouped in two and triple because there are three total groupings. The following time signature in ⁹⁄₈ is compound because the eighth notes are grouped in three and triple because there are three total groupings.

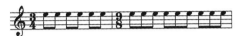

Quadruple time signatures contain four total groupings of beamed notes (simple or compound) per measure. The following example illustrates two options of quadruple time. The first in ⁴⁄₄ time is simple because the eighth notes are grouped in two and quadruple because there are four total groupings. The following time signature in ¹²⁄₈ is compound because the eighth notes are grouped in three and quadruple because there are four total groupings.

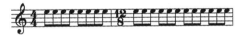

## Musical Road Maps

Following musical road maps involves learning six symbols that dictate where to go while reading music—like directing traffic or following a road map.

The first symbol is the backward repeat. This sign consists of two dots placed on the left side of the bar, between the middle line. The backward repeat tells the reader to go back to the left. In the example below the reader would go back to the beginning after measure three.

The forward repeat is a sign that directs the reader to the right. This sign consists of two dots placed on the right side of the bar, between the middle line. The forward repeat directs the reader to go to the right.

**269**

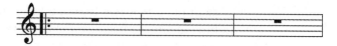

When the forward and backward repeats are used together, the backward repeat directs the reader back to the forward repeat. In the example below the backward repeat in measure three directs the reader back to the forward repeat in measure two. Notice how the numbers indicate the order and flow of the music. After the second and third measures are repeated, the music moves on to measure six.

If a forward repeat is missing the backward repeat returns to the beginning of the piece of music.

First and second endings are also used to direct the musician through a piece of music. The first ending and second ending are always used in tandem. Third, fourth, fifth . . . endings are also possible, but most music uses only first and second endings. The first ending is played when the musician encounters the measure the first time. The first ending will contain a backward repeat that directs the reader back to the beginning or to a forward repeat. When the reader returns to the first ending measure, the ending is skipped and the second ending is played. Notice how the number five moves to the number six in the second ending. First and second endings are like gates that open once then deny entry the second time. The melodic and harmonic material in the first and second ending is usually similar with a slight variation.

D.C. (Da Capo) means "from the head" in Italian. This sign tells the musician to return to the very beginning of the piece. D.C. is usually used along with a Fine sign (D.C. al Fine). When used together the direction becomes go to the beginning and stop at the measure that contains the word Fine. In the example below the D.C. at the end of the piece directs the reader back to the top and then the Fine indicates the end of the piece. The double bar is also an indicator that the piece is over. The double bar is ignored the first time in bar two.

D.S. (Dal Segno) means "from the sign" in Italian and is used if the composer wants the music to repeat somewhere other than the beginning. D.S. is often used along with the Fine sign (D.S. al Fine) and means go to the sign then stop at the measure with the Fine sign.

## Major Scales

Understanding the construction of the major scale is one of the most important concepts when it comes to learning music theory. Major scales have a bright or "happy" sound and are the highly used in Western music. The major scale is the foundation for intervals, chords, and modes. Music theory is abstract without the understanding of the major scale. Major scales are constructed by using half steps and whole steps. Remember that a half step is the smallest distance between two notes. The half step is on key up or down from any note on the keyboard. The whole step is created by moving two half steps up or down.

The formula for creating a major scale is as follows:

| whole step | whole step | half step | whole step | whole step | whole step | half step |
|---|---|---|---|---|---|---|

Breaking this pattern into two parts makes it easier to remember and comprehend: W W H W W W H.

The scale below is a C major scale. The pattern of whole steps and half step is apparent when the construction of the scale is examined. The distance from C to D is a whole step. The distance from D to E is a whole step. The distance from E to F is a half step. The distance from F to G is a whole step. The distance from G to A is a whole step. The distance from A to B is a whole step and the distance from B to C is a half step.

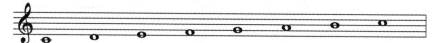

If this same pattern of whole steps and half steps were applied to a scale starting and ending on the note G the note F# would be needed to accommodate the last whole step (E to F#). This is a G major scale.

At this point it becomes clear that a G major scale contains an F#. This is true for the key of G as well—still to come.

When the major scale pattern is applied to a scale starting and ending on F the note B♭ is needed to create the first half step from A.

When creating major scales, the accidental is applied to the note on the right. For instance, if the accidental was applied to the A and not the B, in the example above, the A would become A#. This would then create an interval larger than a whole step from the note G.

Major scales are in introduction to tonality. Tonality is the organization of all the tones and harmonies of a scale or musical work in relation to a tonic or keynote. Tonality is a system used in music that involves giving musical "weight" to a specific pitch. A C major scale has a C tonic or tonality because the C pitch holds the most weight.

## Key Signatures

Key signatures are used so that accidentals do not have to be written on every note, every time. In the G major scale example above, the note F is always sharp. It would look clustered if the F# was written every time throughout a piece of music in G major. The solution is to place the F# in the key signature at the beginning of the piece. This simplifies the notation and makes it so that less accidentals are used. Here is the key signature for the key of G major:

This key signature indicates that every F note played is F sharp, in every octave.

Key signatures are divided into sharp and flat keys. Sharps and flats are never mixed within the same scale. There is a specific order to flat and sharp key signatures depending on the amount of sharps and flats. Sharp key signatures appear in the following order:

| Major Scale | Number of Sharps |
| --- | --- |
| G | 1 |
| D | 2 |
| A | 3 |
| E | 4 |
| B | 5 |
| F# | 6 |
| C# | 7 |

Key:    G    D    A    E    B    F#    C#

The sharps themselves also have a specific order. F# is always the first sharp followed by C#, G#, D#, A#, E#, and B#. The F# is always placed on the top line of the treble clef in sharp key signatures. All other sharps follow in the exact placement as the graphic above.

| Major Scale | Sharps |
| --- | --- |
| G | F# |
| D | F# C# |
| A | F# C# G# |
| E | F# C# G# D# |
| B | F# C# G# D# A# |
| F# | F# C# G# D# A# E# |
| C# | F# C# G# D# A# E# B# |

There is a mathematical pattern in the order of the keys and the order of sharps. The keys move in the interval (distance between two notes) called a fifth. G to D is a fifth (G A B C D). D is five notes higher than G. D to A is also a fifth (D E F G A). This follows all of the sharp keys. The sharps also move in fifth intervals. F# to C# is a fifth (F G A B C). The exact interval is called a perfect fifth (see "Intervals" section). A mnemonic to remember the sharp keys is Grumpy Dogs Always Eat Big Fat Carrots. A mnemonic to remember the actual sharps is Fat Cats Go Down Alleys Eating Birds.

The flat keys have an order as well—both the key order and the actual flats. Flats move in fourth intervals. F to B♭ is a fourth (F G A B♭). B♭ to E♭ is a fourth (B♭ C D E♭). The actual interval is called a perfect fourth (see "Intervals" section). Flat key signatures always follow the same protocol for flat placement. The first B♭ is always on the middle line of the treble clef. All other flats follow as in the graphic below.

F is the only flat key that does not have a ♭ in the name. All other keys contain a ♭.

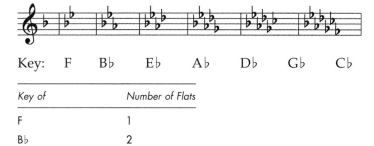

Key:    F    B♭    E♭    A♭    D♭    G♭    C♭

| Key of | Number of Flats |
|---|---|
| F | 1 |
| B♭ | 2 |
| E♭ | 3 |
| A♭ | 4 |
| D♭ | 5 |
| G♭ | 6 |
| C♭ | 7 |

The actual flats are also a perfect fourth away from each other (B♭ C D E♭ ). A good mnemonic to help remember flat keys in order is Five Blue Elephants Ate Delicious Green Carrots. A good mnemonic to help remember the actual flats in order is Blue Elephants Ate Delicious Green Carrots Friday.

| Major Scale | Flats |
|---|---|
| F | B♭ |
| B♭ | B♭ E♭ |
| E♭ | B♭ E♭ A♭ |
| A♭ | B♭ E♭ A♭ D♭ |
| D♭ | B♭ E♭ A♭ D♭ G♭ |
| G♭ | B♭ E♭ A♭ D♭ G♭ C♭ |
| C♭ | B♭ E♭ A♭ D♭ G♭ C♭ F♭ |

There are two tricks when it comes to naming the key if the key signature is available. The flat key trick involves covering up the flat farthest right to find the name of the key. This only works for keys with two flats or more. For instance, if the key signature has two flats (B♭ E♭ ) cover up the E♭ and the letter that is viable is the correct key—B♭. This works with all keys except for the key F.

The sharp key trick works with all sharp key signatures and is very simple. Start with the sharp farthest right then move up a half step. This will provide the name of the key. For instance, if the key has one sharp (F#), move up a half step from F#. The key is G.

## The Circle of Fifths

The circle of fifths (also called the cycle of fifths) is a visual representation of all 15 keys, moving in logical order, from key to key by the distance of a fifth. The fifth interval applies to the circle when moving clockwise (C G D A . . .).

The circle of fifths is used for various reasons: as an aid to remember keys, as a way to visualize enharmonic keys, and as a tool to learn all perfect fifth and perfect fourth intervals.

The circle of fifths contains 15 keys, 3 of which are enharmonic. The keys of C♭ and B, G♭ and F#, and D♭ and C# are all enharmonic to each other.

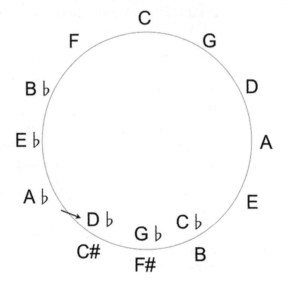

There is an interesting mathematical trick called The Magic Seven that can be used to remember all key signatures in the cycle of fifths. The Magic Seven trick involves the total number of sharps and flats adding up to seven in keys that start with the same letter. For instance, the key of G contains one sharp so the key of G♭ must contain six flats (1+6 = 7). This works with all keys. The table below illustrates all of the same letter name keys and how they all add up to seven.

## Magic Seven

| | | | | |
|----|----------|-----|---------|-----------|
| G | 1 sharp | G♭ | 6 flats | 1 + 6 = 7 |
| D | 2 sharps | D♭ | 5 flats | 2 + 5 = 7 |
| A | 3 sharps | A♭ | 4 flats | 3 + 4 = 7 |
| E | 4 sharps | E♭ | 3 flats | 4 + 3 = 7 |
| B | 5 sharps | B♭ | 2 flats | 5 + 2 = 7 |
| F# | 6 sharps | F | 1 flat | 6 + 1 = 7 |
| C | 0 sharps | C♭ | 7 flats | 0 + 7 = 7 |
| C | 0 sharps | C# | 7 sharps | 0 + 7 = 7 |

### *Intervals*

An interval is the distance between two notes. When intervals are played simultaneously they are considered harmonic intervals. When intervals are play separately they are considered melodic intervals. The interval number is determined by counting the bottom number as one. In the graphic below, the interval from C to D is called a second, counting C as one. The next interval, C to E, is a third (C D E). The last interval, C to C, is an eighth (C D E F G A B C). The intervals below are all harmonic intervals.

Intervals all have qualities or colors. Some adjectives used to describe intervals include bright, happy, dark, sad, tense, dissonant,, and consonant.

The first group of intervals to examine are seconds. When a second interval is only a half step above the bottom note, it is called a minor second. If the second interval is a whole step above the bottom note, it is called a major second. Both are dissonant sounding but the minor second is more dissonant than the major second. When counting half steps in intervals, the bottom number is not counted. The minor second interval contains one half step, and the major second contains two half steps.

Next are the third intervals. Third intervals also belong to the major/minor classification. When an interval is three half steps from the bottom note, it is called a minor third (C Db D Eb ). Remember the bottom note is not counted. When an interval is four half steps up from the bottom note it is called a major third (C Db D Eb E). Thirds have a consonant sound. The minor third sounds sad and the major third sounds happy. Thirds are very important when it comes to studying chords, as chords are all built on thirds.

The next intervals to examine are fourths. Fourths belong to the perfect/augmented/diminished classification. When an interval is five half steps from the bottom note it is called a perfect fourth. This interval is "pure" and consonant sounding. When the perfect fourth interval is raised by a half step, to six total half steps from the bottom note, it is called an augmented fourth. The augmented fourth is tense and dissonant sounding.

Fifths also belong to the perfect/augmented/diminished classification. The diminished fifth interval is six half steps up from the bottom note, just like the augmented fourth. The perfect fifth is seven half steps up from the bottom note and has a pure consonant sound. The augmented fifth is eight half steps up from the bottom note and has a tense dissonant sound.

Sixth intervals belong to the major/minor classification. The minor sixth is actually the same sound as the augmented fifth with a distance of eight half steps from the bottom note. The major six is nine half steps from the bottom note and has a consonant pleasant sound compared to its minor counterpart.

Seventh intervals also belong to the major/minor classification. Both intervals are dissonant although some would hear the major seventh as being more dissonant. The minor seventh interval is ten half steps from the bottom note, while the major seventh is one half step higher.

The final interval is the octave or eighth, and it belongs into the perfect/augmented/diminished category. For the sake of simplification the perfect octave will be the only eighth interval covered. The perfect octave is twelve half steps from the bottom note and has a pure simple sound.

## Interval Summary

| Interval | Shorthand | Half steps |
|---|---|---|
| Unison | P1 | 0 |
| minor 2nd | m2 | 1 |
| Major 2nd | M2 | 2 |
| minor 3rd | m3 | 3 |
| Major 3rd | M3 | 4 |
| Perfect 4th | P4 | 5 |
| Augmented 4th | aug4 | 6 |
| diminished 5th | dim5 | 6 |
| Perfect 5th | P5 | 7 |
| Augmented 5th | aug5 | 8 |
| minor 6th | m6 | 8 |
| Major 6th | M6 | 9 |
| minor 7th | m7 | 10 |
| Major 7 | M7 | 11 |
| Perfect 8th | P8 | 12 |

Two classification groups exist in the world of intervals. Unison (1), 4ths, 5ths, and 8ths reside in one group while 2nds, 3rds, 6ths, and 7ths belong to the other group. The 1, 4, 5, 8 group has qualities that are perfect, diminished, and augmented while the 2, 3, 6, 7 group have qualities that are generally major and minor.

### Triads

Triads are three note chords that are essential to understanding all harmonic concepts. Triads have been the foundation for harmony since the 1500s and are still the foundation for modern popular music.

A triad has three components: the root, the third, and the fifth. Notice in the graphic below how the C note is the root, the E note is the third, and the G note is the fifth. This chord is a C major triad.

Triads are like intervals in that they have inherent qualities: bright, dark, happy, sad, consonant, and dissonant. The four basic interval qualities are major, minor, diminished, and augmented. Constructing triads involves utilizing intervals. There are several approaches to constructive triads; this chapter will focus on one method.

Triad construction starts with measuring the root to the third, then the root to the fifth. The example below constructs a C major triad. The first interval above the root is a major third (four half steps above the root), and the second interval above the root is a perfect fifth (seven half steps above the root). When a major third and perfect fifth are combined, a major triad is created.

The minor triad is created by combining a minor third (three half steps above the root) and a perfect fifth above the root. Minor triads have a melancholy sad sound.

The diminished triad is created by combining a minor third above the root and a diminished fifth above the root (six half steps higher than the root).

Augmented triads combine the major third above the root with an augmented fifth above the root (eight half steps above the root).

## Summary of Triad Construction

| Triad Quality | 3rd | 5th |
| --- | --- | --- |
| Major | Major | Perfect |
| Minor | Minor | Perfect |
| Diminished | Minor | Diminished |
| Augmented | Major | Augmented |

There is a specific protocol when writing chord symbols for triads. The major triad only needs a letter, nothing more. The other chord symbol options are listed in the table below.

## Chord Symbol Protocol for Triads

| Major triad | C | |
| --- | --- | --- |
| Minor triad | Cm | C– |
| Augmented | C+ | Caug |
| Diminished | Cdim | C° |

### Seventh Chords

Seventh chords made up of four notes stacked in thirds and are essentially extensions of triads. Seventh chords are vital building blocks to understanding harmony. These chords are common to all styles of music and have been around since the Renaissance. The five most used seventh chords are major seventh, dominant seventh, minor seventh, minor seventh flat five (also called half diminished), and diminished seventh.

The method of construction used to build seventh chords depends on a thorough understanding of triad structure. It combines the triad with the seventh interval from the root note.

Combining the major triad with the major seventh interval above the root note creates the major seventh chord. Major seventh chords sound bright and consonant.

When the major triad and minor seventh interval are combined, a dominant seventh chord is created. The dominant seventh chord possesses a tense dissonant quality. This tension is created because of the diminished fifth interval from E to B♭ within the chord. The chord symbol for the dominant seventh chord is the root letter and a 7. The word dominant is not a part of the chord symbol.

When a minor triad is combined with a minor seventh interval, a minor seventh chord is created. The minor seventh chord actually sounds bright even though it is created with a minor interval and minor chord. The reason for this is the E♭ major triad that exists within the Cm7 chord (E♭ G B♭). Our ears hear the bright major chord even though a minor triad is present as well. There are many chord symbol options for the minor seventh chord: Cm7, C-7, Cmi7, Cmin7.

Combining a diminished triad with a minor seventh interval from the root creates a minor seventh flat five chord. This chord is also known as the half diminished chord because half of the chord contains a diminished triad. This unique sounding chord is dissonant and tense and is used primarily in minor keys.

**283**

The final seventh chord combines a diminished triad with a diminished seventh interval from the root and is called a diminished seventh chord. This is another dissonant and tense sounding chord. The diminished seventh interval was not addressed in the interval section. The diminished seventh interval is eight half steps above the root note and sounds the same as a major sixth interval. The example below could be written with an A rather than a B double flat.

Here is a list of common chord symbols for seventh chords:

Common Chord Symbols for Seventh Chords

| Chord Name | Chord Symbol | Alternative | |
|---|---|---|---|
| Major Seventh | Maj7 | Δ7 | CMaj7 CΔ7 |
| Dominant Seventh | 7 | | C7 |
| Minor Seventh | m7 | -7 | Cm7 C-7 |
| Minor Seventh Flat Five | m7(b5) | ø | Cm7(b5) Cø Cø7 |
| (Fully) Diminished Seventh | dim7 | °7 | Cdim7 C°7 |

## The Harmonic System

The harmonic system is the model for harmony that has existed since the late Renaissance time period. The system involves constructing triads on each scale degree of a major scale. Chord progressions are extracted from the triads within the key; this is called diatonic harmony (harmony specific to a key).

The example below illustrates the harmonic system in the key of C major. Notice how the bottom note of each triad constructs a C major scale. Each scale degree's triad has a quality: I is major, ii is minor, iii is minor, IV is major, V is major, vi is minor, and vii° is diminished. Roman numerals are used to indicate major minor and diminished chords. Uppercase Roman numerals indicate major chords while lowercase indicate minor chords. The diminished chord is indicated with a lower-case

Roman numeral and the small ° symbol. The Roman numeral system is used exclusively in music theory to indicate harmonic progressions. It is also used when musicians communicate with each other in reference to chord progressions.

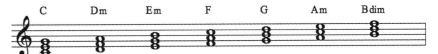

When a major scale is harmonized using triads the order of major, minor, and diminished chords is always the same—I and IV chords are always major; ii, iii, and vi chords are always minor; and vii° is always diminished. For instance, if the harmonic system were applied to the key of G it would look like this:

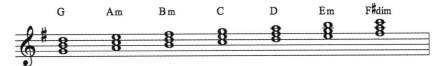

The harmonic system makes it easy to determine all chords that reside within a key by simply knowing the sharps and flats in the key. The key of G has one sharp (F#) that is the seventh scale degree. This means that the only chord with a sharp would be the F#° chord.

## Chord Progressions

There are several common chord progressions used today that have been used for centuries. The first, and most common, is the I IV V I progression. Songs like "La Bamba," "Louie Louie," "Wild Thing," and "Blitzkrieg Bop" use the I IV V progression. This progression would be C F G C in the key of C. This progression is comprised of three major triads. Remember that the I IV and V chords were all major triads. The V chord in this progression is often a seventh chord. The sonority of the seventh chord on the fifth scale degree is dominant seventh. The I IV V I progression would then become C F G7 C.

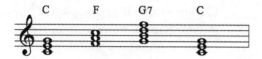

Most chord progressions are not played with the root as the lowest note for every chord. The process of avoiding these "root position" chords is called voice leading: it involves using chords with the third or fifth as the lowest note. These chords are called inversions. Notice how the F chord is notated with a C (the fifth of F) in the bass and the G7 has a B in the bass (the third of G7). When the third of the chord is in the bass the chord is called a first inversion chord. When the fifth of the chord is in bass the chord is called a second inversion chord.

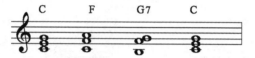

Another common chord progression is the I vi IV V. Songs like "Every Breath You Take," "At Last," "What a Wonderful World," "Penny Lane," and "Stand by Me" use this progression.

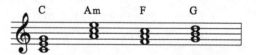

The V chord is often a dominant seventh in the I vi IV V progression. The G dominant seventh chord creates more tension than the G major triad and wants to resolve to the C chord. Here is an example of this progression using the dominant V chord and proper voice leading. Notice how little movement there is between chords. This sound is much more pleasing to the ear than when every chord is notated with the root as the lowest note.

The I V vi IV progression has become one of the most used harmonic progressions in the last 20 years. Songs that utilize this progression include: "With or Without You," "No Woman No Cry," "Don't Stop Believin'," "Let it Be," "Poker Face," and "21 Guns."

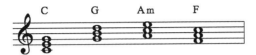

The V chord is commonly not dominant in this progression because it doesn't not resolve to the I chord. Most of the time the V chord is a simple major triad. Here is the progression with voice leading:

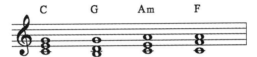

Another type of harmonic system exists for rock and blues type songs. This harmonic system includes three other major chords: ♭III, ♭VI, and ♭VII. These chords are all derived from blues harmony. These chords are sometimes labeled "borrowed" from other keys. All of these chords are actually derived from the key of C minor or C minor pentatonic. The minor sound in the major key created blues/rock tonality.

Here is the harmonic system with the borrowed blues chords:

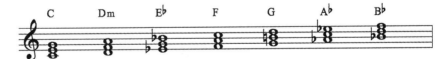

Common chord progressions derived from this progression include the following:

I ♭ III ♭ VII IV
I ♭ VII ♭ III IV
I ♭ VI V

The I♭III♭VII IV progression is commonly played with all chords in with the root in the bass (root position). The parallel movement is common with rock and metal songs. Here are two possible ways to voice the chords for this progression:

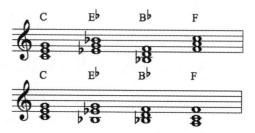

The I♭VII♭III IV progression is a slight variation to the I♭III♭VII IV progression. The ♭VII and ♭III switch places.

The final progression is common to punk rock songs. This song would be played with parallel root position chords or "power chords." Power chords are chords played without the third so that what remains is the root and the fifth. The octave is often doubled so that the chord is notated: root, fifth, root.

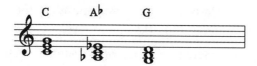

The chord symbol for a power chord is the root letter followed by a 5.

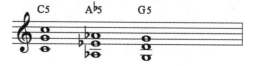

# INTERVIEWS

# 9

## John Swihart

### Bio

John Swihart is a world-renowned composer known for his work on such films as *Napoleon Dynamite*, *Youth in Revolt*, and *Employee of the Month*. John also composed the music for hit television shows such as *How I Met Your Mother*, *Men at Work*, and *Web Therapy*. Swihart got his start in music at the age of eight when he discovered the saxophone. After high school, Swihart was accepted into the prestigious Berklee College of Music in Boston, Massachusetts, where he furthered his musical education. After college, Swihart auditioned and was selected to play zither, chapman stick, bass, and guitar with the Blue Man Group in Boston, New York, and Las Vegas. Soon after departing from the Blue Man Group band, John moved to Los Angeles, where he began scoring independent films before making a name for himself with the hugely successful *Napoleon Dynamite*.

*Q: What is your MIDI controller of choice?*

I have a Fatar that is my main keyboard because I think it's the best weighted keyboard out there but I have 2 LPK 25s, a nano key, an MAudio key rig 49, and an old oxygen hooked up all over the studio. I have a lot of hardware synths so I need controllers all over the room.

*Q: What DAW do you prefer to use when dealing with MIDI?*

I just switched to Cubase 7 after 15 years with Logic. Apple is all about the iPod now so no updates for 3 years is not cool at all. I have had to build my own computers now because I

**Figure 9.1**

cannot work on a laptop and Apple won't make an i7 tower for me. I will probably switch to PCs shortly.

*Q: Have you incorporated the OSC protocol into your studio/live rig at all to replace MIDI?*

I have 3 iPads running touch OSC using Osculator to communicate with my software. I love these things. I have tons of key commands set up and some basic master mix stuff.

*Q: What do you feel is MIDI's biggest weakness?*

I wish it was faster. It's still single file so all the notes line up in a row. Try programming the same beat across 100 tracks and you will see what I mean.

*Q: What do you feel is the biggest benefit MIDI has to offer?*

Undo/redo/quantize. This list could get quite long.

*Q: Do you have any MIDI interconnections in your studio? (besides standard controller into interface)*

I ran out of ports in logic which has 64 ports (63 and one "All" port). Yes is the short answer.

*Q: Do you create your written scores via MIDI or do you create your MIDI via written score?*

Via Midi.

*Q: I agree with your comments about Logic and Apple, and I know it has left quite a few people looking elsewhere. Can you list your top five favorite things about Cubase and why you chose it?*

Cubase is the only sequencer that has been around since the Commodore and Atari computers so it was a no brainer to go with them. I am pretty deep with it all. Everything audio is so much better. More pan laws, two different panners, multiple outputs so I can mix down a stereo mix and a surround mix and six surround stems and eight stereo stems all at the same time taking one pass. Logic only has one surround out and it's a bit of black magic going on there. Likewise, repanning if you want to the left and right channels to the middle of a stereo track you have to use the stereo mixer, which is just weird sounding. Also flipping the stereo image is strange sounding with the stereo mixer plug-in logic.

The pitch transposing and audio stretching algorithms are fantastic in Cubase. I had a producer ask me to lower a cue by a whole step and it took me five seconds to do this. Select all, then transpose -2 and I was done. All the audio sounded great still. Very impressive. Quantizing audio is not perfect but it is superior to Logic's flex stuff by far.

Another big issue with Logic was timing. I would record my synths in and depending on how may plugs you had on buses, the audio would end up in a different location every time. If I set delay compensation to "All" then the midi I would record in was off by about a 16th note. Bazaar and so not cool.

I mixed a film about a year ago that was an action adventure SciFi thing and it took me two weeks to bounce out the stems and with Cubase, it would take me two days. Lots of surround stems that I had to bounce one at a time in Logic. I could have done this in one pass with Cubase.

The MIDI side of Cubase is also fantastic. Editing velocity is great with the curve tool and the ramp selected tool, great stuff for working with film. The MIDI plug-ins are great as well. Track folders, and the way I can set up external hardware processors so they show up like plug-ins is also great. And it's really colorful.

Okay, top five favorite things about Cubase:

1. Audio processing, stretching, pitch, pan, etc.
2. MIDI editing, and MIDI plug-ins and basic engineering of MIDI, very intuitive and useful.
3. Hardware integration. (I have 96 i/o and I use all of it for both external processors and 48 channels output to my Pro Tools machine for delivery).
4. Yamaha is a good music company that will be around for a long time.
5. Great tech support and user forums.

*Q: Your comments about timing are nothing new, but I'm curious if you have had issues in your day-to-day work. Is there anything you have to do to combat its timing limitations?*

Not with Cubase; no matter how may plugs I put on, the program figures out the latency and compensates for its current configuration. Recurring my hardware synths back onto the auto tracks of the session is always perfect. As far as driving external synths with USB MIDI I am under the impression that there are issues with USB that cannot be worked around. I do not understand why there is not a Cat5 MIDI interface? If the Eucon can use MIDI over Ethernet, why have I not heard of a MIDI interface that is Ethernet?

If I have something that is very fast I usually do it on the modular and use the sync gen from innerclock to drive the gate.

*Q: How/where did you learn to use MIDI, and do you have any tips for student composers who are working to develop sequencing skills?*

I bought a synth. Read magazines, forums, and everything.

Keep writing. Learn by doing. There is no substitute for experience.

*Q: Do you have any favorite MIDI anecdotes?*

I remember being on hold with tech support for about half an hour with Digidesign and when the tech person got on the phone I brought up MIDI and they scoffed at me and all I could think was that he was doing tech support and I was writing music for living. I have lots of baggage with Pro Tools because when I was starting out, potential clients would try to qualify you with it because it has the word "Pro" in it. Idiots. I have a friend who bought a Pro Tools rig and I bought a house for the same amount of money. Guess what's worth more now . . .

## George Strezov

### *Bio*

George Strezov has been passionate about music since an early age. Strezov always knew he wanted to be a film composer and began his career at the age of 15. George studied orchestration under one of Bulgaria's most acclaimed composers—Alexander Tekeliev—along with the world-renowned conductor Adriana Blagoeva. Some of Strezov's most notable projects include the movies *Number 1000, The Silence, Short Stop on the Way*, as well as the critically acclaimed short films *Room Number 4* and *Playing Marbles*. Strezov is also known for writing the opening music for 2012's Rhythmic Gymnastics World Championship as well the documentary series *The Path of Human Civilization.*

**Figure 9.2**

*Q: What is your MIDI controller of choice?*

I am currently working on Studiologic Numa Nano and I am using this as my main MIDI controller. Funny thing is that I am still using Evolution MK-149—a very old MIDI controller that was a gift to me by my first mentor. I still keep it and actually it does help me in my work! For controllers, I use Korg nanoKontrol2—suitable both for MIDI data and mixer controller.

Also, sometimes I use the "Pulse controller" for writing down percussion parts. I have had other controllers in the past, but since I play everything by hand I tend to keep things that are really reliable and save me lots of time—because time is of the essence, especially in the music production business!

*Q: What DAW do you prefer to use when working with MIDI?*

Steinberg Cubase. I have worked with other DAWs as well—from ProTools to Samplitude, Sonar, and FL Studio. But

Cubase helps me work with audio and is really, really fast in terms of working with MIDI.

*Q: What do you feel is MIDI's biggest weakness?*

Since I am working with orchestras and lots of live music, I tend to find that lots of people rely on MIDI too much—sometimes the computer can "play" music that is practically unplayable! When doing orchestral mockups you can place the double basses really high and make them sound really soft, while in reality they will have lots of tension and will not sound balanced with the other instrument sections (if they are not in their highest register, of course). And the biggest problem of MIDI—too perfect, no matter what you try doing.

*Q: What do you feel is the biggest benefit MIDI has to offer?*

Definitely the possibility to edit each single note—especially with latest standards when the composer can even edit the different parts of the chord. The sample libraries are developed really fast and today you can basically edit the vibrato, dynamics, and timbre of an instrument, thus making the music sound as real as possible!

*Q: Do you create your written scores via MIDI or do you create your MIDI via written score?*

Both. Depends on what I have to do—when I work for film, I usually compose directly inside Cubase while looking at the video. Composing concert works, arrangements, or library music I usually do within Sibelius and then manually edit all the MIDI data, "adjusting" it to the sample libraries (sometimes I just play the parts manually, especially when dynamics are involved).

## Dr. Noize

### *Bio*

Dr. Noize, or Cory Cullinan, was raised in Silicon Valley, California. Cullinan studied music at the prestigious Stanford University, emphasizing classical music history, electronic

**Figure 9.3**

music, and voice. Cullinan has compositions featured in Brad Pitt's *Spy Game* as well as documentaries shown at Sundance Film Festival and aired on PBS. Cullinan then began teaching high school music at Pinewood School, where he was named the Arts, Communication & Technology department head. Soon after becoming a father, Cullinan began creating inspired music and multimedia learning for children under the pseudonym Dr. Noize. Cullinan had a #1 hit song—"Banana"—on Sirius XM Kids Radio. Dr. Noize currently performs across the country, engaging kids and adults with his innovative performances as well as hosting "workshopz" across the country.

*Q: What is your MIDI controller of choice?*

In the studio: Roland A-90EX, Yamaha Motif, & Roland Handsonic HPD-15. Also the Mackie Control Universal for mixing. They're all pretty old but good; there's probably better stuff available now.

*Q: What DAW do you prefer to use when dealing with MIDI?*

In the studio, I use Logic. Sometimes Pro Tools, but only because my mixer and drummer use that. In live performance, I use Ableton Live.

*Q: What role does MIDI play in your live performances?*

I loop record drums with the Roland HandSonic HPD-10. I also mix and loop record live with the Akai APC20. I used to also play my synth parts through wireless MIDI on the AX-1, but now I have the Ax Synth, which has built-in sounds. I just use those sounds.

*Q: Have you incorporated the OSC protocol into your studio/live rig at all to replace MIDI?*

I don't know. I don't think I even know what that is. Probably answers your question.

*Q: What do you feel is MIDI's biggest weakness?*

Slow and connectivity issues.

*Q: What do you feel is the biggest benefit MIDI has to offer?*

You can quantize stuff. MIDI is great for making fast great demos, or quantizing live loops.

*Q: Do you have any MIDI interconnections in your studio?*

I use the emagic amt8.

*Q: Do you create your written scores via MIDI or do you create your MIDI via written score?*

Written scores via Sibelius. No, I don't create MIDI via written score.

## C. J. Drummeller

### Bio

C. J. Drummeller is a multiple Emmy Award-winning audio engineer. Drummeller owns and operates Follow Happy Productions, an independent production company that specializes in composing, ENG and EFP field mixing, dialog editing, small production, rerecording sound mixing, foley, live broadcasts/recording, and vocal tuning/touch ups. Follow Happy Productions features a full 5.1 and 7.1 production studio that combines modern digital and vintage analog equipment. Besides Drummeller's multiple Emmy Awards, Follow Happy Productions has also been awarded 68 Telly Awards and has worked on both nationally and internationally distributed projects. Besides operating Follow Happy Productions, C.J. has served as supervising sound editor for more than 1,200 broadcasts and syndicated TV shows in the last six years, including one of the longest-running live satellite broadcasts in television history via Daystar Satellite Network.

**Figure 9.4**

*Q: What is your MIDI controller of choice?*

For general use, I am a huge fan of the Novation Impulse series for an all-purpose pad, key, and fader controller. In the studio, I tend to match controllers to the keyboard-weighting type of the sound I am using. For example, when playing a piano virtual instrument, I love to use the Korg SV-1 due to the realistic RH3 keybed weighting. When playing an organ or synth virtual instrument, I'll use one of my waterfall weighted keyboards.

*Q: What DAW do you prefer to use when working with MIDI?*

I have become a big fan of Ableton Live, as it has developed some incredibly creative MIDI tools like audio melody to MIDI and MIDI reverse/invert. That being said, since a majority of my MIDI ends up being mixed to albums, Pro Tools 10 provides the cleanest and quickest workflow with most studios.

*Q: What role does MIDI play in your live performances?*

For example, live performing via MIDI sound banks, MIDI controller triggering clips, etc.

Depending on the performance or group, I tend to stay away from using software when possible. I run an Akai MPC1000 as my main MIDI brain, letting it run click, control my array of synths (Prophet '08, Moog Little Phatty, Dave Smith Mopho, Korg MS-2000), and run vintage drums samples via MIDI input. Recently the live process includes a large amount of modding and FX enabled by the MPC MIDI controlling the simple note on/off and velocity messages. I find this to be truer to the original synths which were designed without keyboards, or piano-based note controllers, allowing me to focus on the musical value of the "mod" just as much as the note. In a way, MIDI allows me to clone myself in the live environment allowing me to focus on what is going to make the show unique to the situation or audience, while keeping the notes the same. At times

I'll record MIDI NRPN parameters (filter sweeps, LFO BPMs, OSC pitch, etc.) directly to the MPC for certain song portions or transitions. This allows for a new level of dynamics in the set. Feats rendered impossible if I were limited to the use of my two hands playing notes. I also use the MPC to send Program Change messages to all my synths triggered on launch of each song in the set. Most of these things could be handled with a laptop or software, but having the hardware is something important to me, and seems to be more stable than trusting the whole show to a fragile laptop processor.

*Q: Have you incorporated the OSC protocol into your studio/live rig at all to replace MIDI?*

Short answer: no . . . but I would like to.

*Q: What do you feel is MIDI's biggest weakness?*

In my opinion, the biggest weaknesses are the speed (latency) of transfer, and the max run length of a MIDI cable. Though not so much an issue when playing live, in the studio environment the latency and MIDI offsets needed to play in real time can be a true pain when sending MIDI through and external instrument and back into the DAW. I've set specific channels for the latency in each synth channel so that the process is somewhat automatic, but even so, it still requires nudging after the take as sometime MIDI pass-through seems a bit unpredictable.

Cable length becomes an issue when you are trying to trigger external components via MIDI. Be it a fog machine, a FOH board snapshot change, or a complete light show controlled by MIDI, the MIDI cable loses much stability when run over 50 ft.

*Q: What do you feel is the biggest benefit MIDI has to offer?*

I'll start with a comparison: MIDI is to performance, what DAW non-linear editing is to music. Before MIDI, when musicians wanted to record a song they got together, hit "record" on the tape machine and did it over and over until they got the take they felt to be "good enough." Now with non-linear editing, the engineer can keep the drums, bass, and guitar track, then rerecord the keyboards on the chorus. Breaking down each take to usable parts. MIDI takes this another step, allowing the edit for each individual note, as well as the velocity, sustain, and timing of that note.

As a performer, I often joke that MIDI is the best and worst thing that's ever happened to me. I can now record an inferior take and edit or even "perfect" it in less time that it would take to practice until I could get it right. On a positive note MIDI allows me to hear my take from a different perspective, especially as I am my own engineer. For example: it is often impossible to listen to myself playing and maintain a sense of listener perspective. Whether I need to "tame" my passionate moments (via velocity and quantization), or excite it (doubling a lead line with octaves perhaps), all this is made possible from a few clicks of the mouse. The creative benefits of MIDI are endless, making your musical canvas something moldable, stretchable, and even random when needed.

At the same time learning to edit MIDI can be like a kid stopping vocal lessons because she started watching auto-tuning tutorials.

And yet, to all the MIDI naysayers I propose a question: at the end of the day what really is the difference from hitting a key on a keyboard and clicking a mouse button? In the end music is music, no matter what's triggering the waves.

*Q: Do you have any MIDI interconnections in your studio?*

I run MIDI I/O throughout my studio via the Digidesign 003R+ and a M-Audio Midisport 8 × 8/s. Usually a take involves a somewhat ritual process, as nerdy as that may sound. I route and connect MIDI IN and OUT to the synth of choice and make sure MIDI clock is being sent from the DAW to that channel. On the first take, I will simply record the MIDI note, velocity, and sustain messages. Then, I'll play back via MIDI OUT, and adjust the sound if needed to find something that fits the song or part better. I'll then take a quick pass at the quantization and notes, making sure everything sounds proper. Once happy with the performance I'll set up a secondary MIDI track, taking the "note" MIDI track out of record mode. This second track will record the second pass of MIDI "mod" NRPN messages. I'll hit "record," and only record the filter sweeps, LFO changes, attack and release envelopes on the notes being read by the MIDI IN on the synth. This maintains the purity of the simple MIDI messages in case I switch analog synths, or want to export MIDI tracks to the MPC with no mods so I can do it in a live environment.

*Q: Do you create your written scores via MIDI or do you create your MIDI via written score*

I am a big fan of the impulsive "write-record-write-record" method. This basically means I'll record a blip of MIDI or something that inspires me, and build a whole track around that inspiration. Many of my favorite tunes are actually mistakes I was able to reconstruct in the MIDI realm and make palatable for the listener. Writing with MIDI opens boundless venues of creative options I wouldn't have otherwise.

## Jonathan Hillman

### *Bio*

Jonathan Hillman got his start in music at the age of 4 by learning to play the piano. He studied composition in college and has dedicated his life to music ever since. Being an avid gamer, it was only natural that Hillman would pursue sound and music for video games. Among many others, Hillman has composed music for such games as "Titans of Space," "Dark Island," "Regardless," "Sneaky Snakes," and "Hamster: Attack!" Aside from composing music for video games, Hillman worked as a product manager for PreSonus for 10 years developing their "Studio One" software, which has become an industry standard. Hillman is also an active member of the Game Audio Network Guild (GANG), as well as a member of ASCAP.

**Figure 9.5**

*Q: What is your MIDI controller of choice?*

I've had quite a few. Right now I have an Alesis QS8 as my main "playing" board. I don't use any of the built-in sounds, just needed the action, as I prefer weighted keys (I'm a keyboard player). I'm actively looking for an old Yamaha KX-88 to replace it.

*Q: What DAW do you prefer to use when working with MIDI?*

Studio One if in the studio, Live for performance/installation stuff.

*Q: What role does MIDI play in your live performances?*

For example, live performing via MIDI sound banks, MIDI controller triggering clips, etc.

When I was still gigging I played VSTs live, preferring the sounds of plug-ins to any workstation. So, I had a bunch of banks setup that I would switch from the controller, either by switching through MIDI tracks, or program changes (rarely).

I also had controls set up for each instrument I would play, to tweak different parameters.

*Q: Have you incorporated the OSC protocol into your studio/live rig at all to replace MIDI?*

I've used OSC with various controller setups I've built with the Arduino platform in conjunction with Max/PD. Outside of that, MIDI is usually sufficient otherwise.

*What do you feel is MIDI's biggest weakness?*

While a lot of progress has been made to abstract the inner workings of MIDI to modern users, MIDI's biggest weakness is now its usability. Users these days do not, do not wish to, and do not need to understand how MIDI works. In fact, in my experience most users would not recognize MIDI if they saw it, even though they use it all the time. MIDI is becoming less relevant every day as a result, as even though a lot of modern paradigms are using MIDI "under the hood," at some point they will evolve away from MIDI altogether.

*Q: What do you feel is the biggest benefit MIDI has to offer?*

Ubiquity. Every DAW supports it, every controller supports it, is documented end to end, inside and out. To this day, I find it amazing that any technology platform that enables creativity achieved such a monopoly.

*Q: Do you have any MIDI interconnections in your studio?*

Only from the controllers to my computer, however I "talk" to/from all of them from there. I also use LoopMIDI to bring in some external stuff like Lemur (the iOS app) controllers and Arduino hardware when necessary.

*Q: Do you create your written scores via MIDI or do you create your MIDI via written score*

When I need a written score, either as real need for the project or as an aid in the composition process, I always write the score first. I'll then go in and produce the score via MIDI in a DAW, which usually involves backflips of all sorts to achieve what's written in the score.

## Matt Moldover

### *Bio*

Matt Moldover is the godfather of "Controllerism." Moldover singlehandedly created an entire subculture of "Controllerists" that are beginning to emerge as the MIDI innovators of the day. Moldover has been designing and building his own custom MIDI controllers for some time now and has gained extreme notoriety for his innovative use of these controllers.

**Figure 9.6** Credit: Marie Jo Mont-Rey.

Moldover has also worked with Visionary Instruments in order to construct a guitar/MIDI controller for mass markets known as the "Robocatser." Moldover is also at the forefront of an emerging movement that brings together fellow Controllerists in order to bring about musical collaboration and live performance—something that has been missing in contemporary electronic music.

**Q: What do you feel is the greatest strength of MIDI?**

Its ubiquitous presence in digital musical instruments made in the last 30 years.

**Q: What do you feel is MIDI's largest weakness?**

In common implementation it still suffers from some antiquated features. Those features made it practical and popular 30 years ago, but now they cause inconvenience, such as the 7-bit continuous controller standard.

**Q: What inspired you to begin creating your own innovative controllers?**

I started performing professionally as a controllerist around 2004. At that time there was a huge gap in the controller market. There were cheap instruments based on legacy musical interfaces, like the old Oxygen 8 keyboard, and expensive instruments offering futuristic musical interfaces like the Haken Continuum. As an independent musician living in New York City I couldn't afford single instruments that cost thousands of dollars. I started buying the cheap ones to combine and modify in new ways to get what I wanted. By 2007, my needs for the instrument had grown beyond what I could do with modification, and I began designing custom controllers.

**Q: Do you ever use standard controllers in the studio or just the ones you have built?**

I use several standard controllers in my studio, but more-so for the legacy interfaces (keyboards and drum pads).

*Q: Can you tell us a bit about your Mojo controller as well as your jam boxes like the Mini-Masher and Octo-Masher and what you set out to create with them?*

The Mojo is the third-generation physical interface for a sample-manipulation and dub-mixing instrument. The software began in early versions of Ableton, was augmented by many custom Reaktor patches, and now includes a variety of Max4Live and 3rd-party VST devices. The Mojo's physical design can be described as a hybrid of a DJ mixer, a keyboard, and a gaming controller. It has an ergonomic layout based on a pair of human hands as they would lay on a flat surface. It utilizes a wide variety of sensors chosen for different expressive gestures and tactile differentiation. It is constructed with high-quality, easily replaceable parts.

Since 2005 I have been creating multiplayer musical instruments commonly referred to as jamboxes. These create the social music experiences I don't normally get on stage, and act as a counterpoint to my work as a solo performer. In creating a jambox, I apply my knowledge of performance instrument design to the very different context of group human interaction. The result is not an elegant and polished piece of musical engineering like The Mojo, but the experience of making music with this instrument and a group of people at the same time is nothing short of phenomenal. Now that Controllerism is a commonly practiced art, and I'm turning my energies to evangelizing jamboxes, it's only a matter of a few years before interest in them explodes, and a new niche is carved in the musical landscape.

*Q: Do you only use Ableton or do you integrate other DAWs as well?*

I don't consider Ableton Live a DAW. It was designed as a live performance instrument, not an "audio workstation." I believe this is one of the primary secrets to its success in the broader category of music software, and the reason so many people wish to use it in the studio as one would use a conventional workstation. I use Live for live performance, and Steinberg's Cubase for studio production.

*Q: Have you incorporated OSC at all into your live or studio setups?*

I have used OSC for brief periods with instruments like the Jazz Mutant Lemur, Reaktor, and the TouchOSC app for iOS. I have not used it extensively.

*Q: Do you believe MIDI will be replaced by OSC (or another protocol) in the future?*

All things change, and I imagine music makers touring the stars will probably not use MIDI as much as I do. Perhaps a good parallel is musical notation. I haven't used notation much at all in the last 10 years, largely because of my fascination with music technology. MIDI sequencing and digital audio recording have replaced my need for such a thing, however plenty of people on the planet are still making music with notation every day. Just the same, I think MIDI will be around for a long time. Most music is and will be made up of sounds which we might call "notes" and "beats," which we might draw as a dot on a piece of staff paper, or encode as MIDI messages. Just because we have new instruments and extended musical vocabularies to explore those things doesn't mean we need a whole new system for communicating our musical ideas.

## Kenny Bergle

### *Bio*

Kenny Bergle got his start in music by banging pots and pans as a three-year-old. In high school, Bergle was beginning to experiment with electronics and was constantly pulling apart old transistor radios to see how they functioned. Bergle eventually went on to study jazz composition, jazz education, and jazz guitar at the University of North Texas. Bergle opened his own recording studio, KCB Studios, in 1979 and formed KCBSystems, an audio/MIDI consulting firm in 1985. While

**Figure 9.7**

operating KCBSystems, Bergle was hired to design and implement MIDI compositional and performance systems for many world-renowned artists, including B. B. King, Kiss, The Grateful Dead, RunDMC, and Ornette Coleman, among many others. During this time, Bergle began gaining notoriety composing and recording jingle for Pepsi, KFC, McDonald's, Pizza Hut, Burger King, Disney, Del Taco, and many others. Bergle then went on to become the technical director at The Caravan of Dreams Performing Arts Center in Fort Worth, Texas, where he worked with most of the jazz greats of the period including Dizzy Gillespie, Ornette Coleman, Joe Zawinul, Pharoh Sanders, Herbie Hancock, Pat Mentheny, and Chick Corea, just to name a few. Bergle now works for Sweetwater, hosting instructional videos and interviews online at sweetwater.com as well as working on Broadway as a technical consultant.

*Q: What is your background with MIDI? How were you introduced to it and what were some of your early experiences with it?*

I was introduced to MIDI like everybody else in the industry at the '83 NAMM show. There was a thing called the MIDI

Manufacturers Association. It was started by Roland and Sequential Circuits and a few others. Surprisingly, all the big name manufacturers got together and actually agreed on something to further the industry by going from control voltage to MIDI. The MMA voted at the January show in '83 on the specifications of MIDI and by 1985 it was pretty well accepted by a bunch of manufacturers.

So that's how it started and it was a big buzz at NAMM. There was a separate kind of meeting—a MIDI branch at NAMM in the early 80s but as soon as it hit the market it took over NAMM and it took over the whole music industry. At first pro-audio said, "well no, no, no that's for consumers and for musicians and that's not for us pro-audio guys." Then they realized the value of control of MIDI and then you saw MIDI plugs on lots of studio devices so you could control and save presets and stuff like that.

So taking a step back, I'm a nutty Avant-Garde musician. The stuff I play is reflective of my world, which is crazy and unresolved and full of conflict. So my music sounds like that. Nobody really cares to hear it and definitely nobody cares to work on it and play with me so I've always been into the drum machines and the keyboards that sit there and play without complaining about what I told them to play while I played guitar on top of it. So when MIDI came out, I saw that as a huge opportunity for me to have a whole orchestra or a whole band that didn't show up drunk and didn't complain. So I went into it wholeheartedly just to be able to compose my own whacky mess.

Soon, I found that as MIDI devices started coming out, I started buying tons of that stuff. I had inherited a bit of money and I used that money for music school, which I was going to at the time, and for gear to put a studio together so I could create my own stuff. I started buying the stuff and realized quickly that the manuals were lying, the advertisements and magazines were lying, and basically the manufacturers were pulling over the public and musician and consumers by saying this works with this and it will all work together. It wasn't true at all. The fact is that many pieces by manufacturers, who will go nameless, didn't work within just the manufacturer themselves. One piece wouldn't talk MIDI to the other piece—they didn't have the same time base. We didn't understand back then that things had to be clocked and synced in a clock sense and a timing sense. Some of these larger manufacturers that had different branches of development were designing instruments that supposedly worked with each other and they didn't.

Since I had been spending all my money on this MIDI stuff, I literally had no money to eat and I was desperate to make this stuff work or sell it to eat. So I would, with that kind of desperation, stay on the phone with all the manufacturers—all of them—Yamaha, Roland, Korg, Akai, and Sequential Circuits. I would stay on the phone with them and many times they'd hang up and I would call back and keep calling back until I would at least talk to somebody that would know something about the design of the piece of gear and tell me the truth as opposed to what was in the manual and what was in the adds.

Enter B. B. King. At the time he was playing in Dallas at the Fairmont Hotel, which was just an hour north of me. B. B. was very intelligent, very hip on technology, and he had a ton of gear in his hotel room, none of which worked. He asked the head of the house band in Dallas if he had any knowledge about the MIDI stuff and if he could help him with it. That guy was my client and even back then he would call me and I would straighten his MIDI sequencer stuff out and his computer stuff. Anyway, he said "no, really you should call Kenny Bergle." So believe it or not, at four o'clock in the morning, I got a call and it was B. B. King. At first I was like "no, no who is this really" and I was cussing and he told me it was really him and that the head of the house band gave him my number. I shot up in bed and started apologizing. He said, "Look, I need your help. I've got all this gear and none of it works" and then we talked for about 15 minutes and I, at that moment, got out of bed, threw on my clothes, and went the hour down to Dallas. I got to Dallas, right at sunrise and got up to his room which was completely littered with computers and MIDI interfaces and synthesizers and all this wild electronics. He started telling me that "this didn't work and that didn't work" and I said "yeah, that doesn't work and that doesn't work" and then he said, "what does work?" I proceeded to sell him, over the next three years, a whole kind of rig to where he could play Lucille into the computer and spit out sheet music for the band to rehearse off of. And when I did that, successfully, he basically told everyone in show business. And then I was getting calls from everybody—The Grateful Dead, The Who, Kiss, and all of the big names. Everybody called because they were all trying to integrate MIDI into their deal but nobody really knew anything. No one had been persistent enough to sit on the phone like me and amass all these data across manufacturers.

Anyway, that's how I kind of got into MIDI and then by that time I realized that there was a huge call for this and I was working on other people's problems 100% of the time and not working on my music at all. It was good, but it was just one of those deals that I could only take for a while because I started all this to foster my own creativity. So I quit doing the studio and quit doing the MIDI support thing and joined on as a technical director at the Caravan of Dreams, which is this beautiful performing arts center in downtown Fort Worth, Texas, and basically ended up doing the same thing for all of the touring acts that came through (laughs). But at least I was in a creative atmosphere and I ran a studio where I did a ton of tremendous recordings, which was really a dream come true for me, as well as working on my own stuff. So that was a long, long answer but that's kind of how I got into MIDI.

*Q: How much do you use MIDI on a weekly basis these days?*

I wish I could say I used it a lot but I don't. The fact is with a 10- and a 12-year-old, it's all I can do to play piano and play guitar. The cool thing about MIDI now is it's just such a no brainier—like with virtual instruments you know, you don't really have to think much. It used to be that I had to think all the way through from the controller to the virtual instrument and to the D/A converter and back out and all that mess in Pro Tools or Cubase or Cakewalk or any of them. And now, they all pretty much have it down to where it's just another track and it takes care of all that thinking internally inside of the computer. I do use MIDI for instance, because I use Superior Drummer for a drum track to play with but I'm just getting back into it. Just so you know, for my new act, I'll use MIDI to trigger a projector for the different Keynote slides as well as trigger the presets of all my sounds on my guitar rig and the looper and trigger loops and stuff in Ableton. So, I'm working that up again but the fact is, I've been pretty damn dormant. When I had a studio though, I used it all the time.

*Q: What do you consider are the strengths and weaknesses of MIDI as it currently stands?*

Control is a big strength for stuff that doesn't have to be super-high timing resolution. So lights and projectors, its tremendous for that stuff. I really like it for lights because it has so many more channels and translates to DMX really well. And the other strength for it is the whole virtual instrument world and the ability to run the virtual instrument from a MIDI controller. One weakness is that the timing is too rough of a resolution. We need an open source protocol that has the resolution of Ethernet-16million levels of resolution to where we can mix on a better protocol than MIDI. I think that's a big limitation. I'm not one that thinks the 16 channels is a limitation though. I think that's plenty—especially today. A lot of people say they need 32 or 40 channels on a single cable—I don't think that.

*Q: What do you think the future for MIDI is? Do you think it's going to evolve or do you think they're going to replace it?*

People always want to reinvent the wheel. I personally think that it's not going to happen. Just like a Strat, in 60 years we're going to have MIDI. And we'll still have strats. It just works and it works well enough to the point where MIDI chips are so cheap and you can put something together and put it in a keyboard or a drum machine or a guitar really inexpensively. I bet that MIDI, the way it is, is going to be the way it is for quite a while. Audio over Ethernet, though, is kind of where the whole industry is going so I imagine MIDI will just tag onto that. It's such a great control system. And it's cheap.

*Q: Do you have a favorite piece of MIDI gear?*

Well, as a guitarist, the thing that opened my world and my mind to MIDI guitar was being able to play string patches on the guitar and being able to play clarinets and oboes on a guitar which made me, composing wise, so much smarter by being able to play all the parts and hear how it might sound rather than having to try and imagine it. So I think probably MIDI guitar is my favorite because I love guitar, I love keyboard, and I love the orchestral stuff. Yeah, I would probably say MIDI guitar. To be honest, I would say the sequencer itself as well. The MIDI recorder also changed my life and allowed all of this stuff.

*Q: Which MIDI guitar do you use?*

I have a Fender Strat that has a Roland 13 pin in it, I have a Brian Moore that has the Roland GR System built into it. Then I have a MIDI pickup on a Paul Reed Smith that's killer. On a side note, it's interesting because there's been a huge resurgence of MIDI because in the 90s, MIDI was kind of the stepchild to Audio. Digital Audio was new, and it was just coming on the scene and it was developing and getting better and better. And MIDI was matured at that point really. And so everyone was into Digital Audio. But when Apple started putting Garage Band in every Mac for free, and there's all these MIDI loops in there, MIDI started making a comeback. And to be honest Ableton completely changed the entire landscape. When Ableton came out, and people could do these audio loops and sync them tempo wise so MIDI and audio loops could play together and it didn't matter what the tempo was, that was a huge thing and then all over the world people rediscovered MIDI. All the ravers and the DJs and the techno and dub guys and all this electronica is all MIDI based. And now, DJs, are a huge MIDI market.

*Q: What do you know about OSC? Do you know what that is?*

Yeah, it's kind of a protocol that allows iOs to talk MIDI. It's also a protocol that people can use to build their own programs like TouchOSC.

*Q: Do you see that getting any traction?*

Well, it's a big download; a lot of people have it on their iPhones and iPads and stuff. TouchOSC was the first app to control pro tools. So that was a big indicator that it's useful. But honestly, I'm so far from that side of development. I'm on the other side where everything has already been developed and marketed. But a lot of my customers use it and are developing all kinds of stuff.

*Q: Do you have any stories where MIDI let you down? Crashed and burned?*

Hmm. Not let me down but this is a classic story about this huge mega-rock band of the 70s and 80s who will go nameless. They had a whole drum set recorded on 8 tracks of reel-to-reel tape and they had a Yamaha DMP7 mixer that was MIDI controlled. They were supposed to automate the mix so that the front of house guy could just run the tape and the drums would mix themselves while he mixed everything else live. The drummer would play the drums which had mics on them, but the mics weren't on. But it didn't work, that desk didn't do what it was supposed to do—it failed miserably. I got called to come fix it and when I got there, I told them it wouldn't work to do what they wanted and the main member of the band fired me right there on the spot and called me a liar. Well a few weeks later I got a call from his office apologizing because they figured out I was right. They asked me to come back out and put together a system that does work but I had to decline though because I was working with The Grateful Dead putting together the first MIDI marimba.

Here's another story that's really cool—I was working with the keyboardist for Weather Report and at one point his Korg M1 got damaged on a flight. The Korg M1 was one of the keyboards that really made MIDI acceptable on stage—it had such great sounds that artists thought it was worthy to play with on stage. But anyway, he comes to me five minutes before curtain and told me he couldn't do the show without the M1. I told him I wasn't a keyboard tech but I'd take it apart and look at it for him. When I got the top off, I found four or five screws rolling around the bottom of it and I took those out and put the keyboard back together and low and behold, the son of a gun worked. So the screws were doing some kind of short—they were shorting something out somewhere. I brought it back up stairs and gave it to him and told him I got it to work and he literally got on his knees and told me I was his hero.

## Jay Smith

### *Bio*

Jay Smith began his musical and electronic career while studying at the University of the Arts in Philadelphia. During his studies at the university, Jay built his first innovative controller—"The Editar" and its corresponding software—in his parent's basement. The following year, "The Editar" was transformed into "The Viditar," which incorporated innovative

**Figure 9.8**

video control. Jay started playing live with his group "Sinch," combining music and video. During a show in Houston, Texas, Jay met Travis Redding, an innovative instrument maker, and the two began collaborating together in order to create state-of-the-art innovative controllers and instruments. Soon after, the two started Livid Instruments and began creating controllers and software for the public. Livid Instruments is now the leading company creating unique and creative control surfaces as well as DIY equipment that consumers can utilize while building their own instruments and controllers.

## Q: What got you into MIDI?

I went to college in Philadelphia in a fine arts program for experimental media. I was working on a lot of physical installation work with video and audio. Back then, I wasn't in an engineering program and there wasn't much MIDI available and the DIY market was pretty small. I started building and experimenting with a controller I ended up calling the Viditar. It was an audio/video mixing instrument. I developed that in college. The first MIDI interface I used was the Doepfer CTM, which was the original DIY MIDI interface

I built my first instrument and I joined a rock band. It was kind of a conceptual thing with me playing this instrument in a five-piece rock band with video screens and audio samplings. It was pretty interesting. It was in '99 when I was doing that. So I had to run a number of instruments in that band and I just kept tweaking and modifying my interfaces. We ended up getting a record deal during my senior year in college and I took my little invention and went out on the road. I was playing this experimental, fine art, MIDI instrument in a pretty heavy rock touring setting, which was really interesting because my history was with experimental performance art and I was taking that into a mainstream setting. From there I met Travis, my business partner, at a show in Houston. After the show he came up to me, and told me that he was making these MIDI bass guitars, which had MIDI triggering systems in the fret board and an analog control in the body. I was a novice builder and my stuff was really crude but his basses had these beautiful bodies. He was living in Austin, Texas, and since I was speaking at South-by-South West that same year, he told me to come by and we'd build something. We started collaborating and here we are 10 years later still doing the same kind of stuff. That's kind of how I fell into it.

*Q: Do you still play quite a bit?*

Um . . . I play boss! Hahahah. No, I don't play anymore. Running the business is as much as I can handle. I demo our products and I like to experiment with other people's products too. Just seeing what people are doing. I still build my own stuff every now and again. But no, I don't play out, hardly ever.

*Q: Do you miss it?*

Yeah I do, absolutely. If I had time I would love to, I just don't have time.

*Q: What else do you see that's out there that's kind of impressed you lately? From other people's designs and companies.*

Yeah, like I said, when I first started I was not an engineer at all. I went to school for fine art and I was interested in creating things that didn't exist from a creative and artistic standpoint. I absorbed all the cool new tech. But at the time, Doepfer was the only company making the DIY things and I pledged that when I started a company I was going to do that. So we've championed the DIY market. It's still a small market but it's my pet project. One of my partners is in town and we went to Radio Shack and saw Arduino builder kits and I was like, wow. So the Arduino thing is interesting its maybe a little too technical—I like stuff to be simpler because I don't think you have to be an engineer to make something cool.

But definitely Arduino is pretty cool stuff. Doepfer kind of got out of the game there still doing cool things but not necessarily in that realm. But with our stuff, in particular, I've seen some really cool stuff. There's this guy—Matt Moldover—I don't know if you've heard of him. Have you heard of Moldover? He's pretty well known in the electronic music and DIY scene. He's created some really amazing instruments using our DIY products. His work is just really, really cool. Are you speaking about who's doing cool things in general? Or from a DIY or commercial standpoint?

*Q: I was thinking more of the DIY stuff*

It's funny, you know we create these products that you can make your own MIDI controllers with and over the past year Ableton had been ordering various DIY parts and they came out with their Push controller. Then we found out at NAMM that that's what they had been purchasing our products for the whole time. There were using our DIY stuff to make this commercial controller, which was just super awesome to find that out. There's just so many cool controllers that were made by using our stuff. I couldn't tell you off the top of my head, I'd have to send you links to them. I'm more impressed by the people that are building stuff really than I am about the people that are making commercial kits or anything like that. I think Arduino has done a lot for the community just in terms of physical computing interfaces and making things. But yeah, I'm more impressed with the people that are building things. There's this guy— Nick Francis—who created this instrument called the chopper-tone. He's an older guy—never built anything in his life and he had this idea for this instrument and he looked on our wiki, bought a couple of Brains and built this really cool instrument that he does jazz remixes with. It's things like that—someone who's never built anything in their life who suddenly have created a MIDI controller for their own language of performing music based on this little microcontroller that we sell.

*Q: What about things like OSC? Have you been looking at incorporating that at all or any other formats?*

MIDI is just convenient. It's my personal opinion, I mean I don't care, it's just a protocol. Whatever makes it easy. Whatever makes it easy for the end user is what I'm really concerned about. OSC is interesting but it's not really viable for a hardware product. People like OSC because it has this high resolution but to manufacture hardware that has that high resolution is very, very difficult and probably not viable. Which is why there's never been an OSC hardware device. I mean, you have some people like Keith McMillian, they have some OSC drivers—they're not really OSC it's just a driver that turns into OSC—I don't really see the point in that. I mean it's great as a protocol from one computer to the next—especially for people who are doing visuals and who connect multiple computers to networks—then it's great. But when it comes to hardware, it's new, it's unsupported, and there's no hardware devices that actually are OSC. People are excited about it but if people like Ableton and Native Instruments started supporting it, then other people would jump on board. But the nice thing about MIDI is that it's just been around for so long. I mean it's been the same protocol for 30 years—it's still 1.0. It's not like its super high tech it's just easy and people get it. So I'm interested in other protocols but it's really up to the software companies to support it. Because hardware really can't support it until software does.

*Q: Yeah, well your views are pretty much spot on with everyone I've talked to. So I'm getting the same message from everybody.*

Yeah, people keep saying "make an OSC driver" and I say for what? Why would I do that? What's the point? I think it's almost a marketing gimmick. If you're using an iPad maybe that makes sense but from a hardware standpoint it doesn't really do much for the end user. I'm all about making it easy. My thing is that I think people should spend less time being techno geeks and technology junkies and spend more time being artists. So whatever makes that easier for the artist, I think is what's important.

Q: *Describe your experiences with MIDI over the years.*

For me personally, I didn't start using MIDI until it was well established. And I didn't really know what it was when I first started using it. I knew that CC7 was volume and that was the first time I really understood the correlation between MIDI numbers and music. Because now for me, I think in terms of numbers and how it turned from this musical format into this technology format. And when you have a company like ours, your thinking controllers that are doing new musical things where C2 isn't actually a note—it's a number and it does something different for everyone. I'm thinking back to MIDI and MIDI files and the web and the first time I ever used MIDI. The first time I ever used it, I was actually using it to do a video installation. I had been sending these note messages but I didn't care about the note messages I just needed the values to trigger the sensor.

One thing that actually does come to mind is my first MIDI controller was a MAudio MIDIman oxygen 8 and I just remember being able to take that controller, hook it up to Max/MSP, and use something called NATO, which was a quick-time program for MAX, and being able to play a keyboard note and trigger a visual. And I just thought that was a cool thing. It was the first MIDI controller I ever had—the oxygen 8, I still have it. For me the first portable MIDI controller was the Maudio oxygen 8. That was a huge light bulb that went off for me and I realized how simple what I wanted to do could be.

Q: *And that's another great example, too, of just talking about how Max/MSP has made such a big difference in it as well.*

Yeah, I mean, if anybody is at the cutting edge of technology with music and media interactions and stuff it's the guys over at Cycling 74. You know, I said nobody supports OSC but

Max does. I was thinking that back in my mind but I didn't say it. So yeah, Max/MSP was literally my first time ever using MIDI from an I/O standpoint you know, with an input and an output.

And those guys have been really significant for us—the guys over at cycling have been huge supporters of what we do and a lot of the stuff we do, we rely on Max, especially in the early days.

*Q: Any last thoughts?*

Sure, well you have guys like Dave Smith who was obviously one of the pioneers of MIDI and he's using it on his new products on a very modern level. That's a really good kind of history lesson there. It hasn't changed much but look at the products, they've changed a lot. For me, MIDI isn't about music, it's about numbers—it' s about an easy protocol and that's what I really love about what our users end up doing with the DIY stuff—there doing things way beyond a notation system. I just saw a video of a guy doing a mind control visual thing with one of our MIDI brains. It was like a Star Wars mind Jedi trainer thing that you put on your head and you can make things go up and down.

I think the most significant thing that's happening to MIDI even in the past five years, is that it's no longer a musical system—it's really just a protocol for people to interface with computers and vice versa. That's the biggest change. A lot of people that use it don't even know that its related to music.

## John Staskevich–Highly Liquid
### *Bio*

Figure 9.9

Beginning in 2004, Highly Liquid has provided MIDI electronics for DIY consumers for custom projects. Through innovative design, Highly Liquid's products have allowed musicians, artists, and hobbyists a means to rapidly build unique MIDI devices without a tedious understanding of circuit board design and embedded software work. John Staskevich is the leading designer behind Highly Liquid's products. Some of their products include an instant DIY MIDI controller/MIDI encoder, a MIDI decoder with 24 Logic/Servo outputs, and a MIDI Decoder with 8 Reed Relay Outputs. All of Highly Liquid's circuit board fabrication and assembly take place completely in the United States.

*Q: As a start, can you tell me a little bit about yourself and how you got into doing what you do with MIDI?*

The background is that I have been a fan of synthesizers and programming since I was a kid. I earned a BSCmpE in 1998 and specialize in embedded software.

Around 2001 I wrote a Linux-based MIDI sequencer for my own use. A couple of years later, I found an old Casio SK-1 at a garage sale and thought it would be cool to control it via MIDI. Sometime in the 80s or 90s, a Casio SK-1 MIDI retrofit was commercially available, but had been discontinued. So I decided to take a crack at designing my own. That was my first MIDI hardware design.

I decided to put the retrofit kit up for sale on eBay and surprisingly, there was enough demand to justify manufacturing a small batch. From there, I ended up creating some additional products based on my own project needs and customer suggestions.

While the kickstarter projects are not directly related to MIDI, how did they come into existence? BTW, they look really interesting!

The NTHSynth projects (NTH Music Synthesizer and Luminth) are the result of a collaboration with Kevin Holland. Kevin is a musician/programmer and fellow synthesizer enthusiast. Our goal so far has been to create fun and easy-to-use products. The collaboration is part time and just a couple of years old, so it's still in a very experimental phase.

*Q: Do you perform or compose? Do you have a MIDI studio?*

After I discovered the SK-1, I did some experimenting with circuit bending. This led to some additional products like the MSA* ("MIDI switch array") that I used to modulate circuit bends via MIDI. Another product was the MIDISpeak, which allows a Speak & Spell to be used as a MIDI sound module.

For a while I did have a collection of modified keyboards, drum machines, and other devices that all accepted MIDI input. I sequenced it all together using Ableton Live.

Composing is fun but I find it to be a giant time sink. I have given it up in recent years.

Interestingly, the MSA subsequently was used by Rock Band aficionados to retrofit their game controllers to accept MIDI input from proper instruments like e-drums and keyboards. (Originally, there were no game controllers manufactured with an integrated MIDI port.) The MSA has evolved since then and is now used for guitar effect loop switching and miscellaneous other things. Kind of an interesting range of applications.

# HISTORY OF MIDI     10

Musicians and instrument builders have long been interested in creating musical instruments that can play themselves. From the music box to the player piano and on to MIDI, a variety of technologies have been used to create mechanical instruments. Each of these instruments have a way to program the music it plays, and each system is unique from each other.

Some instruments use perforated paper in conjunction with an air system to trigger notes while others use metal spokes on a rotating cylinder. In all the years of mechanical instruments, there were very few standard performance specifications and so each designer built his own. This means that instruments couldn't sync together to create a larger ensemble, and it limited the scope of what they could accomplish.

Some of the more well-known automatronic instruments include player pianos, the orchestrion, music boxes, and the Ampico piano. The Ampico reproduces piano works in such realistic fashion that it is indistinguishable from an actual performer. Several well-known composers in the 1920s recorded performances for the Ampico and these are still available. Why, then, did the development of reproducing instruments halt? The reason that much of the forward momentum ceased concerning reproducing instruments was because of the invention and proliferation of audio recording. It was certainly cheaper to buy a disc than an entire piano.

The invention of electronic instruments started an avalanche of innovation and paralleled the growth of the music industry as it grew into a multibillion dollar business. Concerts became bigger and musicians used more and more equipment on stage, but they were limited as to how they could

**Figure 10.1** Ampico
Reproducing Piano

connect them. In the beginning one synthesizer couldn't control another and each had to stand alone, but with the further development of control voltage and shared voltage specs, synthesizers could share things like pitch control, gate triggering, and envelopes. Digital advances brought new ways to make synthesizers, hardware sequencers, and the foundation for creating bridges between devices.

Much has been written about the history of music technology and the events that led up to the full integration of MIDI in the production process, and so let's do something a little different. While many of the important dates are still listed here and the key developments are still credited, the history of MIDI is explained in five scenarios that demonstrate in practical terms the context of MIDI.

## MIDI—The Early Days

It seems like such an unlikely situation considering the continued success of MIDI, but at the beginning it took some time to get things working between the various manufacturers. Some didn't believe it would be accepted, others believed it wasn't good enough, and others didn't fully understand how to implement it. In the beginning, MIDI was only designed for live connections and could do things like allow you to control multiple instruments from a single keyboard or control multiple instruments from a computer in a multi-track setting.

Most of the history of MIDI revolves around NAMM meetings and some very passionate individuals who kept trying and trying to make a system work. The leaders of development were companies based in Japan such as Roland. A list of MIDI specifications was agreed upon before the January NAMM meeting in 1983, and several instruments were demonstrated working together. The first public connection of two MIDI instruments happened between the Prophet 600 and the Jupiter-6. Over the next months, MIDI was changed and tweaked and came dangerously close to imploding as different companies starting taking things in different directions.

**Figure 10.2** Prophet 600—The Original MIDI Synth
*Source:* Photo courtesy of www.perfectcircuitaudio.com

As a result of the early growth, MIDI 1.0 was announced and formalized to prevent continuous changes and to allow MIDI to begin to mature. Some manufacturers didn't adopt MIDI in the beginning because they were working on alternate systems. Oberheim had a parallel interface that promised to be much faster and initially refused to implement MIDI into their designs. Of course, once MIDI took over, Oberheim traded their system for the more popular system that was full of compromises.

Another issue that some manufacturers had with MIDI was the use of the 5-pin DIN connector, which was a decision made by the organizing body in an attempt to follow one prime directive: make the design simple and affordable to implement. There were a thousand ways to make a better communication protocol than MIDI, and using higher quality connectors might have made a better product, but that didn't fit into the plan.

Since the very beginning, there have been 16 channels per MIDI cable and multiple modes to determine how a source and destination send and receive MIDI. The 10-page MIDI spec had dictated 3 modes: omni, poly, and mono.

This example includes a keyboard (A) that is connected to two (B & C) MIDI-capable synthesizers. Controller A has two keyboards that are able to transmit over independent MIDI channels so that you can control both B and C. The ability of B and C to take advantage of the full MIDI spec is dependent on the available features of each instrument. In this example, A has hardware that is velocity sensitive and keys that generate pressure data (aftertouch). Instrument B responds to both velocity and pressure, but instrument C isn't designed to work with either. The difference in features directly affects the use of each instrument. C would likely be used for bass sounds or some other track that doesn't need a lot of dynamic range. Instrument B would be used for the more expressive tracks.

## The First MIDI Instruments

Creating a MIDI specification is all well and good, but it wouldn't have meant anything without having instruments to use it. The first keyboard to implement MIDI was the

**Figure 10.3** Yamaha DX-7—FM Synthesizer
*Source:* Photo courtesy of www.perfectcircuitaudio.com

Sequential Circuits Prophet 600. Dave Smith was the co-inventor of MIDI and also the founder of Sequential Circuits, and it is only fitting that his instrument would be the first to incorporate MIDI. While MIDI on the early instruments was fairly rudimentary, its success paved the way for more and more instruments to use the spec. It was not the Prophet 600 or the Jupiter-6, but it was the Yamaha DX-7 that cemented MIDI as the format of choice.

The DX-7 is an enigma because it was very popular but difficult to program. Its sound engine uses FM (Frequency Modulation) synthesis and could create much different sounds than its analog counterparts. From bright and clear patches to metallic pads, the DX-7 was popular because it could mimic real instruments and also reach into the world of space-like sound design. It could also be used as a controller to send MIDI to other instruments and presets were relatively easy to access. In spite of being difficult to program, the DX-7 was popular enough to make MIDI a permanent fixture in the music world.

Other instruments followed and have continued to follow 30 years after the birth of MIDI. In situations where the MIDI spec was limited, many instruments made up the difference. The E-mu Virtuoso 2000 is an example of such an instrument because it wanted to do more with MIDI and so it had multiple inputs for a total of 32 channels instead of 16 and over 1,000 sounds. Previously an orchestral module such as the Proteus One would have to be paired with several other modules to do the same thing.

MIDI started with synthesizers but quickly moved to samplers. In the 1980s and early '90s samplers were very limited in their storage capacity but as their abilities grew so did their use. Musicians often preferred them on stage because they could reproduce the exact desired sound without having to tweak knobs and a sampler could load wildly varying sounds in a way that a single synth could not. Two examples of such a module are the famous Fairlight CMI and the Akai S900. These two demonstrate the range of samplers. The Fairlight IIx, the first Fairlight to incorporate MIDI, was expensive and did much more than just sampling but showed the world what a sampler could accomplish. The Akai, on the other hand, came later and without such a distinguished pedigree, even though it had its own important history. The Akai is a rack unit that was considered professional in quality and design. Sounds are loaded off of 3.5-inch floppy discs, and you can easily create new instrument with audio inputs and built-in editing features. Both samplers helped shape what MIDI could do outside the realm of synthesizers and push forward the use of MIDI in both the studio and on the stage.

## MIDI—Early Computers

Instrument-to-instrument connections was a great first step for MIDI but there had been previous efforts using control voltage and other proprietary systems and so by itself it wasn't enough to make it a "universal" format. The draw to MIDI really took off with the integration into personal computing systems. The two platforms that made an early difference were Apple and Atari. While not alone, these two

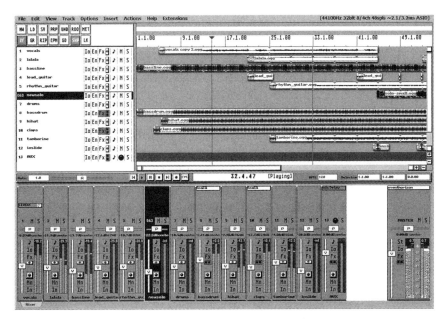

**Figure 10.4** Cubase on the Atari ST

companies made an effort to develop MIDI functionality. Atari consoles had something that has never existed since, which is a set of built-in MIDI ports. Using an Atari as a sequencer has endured long past a normal tech life cycle, and there are still people using them today. Several MIDI sequencers that were created for the Atari ST are still around, including Logic Pro and Cubase.

A setup using the Atari ST as the sequencer is relatively straightforward because of the MIDI ports and the available software. The primary limitation is due to only having a single MIDI Out, but it is possible to send 16 MIDI tracks at a time and there are several additional hardware expanders that use the printer port for up to 4 or 8 MIDI Outs. The Cubase sequencer could handle up to 64 tracks and had modules such as an arpeggiator, a score editor, and other various editors. While the editing capabilities are limited by today's standards and there are no built-in sound generators, which means that all sounds will come from external MIDI instruments and then have to be mixed on an audio mixer. Until the MIDI spec was updated with a file format, every sequencer had to save the MIDI in its own way.

As an interesting side note, Windows joined the MIDI party a little later after Windows 3.0 was released in the 1990s. For many years it was MIDI software that was the primary innovator in the music technology realm, but things have flipped due to the power and popularity of audio software. What started first as separate applications has now become a single DAW entity with both audio and MIDI capabilities.

## MIDI Interfaces

The 5-pin DIN connector was the original MIDI interface, but with computers there had to be a method of connecting MIDI cables. Various components were used to connect MIDI devices including parallel, printer, and joystick ports,, but the MIDI stream was essentially the same in each case and it was always serial. The software on each computer had to be able to work with the incoming MIDI and required additional software managers. Opcode Systems Inc. was founded in 1985 and played an integral role in the interfacing of MIDI and sequencing software. Among all of Opcode's achievements, perhaps its flagship sequencer Vision is the most noteworthy and rivals in many ways the sequencers of today. Remnants of Studio Vision can be seen in most modern sequencers such as the rhythm programmer and the style of controller editing. Opcode's interfaces also helped move MIDI forward, and they made the MIDIPort, which used USB. Opcode closed its doors in 1999, which upset a lot of tech savvy musicians.

## MIDI—GM and the Web

The initial MIDI spec was not without hiccups, and the MMA set about to add additional refinements and increased oversight to make sure they could keep up with the quickly expanding world of computers. In addition to general improvements to the basic MIDI spec, the MMA added General MIDI (GM), which includes a MIDI file standard. With a universal file format it is possible to share your sequences with other musicians on any sequencer. As the Internet began and gained in popularity, MIDI was a large part of the audio capabilities. The early Internet was limited in its maximum speed, and it wasn't possible to stream audio files because of the bandwidth required. Downloading audio was also very time consuming. MIDI files were much easier to handle because of their small size, which made them a solution to the bandwidth issues.

Due to the fact that MIDI doesn't transmit sound, MIDI on the web relies on the hardware and software of the receiving computer. In the 1990s it became important to upgrade your sound card because that was the component that was used to turn the MIDI into audio, using samples that were stored on the card. Soundblaster by Creative Labs is an example of a sound card that could be purchased and installed to increase the quality of sound and MIDI realization. E-MU and Creative Labs created a new format called the Sound Font that could be used in conjunction with General MIDI and as a stand-alone music production tool.

While having MIDI on the web was a good solution because it helped overcome the bandwidth limitations, the quality of the reproduction could not be guaranteed because every sound card is different. Many people would hear different things because of varying hardware. GM allowed the correct instruments to be triggered and MIDI data set the levels, panning, and other performance data, but it doesn't have the ability to differentiate between sounds and playback options. When sequencing for a GM destination it became important to test out the production on various cards to test for compatibility and maximum playability.

GM was also used for playback of music and sounds in video games because including audio for the entire score wasn't practical in early video games. Once the storage formats increased, it became easier to include full audio scores and gaming platforms continue to increase their content storage capacities.

An example of using GM on the web would be posting a sequence to a site that could be downloaded by anyone who would then subsequently play it back on his or her computer using the computer's sound card. Perhaps you are hosting a classical music archive and instead of spending thousands of dollars paying orchestras to record the music you sequence it using MIDI. Perhaps your site is designed for researchers to study music and so MIDI creates an affordable way to post the music. The GM file includes all of the instrument tracks and automatically triggers the correct sounds.

## MIDI—Implementation Charts

With so many different devices, all of which follow the MIDI spec to varying degrees, the idea for a chart to list MIDI capabilities has proven to be very useful. The chart lists the MIDI messages that a piece of gear can recognize. This is where you look if you need to know if a device can send or receive certain channel or system messages. Some examples of data that are useful would be whether a sound module can use aftertouch or which SysEx numbers are enabled and for what purpose.

With a standardized chart format you can easily compare equipment and features to make sure you are able to get the most from the connections and MIDI features. If you have two charts lined up next to each other you can learn a lot about how they will and won't work together. If you are using a controller without aftertouch capabilities to control a synthesizer that has after-touch capabilities then you are going to be missing out on performance techniques because you won't be able to harness the full ability of the synth. The connection will still work and you'll be able to control the synth but not everything will be operational.

Using an Implementation Chart is less common with software synths but it is still important to know the available MIDI options but you may have to dig a little bit further. You certainly can't assume full MIDI spec functionality in any situation. Most sequencers follow the spec as a MIDI source, but it is the sound generators that will implement specialized MIDI spec options as needed and not universally use every part of it. You can find examples of charts in the appendix at the end of the book.

As an example, you might pull up the Implementation Chart for the DX-7 when controlling it via Logic Pro. If you look at the control change list you can see the data values for each controller input. Should you want to set up a custom environment layout and use faders and knobs to control various parameters, then knowing the appropriate control numbers is the place to start. According to the DX-7 chart control change, #5 is linked to the portamento time. In Logic it is possible to create a virtual fader that is attached to the MIDI channel of the DX-7 and the control value of 5. Adjusting the created fader sends data to that parameter. You can essentially create an entire virtual control surface that is set to control the various parameters on the DX-7 and then manipulate the instrument without touching it at all. A patch editor for the DX-7 is nothing more than a software implementation of the Implementation Chart. This example mirrors exactly what you would do with any sound modulate that is controlled via MIDI although many sound generators have a much simpler implementation and cannot be completely controlled with MIDI.

## Drum Machines

One of the most popular MIDI devices is the drum machine and there have been a number of successful machines over the years. In many ways the drum machine solved a number of problems with MIDI percussion because you can program patterns using a dedicated device that has accurate timing and access to custom sounds.

Among the very earliest drum machines is the Chamberlin Rhythmate, invented in the 1940s, which used tape loops to create 14 drum patterns and had an adjustable speed control. This machine paved the way for future devices, but it wasn't until the 1970s that drum machines began to be programmable and in the 1980s MIDI was incorporated. An early drum machine that used MIDI was the Yamaha RX11, which had basic controls and pads that aren't velocity sensitive. The "retro" sounds of the RX11 still stand up against modern drum machines and while its abilities are limited it is still fully functional.

One of Sequential Circuits's last instruments, the Studio 440 drum machine, is often considered the first of the modern sequencing and sampling drum and music production machines. With 520kb of memory for sampling you couldn't sample much but at 12 bits you could record basic percussion sounds.

**Figure 10.5** MPC-60

*Source:* Photo courtesy of www. perfectcircuitaudio.com

The drum machine with perhaps the most well-known legacy is the MPC. First released in the late 1980s, its simple design, great sounds, and features like its swing made this the go-to drum machine. There are have been new releases every couple of years, including a tablet version for iOS.

A modern instrument of interest is Dave Smith Instruments Tempest, which combines a drum machine with a synthesis engine. Even though software instruments seem to be very popular, it is still refreshing to see innovative instruments being released. There is no question that software instruments have taken over and there are some very powerful and great-sounding instruments.

## Software Instruments

MIDI started with synthesizers in the '80s and moved into samplers in the '80s and '90s. In the '90s computers began to mature and by the early 2000s the digital audio workstation (DAW) had begun to reach maturity as well. Virtual synthesizers depended on the development of RAM and processor speed while software sampling depended on the development of RAM and hard drive speeds. One company named Nemesys found a way to overcome the limitations of the computers in the '90s and created an application called Gigasampler. Loading only enough of each sample in memory so that if a key is triggered then the rest can be read off of the hard drive while the file in memory is being played allowed larger sampled instruments to be loaded. Larger files typically mean more detailed and professional-sounding instruments. Gigasampler lasted for a few years before being bought and then closed by Tascam. Other virtual instruments took over and several continue to this day, such as the EXS-24 in Logic Pro and Native Instruments's Kontakt.

Modeling also became popular as instruments that are a combination of sampling, synthesis, and programming. The fascination with modeled and sampled instruments is to sound exactly like a specific instrument sounds in the real

**Figure 10.6** Giga Sampler

world, which is both useful but also frustrating because on one hand you have the ease of using a particular instrument where ever you are but on the other hand you don't have the personal interaction with a living and breathing instrument. One set of instruments that are very good are the synth emulations from Arturia. If you have the opportunity to compare these with the actual hardware units, you would see just how accurately reproduced and useful these instruments are.

## MIDI—Mobile Revolution

Up until smart phones took over, MIDI on mobile devices was limited to basic key tones, ring tones, and melodies. As had happened before with the web and gaming, phones grew in power and most of the original MIDI functionality switched to audio. It was just a matter of time before the full power of MIDI sequencing came to mobile devices. The early device leader was the iPhone, but not at its initial release. Several iOS versions had to come before MIDI was introduced and when it came it was pretty basic. In many ways mobile MIDI was like MIDI 1.0 and could just send and receive real time but there wasn't a structure for MIDI files and sequencing. With

**Figure 10.7** Korg iElectribe

the release of the iPad and other tablets, more and more MIDI capabilities were incorporated and the line between mobile and desktop/laptop platforms became completely blurred. The primary limitation of mobile sequencers is the inability to connect to multiple devices and so it becomes the equivalent of the Atari console or instead partners with bigger setups.

> The following instruments showcase important advances in the progression of MIDI through the years. This information is reproduced with permission of Vintagesynth.com.

## Sequential Circuits Prophet 600

This is the first commercially available synth to implement MIDI!! It's a fun synth. Its big brother is the legendary Prophet 5. The P600 is very affordable today and is a great buy. Models with the newest software will enjoy polyphonic MIDI implementation and up to 100 memory patches to store their own sounds! The sound of the Prophet 600 is brighter and harsher than that of a Juno 106 but still just as funky.

The P600 has two oscillators per voice with sawtooth, triangle, and variable pulse waveforms. The oscillators can be individually tuned or synced together. Similar quality VCF and VCA sections from the Prophet 5 can be found here too! The P5's Poly-Mod section has also been passed onto the P600.

The P600 is extremely versatile and easy to use! Its best functions include the on-board arpeggiator, 2-track sequencer, and poly-modulation. The P600 is great for creating analog effects, swells, and drones. It has a cool glide effect and has very flexible modulation possibilities! It is used by Hardfloor, The Higher Intelligence Agency, and Eat Static. Perfect for Ambient, Dub, and other electronic music.

## Roland Jupiter-6

The Jupiter-6 is an incredible analog synth. All of the Jupiters have a sound that was unlike any other synthesizer and the Jup 6 is no exception. This sound is due in part to classic analog Roland technology in its filters, modulation capabilities, and a thick cluster of 12 analog oscillators at 2 per voice. Easy and intuitive programming via front panel sliders, knobs and buttons for all your tweaking needs.

The Jup 6 is a scaled-down version of the Jup 8 in terms of programming and polyphony. However the Jup 6 has some major improvements of its own such as newly added MIDI control and better tuning stability! While the Jup 6 does have MIDI, the implementation is very rudimentary and hard to control. The Jup 6 was one of the very first (along with the Sequential Prophet 600) synths to use the then new MIDI protocol, and the implementation on the Jup 6 is far from complete.

Synthcom Systems, Inc. offers the Europa firmware upgrade for the Jupiter-6, which gives it an up-to-date and comprehensive MIDI implementation. All parameters are controllable via Continuous Controller or SysEx. Europa also features an extensive arpeggiator that will sync to MIDI clock with programmable clock divisors and rhythms, and has about 50 more playback variations than the JP-6's original Up, Down, Up/Down, and Down/Up. A Europacized Jupiter-6 is a thoroughly modern synth with a classic sound.

The Jupiter-6 is excellent for ambient drones, pads, blips, buzzes, and leads. The Jupiter-6 is known for being a very reliable, programmable, polyphonic, analog monster of a synthesizer! It is used by Orbital, Moby, Überzone, Devo, BT, The Prodigy, Vangelis, The Chemical Brothers, The Crystal Method, ZZ Top, Duran Duran, Moog Cookbook, and Blur.

## Yamaha DX7

One of the most popular digital synths ever was the DX7 from Yamaha, released in 1983. It featured a whole new type of synthesis called FM (Frequency Modulation). It certainly is not analog and it is difficult to program but can result in some excellent sounds! It is difficult because it is non-analog, and thus, a whole new set of parameters are available for tweaking, many of which seemed counterintuitive and unfamiliar. And programming had to be accomplished via membrane buttons, one data slider, and a small LCD screen.

Still the sounds it shipped with and that many users did manage to create were more complex and unique than anything before it. Percussive and metallic but thick as analog at times, the DX7 was known for generating unique sounds still popular to this day. The DX7 was also a truly affordable programmable synth when it was first released. Almost every keyboardist bought one at the time, making the DX7 one of the bestselling synths of all time! It also came with MIDI, which was brand new at the time—Sequential had already released the first MIDI synth, the Prophet 600. Roland had just released the JX-3P with very basic MIDI implementation and wouldn't get around to adding full MIDI for another year with the Juno-106, and it would be three years before Roland could counter the popularity of the DX7 with a digital synth of their own, the D-50.

The DX7 has been used by the Crystal Method, Kraftwerk, Underworld, Orbital, BT, Talking Heads, Brian Eno, Tony Banks, Mike Lindup of Level 42, Jan Hammer, Roger Hodgson, Teddy Riley, Brian Eno, T Lavitz of the Dregs, Sir George Martin, Supertramp, Phil Collins, Stevie Wonder, Daryl Hall, Steve Winwood, Scritti Politti, Babyface, Peter-John Vettese, Depeche Mode, D:Ream, Les Rhytmes Digital, Front 242, U2, A-Ha, Enya, The Cure, Astral Projection, Fluke, Kitaro, Vangelis, Elton John, James Horner, Toto, Donald Fagen, Michael McDonald, Chick Corea, Level 42, Queen, Yes, Michael Boddicker, Julian Lennon, Jean-Michel Jarre, Sneaker Pimps, Lynyrd Skynyrd, Greg Phillanganes, Jerry Goldsmith, Jimmy Edgar, Beastie Boys, Stabbing Westward, and Herbie Hancock. Pretty impressive for just a partial listing!

Following the monaural DX7 came the stereo DX7 mkII—just as popular and much more advanced. Its unique sounds are very popular for industrial techno type music as well as ambient and electro. The TX-7 is essentially a desktop module form of the DX7 but is even harder to edit or program since it requires external editors or software. The monolithic DX1 and DX5 models, which packed two DX7 synth engines into one instrument were the epitome of the DX line of synths created by Yamaha. There have also been a few budget spinoffs like the DX9, DX100, DX21, and DX27. FM synthesis has also made its way into the TX-81Z & TX-802 and software synthesizers like Native Instruments FM7.

Still the DX7 has remained the all-around best and most popular DX synth due to its affordable price, professional features for studio and live performance, and its excellent range of sonic possibilities and extensive programmability. In fact the reason the DX7 is always so affordable (usually under $500 secondhand) is because there are so many of them out there, still being used and traded! And they are reliable, still functioning well over 20 years later, unlike older analog gear.

## Akai S900

The S900 sampler was Akai's first truly professional sampler, released in 1986. Its sampling specifications were pro-quality at the time: 12-bit stereo sampling, 7.5kHz to 40kHz variable sampling rates, and a maximum of 63 seconds of sample time at 7.5kHz. Up to 32 samples can be created and stored to disk along with any edit settings. This was one of the first rack-mount samplers to use a built-in disk drive. Although the drive could load sounds while you play, it was still a very slow process.

Editing and programming the S900 is a very good precursor to the advanced S3000 series. There are lots of advanced edit capabilities for looping, truncating, velocity crossfading, tuning, and even analog-like parameters to control. Individual outputs for each of the eight voices, stereo mix out, stereo input, MIDI, and trigger inputs round out this machine as a professional vintage-status sampler that still proves to be very useful even for today's musicians!

The S950 soon followed the S900 and offered increased memory and sampling rates. The sample rate was now variable from 7.5 to 48kHz and it could hold up to 99 samples in memory. Memory could be expanded from 750KB to 2.25MB. The S950 is used by Fatboy Slim, Moby, Skinny Puppy, Depeche Mode, Future Sound of London, Sneaker Pimps, The Bomb Squad, Dr. Dre, DJ Premiere, Prince Paul, Vangelis, Digable Planets, and A Guy Called Gerald.

## E-mu Virtuoso 2000

The Virtuoso 2000 is a 128-voice orchestral sound module with over 64 MB of sounds—an entire orchestra in a single rack space! Featuring the "Orchestral Session" soundsets 1&2 from E-mu, the sounds are great, and they include violins, violas, celli, double basses, trumpets, French horns, trombones, bass trombones, tubas, piccolos, flutes, oboes, English horn, clarinets, bass clarinets, bassoons, contra bassoons, harp, orchestral bells, tubular bells, bell trees, celeste, xylophone, marimba, and a percussion battery with over 20 instruments! With 128 voices, 32 MIDI channels, lightning-fast MIDI response, and over 1,000 sounds, you can create the largest of orchestral ensembles!

Additional professional features worth mentioning include the 12 assignable real-time front panel controls, 6 analog outputs plus an S/PDIF digital output, 2 additional internal ROM expansion slots, ability to play back Flash ROMs authored on E4 Ultra Samplers, and an advanced synthesis architecture based on the Proteus 2000. The Virtuoso 2000 is likely the best all-in-one orchestral sound module ever!

With these expansion options, you could buy a PK-6, then add the sounds of the Orbit 3, XK-6, and the MP-7 . . . or any other combinations you may want. If you like desktop synths, you can start with an MP-7 or XL-7, and then add these same expansion card options to add Proteus, Orchestral, or the new Halo sounds to them. E-mu/Ensoniq's interchangeable sound cards and a variety of keyboard/sound-module options means that there's a model out there for everybody now.

## Fairlight CMI (Series I–III)

The Australian Fairlight Computer Music Instrument (CMI) is a vintage but state-of-the-art synthesizer/sampler workstation. An incredible sampler with 28 megabytes or more of memory! One or two full 73-note velocity sensitive keyboards! Complete synthesis and editing of digitally sampled sounds. Three different on-board SMPTE Sequencers and storage to various disk mediums. The processor itself is housed in a 24-inch module. It was also the first digital sampler to hit the market back in 1979 and has endured throughout the '80s and '90s.

From 1979 to 1985 several versions of the Fairlight were produced, with the Series III being the last of them. Each new series added updates to the Fairlight as technology developed through the early '80s. The Fairlight 1 and 2 had only 16 kByte of memory per voice, and only 8 voices but expanded to several megabytes and double the polyphony by the Fairlight III. The IIx was the first Fairlight to offer MIDI. The Series III added aftertouch capability to the keyboard. They all had pitch/mod wheels, an 82-key alphanumeric keyboard, 15 function keys, a Graphics Tablet for drawing sounds, and a video monitor for seeing what you're doing while editing.

The sampler is the heart of the Fairlight. It's a 16-bit resolution digital sampler with variable sample rates up to 100kHz! Original Fairlight models used two standard 8-bit 6800 processors, updated to the more powerful 16-bit 68000 chips in later versions (the IIx had updated 6809 processors, which is what designated it a IIx over a II, and raised the sampling resolution to 32kHz, from the I & II's 24kHz). In the Fairlight III, sample memory (RAM) comes in 28MB chunks per 16 voices of polyphony—wow! That's plenty of room for creating stereo or mono samples. Edit them using various hi-tech functions and at a "microscopic" level using the large monitor screen. Samples can be looped, mixed, and resampled with processing for sweetening. As for synthesis, create your own waveforms by sampling and applying Fast Fourier Transform and Waveform editing functions. Storing samples and synthesized waveforms can be done to hard disk or 8-inch floppy disks.

As for sequencing, there are three sophisticated methods. There's CAPS (Composer, Arranger, Performer Sequencer), an 80-track polyphonic sequencer. The complicated MCL (Music Composition Language) is like a text-based step time sequencer. And finally, the Rhythm Sequencer, which functions like a classic drum-machine style sequencer. All sequencers are SMPTE syncable.

The Fairlight is a horribly expensive music production center and is rivaled only by the NED Synclavier. Although current samplers, sequencers, and synths can blow away the Fairlight at a fraction of the cost, the Fairlight is a historical, prized piece of vintage digital synthesizer and sampler technology.

It still holds up today, over 20 years later and is still a high quality and professional instrument. The facilities provided by it benefit hardcore synth programmers, wealthy musicians, sound designers, film composers, and wealthy vintage synth collectors.

It has been used by Jean-Michel Jarre, Heaven 17, Hardfloor, ABC, Hall & Oates, the Buggles, Supertramp, Thomas Dolby, Jon Astley, Michael Jackson, Yes, Trevor Horn (Art of Noise), Geoff Downes, Stevie Wonder, Vince Clarke (Yazoo), Peter Gabriel, Paul McCartney, Devo, Julian Lennon, The Cars, Yellow, Lindsey Buckingham, Jan Hammer, Herbie Hancock, David Gilmour, Elvis Costello, Scritti Politti, Starship, Teddy Riley, Brian Wilson, Foreigner, Madonna, Debbie Gibson, Jane Child, Eurythmics, Mike Oldfield, Prince, OMD, Steve Winwood, Duran Duran, John Paul Jones, Paul Hardcastle, Kate Bush, Queen, Keith Emerson, Alan Parsons, Fleetwood Mac, B-52's, Pet Shop Boys, Depeche Mode, Soul II Soul, and Stewart Copeland.

## Akai MPC60

The MPC60 is the music production studio that has single-handedly taken over the Rap and R&B music genres as the main instrument of HipHop production. Designed by Roger Linn (Linn Drum), the MPC60 is a one-box-does-it-all sequencer-sampler workstation.

The built-in sequencer is very complete and professional. There are 99 tracks per sequence, 99 patterns, and 99 sequences that can be created, edited, and stored in the MPC60 with ease. Most artists create their patterns in real time adding drum parts to a beat-loop spontaneously creating a groove that captures the vibe. These patterns are varied and chained into a sequence. Full MIDI, SMPTE, and various other forms of external control prepare the MPC60 for any studio situation.

The sampler section is lo-fi but highly respectable. Its 12-bit sampling at 40KHz is pretty good. Sample editing, looping, and transforming is simple to do. And finally, there's even a built-in drum machine for extra groove! Finally, the 18 voices of polyphony should be plenty of room for anyone who wants to create HipHop on the machine of professional artists worldwide including Apollo 440, BT, Jean-Michel Jarre, Jimmy Edgar, DJ Shadow, Jermaine Dupri, and A Guy Called Gerald.

In 1991 the MPC60 mkII was unleashed. It wasn't much different: the casing and a head-phone jack were new and either machine is still very useful for today's aspiring musicians.

## Sequential Circuits Studio 440

The Studio 440 is like the granddaddy of sequencing/sampling drum and music production machines. You may have heard of the Akai MPC60, MPC2000, MPC3000 and E-mu SP1200 machines. Although some of these exceed the limits of the Studio 440, it is still very much worth checking out! The major difference between the modern Akai MPCs and the Studio 440 is that its sampler is 12-bit. A little lo-fi in comparison to the 16-bit MPC. The Studio 440 also has a slim 520kb memory so you won't have much time to sample any more than some short percussion and drums.

Similar to the MPC60, the Studio 440 has an analog low-pass filter that is always fun. Unfortunately it is not resonant. The sequencer is intuitive and quite functional with a capacity of 50,000 notes, 8 separate tracks, and a swing function. But unlike its contemporaries, the 440 has some visionary features for its time. MIDI data from the sequencer can be transmitted out so that it can play external MIDI instruments. There is also built-in SCSI for external drives and storage.

The 440 is pleasant to look at, even today. It's simple to use and sounds pretty darn good despite its lo-fi 12-bit sampler. Though an MPC is likely a better buy than the 440, these days the 440 still commands quite a high asking price. It was, after all, one of Sequential's last products. It was way ahead of its time and was also very hip! They are rare and difficult to have serviced—what else would you expect from a vintage instrument!

# EXPLORING THE FUTURE OF MIDI          11

*A reflection on the future of MIDI by Nathan van der Rest, masters student at the University of Colorado Denver.*

It is astonishing to think that after 30 years, MIDI is still as relevant today as it was when it was first introduced. What is even more astonishing is that in the 30 years that MIDI has been around, it has changed only slightly. MIDI has been able to stay relevant through all of the major changes in the music industry without having to go through dramatic changes in order to adapt. The original MIDI Spec, which is still in implementation today, is largely the same as it was in the first few years of development. Not many other forms of technology have achieved the same overall success that MIDI has.

Despite MIDI standing the test of time, it has not been completely devoid of criticism. Many users feel that MIDI is not only an antiquated protocol but that it also produces limitations in which their music suffers. Several companies have tried to combat the shortcomings of MIDI by trying to implement their own protocols. One of these other protocols is known as mLAN. mLAN was first introduced in January of 2000 and was initially designed as a replacement for the antiquated MIDI protocol. One of the biggest benefits that mLAN offered was its implementation of the FireWire connection allowing for much faster transfer rates. mLAN was initially released under a royalty free license so that everybody could use it in their products.

mLAN seemed promising at first with a wealth of companies agreeing to include the protocol on their new products but mLAN ultimately never caught on. One of the biggest complaints users had about the mLAN protocol was that, although it was a huge benefit to utilize a FireWire connection, the mLAN protocol consumed the entire bandwidth of the FireWire port it was connected to—meaning that users needed multiple FireWire connections in order to run hard drives and audio interfaces along with the mLAN protocol. By early 2008, mLAN was almost nonexistent and the companies who originally planned on introducing the protocol to their products never ended up releasing these new mLAN devices. Even Yamaha stopped incorporating mLAN into their devices as well as ceasing to release updates to the protocol and drivers. However, new Yamaha products, which include FireWire, are compatible with old mLAN devices so that the original mLAN devices are not completely obsolete.

Another attempt at introducing a new protocol to replace MIDI was the Zeta Instrument Processor Interface, or ZIPI. ZIPI was first created by the Center for New Music and Audio Technology department at the University of California Berkley in 1994. ZIPI was introduced mainly as a new transport protocol for digital musical instruments. The engineers at the University of California Berkley wanted to combat the perceived limitations that arose from MIDI using a peer-to-peer serial port connection. Therefore, ZIPI was designed to run over a star network with a hub in the center. This new type of connectivity allowed for much faster connection and disconnection due to their being no need to daisy chain multiple devices as is the case with MIDI. Although the ZIPI protocol was not reliant on any type of physical implementation, Ethernet 10Base-T was mainly used when implementing ZIPI. The ZIPI protocol differed from MIDI in a number of ways. Instead of individual MIDI channels, ZIPI utilized three-level address hierarchies of 63 families that consisted of 127 instruments—each having 127 notes. This type of three-level address hierarchy allowed for a total of 1,016,127 individual note addresses resulting in much more depth than is available to MIDI. Users could also assemble instruments in a family from different physical devices allowing for extremely fine per-note control of synthesis parameters, which proved extremely useful for nonstandard controllers such as wind and guitar controllers. The resolution of ZIPI messages was much higher than MIDI messages due to the fact that message parameters could be any multiple of 8-bits. Some of the ZIPI messages were directly borrowed from the MIDI protocol such as note on/note off as well as loudness and amplitude; but the vast majority were entirely new and based on a different innovative control logic.

Like mLAN, ZIPI never caught on to the general public. Companies were hesitant to begin producing devices that included the ZIPI protocol. Among the main complaints of ZIPI was its inability to communicate properly with traditional MIDI equipment. Although ZIPI was never intended to communicate with MIDI, companies didn't want to introduce this new technology and singlehandedly make all of their other instruments and hardware completely obsolete. Another major complaint was that although ZIPI was capable of 1,016,127 individual synthesis states, synthesizer hardware at the time could not handle this huge amount of data. Finally, the unusual addressing scheme proved to be extremely complex and ultimately was too hard to implement. Therefore, like mLAN, ZIPI was never widely implemented. The engineers who first worked on ZIPI however, are the same people that have developed Open Sound Control, or OSC—the current contender to MIDI.

Although not necessarily designed to replace MIDI, Gibson developed a similar protocol known as MaGIC, or Media-accelerated Global Information Carrier. MaGIC is an Ethernet-based protocol that allows for bidirectional transmission of multi-channel audio data, control data, and instrument power. MaGIC is mainly used in Gibson Digital Guitars and has been used in conjunction with MIDI. Gibson's MaGIC protocol was mainly developed as a means to improve upon the weaknesses perceived in most MIDI guitar systems. The MaGIC protocol implements both proprietary network and application layers that can be used with a multitude of physical layers like Gigabit Ethernet and optical media.

As was mentioned earlier in the book, OSC is currently the most promising replacement to the MIDI protocol. OSC effectively fixes all of the weaknesses that MIDI poses and allows for extreme creativity and control along the way. OSC is not free from shortcomings and as has been discussed, would be extremely hard to implement as a full replacement for the MIDI protocol. Although MIDI seems to be safe from being replaced, the fact that so many companies have introduced protocols of their own in order to improve upon or replace the MIDI protocol is something that needs to be addressed. The shortcomings of MIDI must be examined in order to help improve upon the technology. Although each user will have different ideas as to what is the largest shortcoming of the MIDI protocol, some of the main issues are detailed below.

## Known MIDI Issues

1. One of the biggest complaints about MIDI is its 7-bit Continuous Controller standard, meaning the user is only able to utilize 127 individual values at any given time. Many users feel that 127 values is not sufficient in order to properly translate their playing. By limiting the user to only 127 values, the amount of expressiveness available to the user is a predetermined factor. Any aspect of their playing, such as velocity, modulation amounts, and anything else, is limited to 127 continuous values. In most instances, 127 independent values are more than sufficient but in certain aspects, it is extremely limiting. One such instance of the limitations of 127 values is when re-creating continuous pitch instruments such as the Theremin. With a continuous pitch instrument like a Theremin, more steps than 127 values are needed to create a smooth pitch shift over many octaves. Therefore, many users feel that a higher resolution bit rate, such as 10 or 14 bits, is needed in order to improve upon the technology. This limitation can be overcome through careful instrument design and how they interpret incoming pitch data, but history has shown that too many rely on a literal 128-step data stream. As has been mentioned earlier, OSC offers the user almost unlimited amounts of depth; which is one of the main reasons people are making the leap from OSC to MIDI.

2. Many users are unhappy with the MIDI clock. Due to the MIDI beat clock being of such low resolution, devices that are synchronized via the MIDI clock are subject to jitter, or clock drift. This problem has mainly been combated through the use of external clocking for MIDI devices but it is still an extremely relevant problem for musicians who do not want to incorporate a computer or other external clock sources into their live setups.

3. Another major drawback to MIDI is the limitation it poses due to its note on and note off nature. Because MIDI was designed around keyboards, it was only natural to trigger MIDI notes with a specified "on" or "off" command meaning. The notes are triggered when keys are depressed and the notes are terminated when the keys are let go. This type of triggering system poses a major problem when trying to play non-keyboard controllers such as breath controllers when the exact moment that the note should be triggered is not as clear cut. Although this note on-note off limitation can be pseudo-combated with envelope manipulation and volume sweeps, the amount of expressive control some artists desire cannot be achieved with the traditional note on- note off nature of the MIDI protocol.

4. Another major complaint that has sprung up about the MIDI protocol is the slow speed in which it is transferred from device to device. MIDI in its current form is limited to a 31.25k baud transfer rate. Although most users will not feel that this is a major limitation, in certain aspects, such as the connection of an extreme amount of devices, which need to communicate simultaneously, this transfer rate can prove to be too slow. In more modern times, MIDI can be transmitted over USB, which is capable of a much faster connection, but due to the fact that the MIDI information needs to be converted back to traditional MIDI when reaching the device, the extreme speed of USB is not able to be fully utilized by MIDI equipment. Again, OSC offers users a much faster transfer rate due mainly to the fact that it is usually transmitted over an Ethernet connection.

These aforementioned limitations are among the many which inspired companies to begin experimenting with their own protocol. As has been mentioned earlier, OSC is the most promising contender to the MIDI protocol. Many people feel that OSC will eventually replace MIDI as a protocol due to its major improvements over the aforementioned weaknesses. Another reason people feel OSC has a chance is that it has gained more popularity than the previous alternatives such as mLAN and ZIPI. However, as was outlined in the Live Performance section of this book, OSC has its own limitations and shortcomings, which makes it extremely difficult to implement commercially. Therefore, in order to fix the limitations of MIDI, it is only logical that the original MIDI protocol be updated and improved upon in order to address the major problems of the protocol while still keeping older MIDI equipment both relevant and functional with the new updated protocol.

In fact, a new, updated MIDI protocol has been in the works since 2005, perhaps even earlier. This new version promises to be an updated, higher-resolution, version of the original MIDI protocol. This new version is known as "HD-MIDI," and finally has been introduced and demonstrated at the January 2013 NAMM show. The HD-MIDI protocol seems to be extremely promising and also seems to combat most, if not all of the major problems users have with the original, 30-year old technology.

## HD–MIDI

The new HD-MIDI protocol is said to be transmittable over either a wired or wireless Ethernet connection. This is a major step forward as most people will agree that the traditional 5-pin DIN connectors are indeed antiquated. The new HD-MIDI protocol also introduces a wealth of significant improvements over traditional MIDI such as faster speeds, thanks to the Ethernet connection as well as support for more MIDI channels—ultimately allowing users more depth than the traditional 16-channel format. Next, HD-MIDI is designed to let users specify a direct pitch for transmission rather than the note numbers that traditional MIDI systems sent.

The introduction of user specified pitches allow for alternative tunings—something that was extremely difficult to implement with traditional MIDI. Although most people are content with the standard tuning MIDI allows, many avant-garde and experimental artists require alternative tunings for their work. Finally, HD-MIDI introduces "Note Update" messages, which allow for parameter changes during the lifetime of any given note. This means that a user can affect how the note plays out with much more control than a typical ADSR, or attack, decay, sustain, release envelope generator allows for.

## HD–MIDI vs. OSC

Although HD-MIDI does not offer all of the features present in OSC, some of the most popular aspects of OSC have been incorporated into the new HD-MIDI protocol. For example, one of the most significant benefits to OSC was its speed and wireless capabilities. Since HD-MIDI can have either a wired or wireless Ethernet connection, HD-MIDI is able to utilize the extreme transfer speeds of Ethernet, effectively solving the slow speed grudge some users hold toward traditional MIDI. Next, users of HD-MIDI have many of the same customizable features that made OSC so appealing; such as the ability to specify the tunings of their systems in whichever way they wish as well as the ability to control how a note plays out with more precision.

Due to the HD-MIDI protocol being a continuation and an advancement of the standard MIDI protocol, HD-MIDI is able to freely utilize the traditional MIDI protocol, meaning that HD-MIDI will be fully compatible with older MIDI systems—something that OSC simply cannot do. The simple ability to interface fully with all previous MIDI devices is perhaps the main reason that HD-MIDI will most likely succeed. It was the inability to interface with MIDI devices that ultimately led to the failure of protocols like mLAN and ZIPI. Also, because the same people who first developed MIDI are developing HD-MIDI, it will act as an "upgrade" to the protocol rather than a complete replacement, which will be much more easily utilized by the end user.

However, the original circumstances that brought all of the major keyboard companies together to first develop and implement MIDI, will prove extremely hard to recreate in the future. Not only are there substantially more commercial companies producing equipment in today's day and age, but also the competitive climate has shifted. In the early '80s, introducing a standard, which allowed for all keyboards and equipment to communicate with each other, promised to increase sales across all companies, as users would want this new equipment that would be able to communicate across platforms.

Users are not going to flock to stores to purchase HD-MIDI equipment. The lack of commercial enthusiasm that will likely arise for HD-MIDI is due mainly to the fact that users are spoiled by traditional MIDI. It must be understood that when MIDI was first introduced, it was a completely new idea. At that point, no standard was available that would allow users to communicate across device platforms.

It is true that all synthesizers at the time utilized control voltage and many different synthesizers could communicate with each other via control voltage, but no standard was in place ensuring the synthesizers would communicate accurately. For example, Moog used the 1 volt/octave standard, which meant that all the notes in an octave would be equally divided across one volt. Korg however used a slightly different volt/octave standard, which meant that if you connected the two synthesizers via pitch control voltage, not only would the notes not match up but the keyboard tracking would also change across the length of the keyboard for each separate unit. Therefore, the introduction of a completely universal standard such as MIDI was groundbreaking.

The need for a universal standard has already been answered by MIDI so the desire to run to the store and buy equipment that utilizes HD-MIDI will not be as great as it was when MIDI was first introduced. Therefore, the shift to include this technology into every new device that is produced will not be as instantaneous as it was in the early '80s. Companies will be hesitant to pay more to include the new protocol when an increase in sales to compensate the higher cost will not be as guaranteed. That being said, HD-MIDI will, in fact, most likely succeed and be included in all new devices. Unlike when MIDI was first introduced, however, the evolution to incorporating HD-MIDI will take place over a much longer period.

# APPENDIX

## Section 1—Musical Instrument Ranges

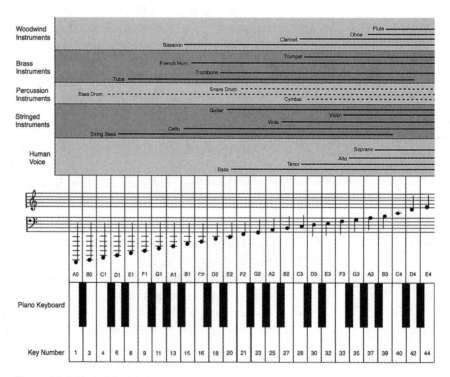

**Figure 12.1** Musical Correlations

**Figure 12.2** Brass

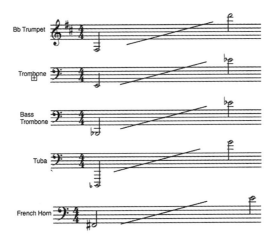

**Figure 12.3** Keyboards

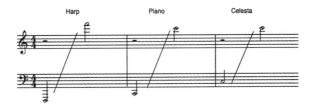

**Figure 12.4** Percussion

**Figure 12.5** Strings

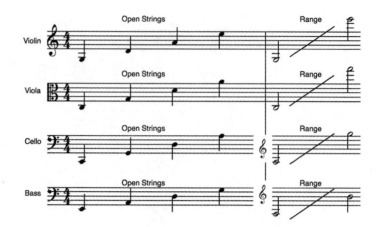

**Figure 12.6** Timpani

**Figure 12.7** Woodwinds

## Section 2—GM Assignments

| | | |
|---|---|---|
| 1. Acosutic Grand Piano | 50. String Ensemble 2 | 99. FX 3 (Crystal) |
| 2. Bright Acoustic Piano | 51. SynthStrings 1 | 100. FX 4 (Atmosphere) |
| 3. Electric Grand Piano | 52. SynthStrings 2 | 101. FX 5 (Brightness) |
| 4. Honky-Tonk Piano | 53. Choir Aahs | 102. FX 6 (Metallic) |
| 5. Electric Piano 1 | 54. Voice Oohs | 103. FX 7 (Echoes) |
| 6. Electric Piano 2 | 55. Synth Voice | 104. FX 8 (Sci-Fi) |
| 7. Harpsichord | 56. Orchestra Hit | 105. Sitar |
| 8. Clavichord | 57. Trumpet | 106. Banjo |
| 9. Celesta | 58. Trombone | 107. Shamisen |
| 10. Glockenspiel | 59. Tuba | 108. Koto |
| 11. Music Box | 60. Muted trumpet | 109. Kalimba |
| 12. Vibraphone | 61. French Horn | 110. Bag Pipe |
| 13. Marimba | 62. Brass Section | 111. Fiddle |
| 14. Xylophone | 63. Synth Brass 1 | 112. Shanai |
| 15. Tubular Bells | 64. Synth Brass 2 | 113. Tinkle Bell |
| 16. Dulcimer | 65. Soprano Sax | 114. Agogo |
| 17. Drawbar Organ | 66. Alto Sax | 115. Steel Drums |
| 18. Percussive Organ | 67. Tenor Sax | 116. Woodblock |
| 19. Rock Organ | 68. Baritone Sax | 117. Taiko Drum |
| 20. Church Organ | 69. Oboe | 118. Melodic Tom |
| 21. Reed Organ | 70. English Horn | 119. Synth Drum |
| 22. Accordian | 71. Bassoon | 120. Reverse Cymbal |
| 23. Harmonica | 72. Clarinet | 121. Guitar Fret Noise |
| 24. Tango Accordian | 73. Piccolo | 122. Breath Noise |
| 25. Acoustic Guitar (Nylon) | 74. Flute | 123. Seashore |
| 26. Acoustic Guitar (Steel) | 75. Recorder | 124. Bird Tweet |
| 27. Electric Guitar (Jazz) | 76. Pan Flute | 125. Telephone Ring |
| 28. Electric Guitar (Clean) | 77. Blown Bottle | 126. Helicopter |
| 29. Electric Guitar (Muted) | 78. Shakuhachi | 127. Applause |
| 30. Overdriven Guitar | 79. Whistle | 128. Gun Shot |
| 31. Distortin Guitar | 80. Ocarina | |
| 32. Guitar Harmonics | 81. Lead 1 (Square) | |
| 33. Acoustic Bass | 82. Lead 2 (Sawtooth) | |
| 34. Electric Bass (Finger) | 83. Lead 3 (Calliope) | |
| 35. Electric Bass (Pick) | 84. Lead 4 (Chiff) | |
| 36. Fretless Bass | 85. Lead 5 (Charang) | |
| 37. Slap Bass 1 | 86. Lead 6 (Voice) | |
| 38. Slap Bass 2 | 87. Lead 7 (Fifths) | |
| 39. Synth Bass 1 | 88. Lead 8 (Bass + Lead) | |
| 40. Synth Bass 2 | 89. Pad 1 (New Age) | |
| 41. Violin | 90. Pad 2 (Warm) | |
| 42. Viola | 91. Pad 3 (Polysynth) | |
| 43. Cello | 92. Pad 4 (Choir) | |
| 44. Contrabass | 93. Pad 5 (Bowed) | |
| 45. Tremolo Strings | 94. Pad 6 (Metallic) | |
| 46. Pizzicato Strings | 95. Pad 7 (Halo) | |
| 47. Orchestral Harp | 96. Pad 8 (Sweep) | |
| 48. Timpani | 97. FX 1 (Rain) | |
| 49. String Ensemble | 98. FX 2 (Soundtrack) | |

**Figure 12.8** GM Instruments

**Figure 12.9** GM Percussion

| |
|---|
| 35. Acoustic Bass Drum |
| 36. Bass Drum 1 |
| 37. Side Stick |
| 38. Acoustic Snare |
| 39. Hand Clap |
| 40. Electric Snare |
| 41. Low Floor Tom |
| 42. Closed Hi-Hat |
| 43. High Floor Tom |
| 44. Pedal Hi-Hat |
| 45. Low Tom |
| 46. Open Hi-Hat |
| 47. Low-Mid Tom |
| 48. Hi-Mid Tom |
| 49. Crash Cymbal 1 |
| 50. High Tom |
| 51. Ride Cymbal 1 |
| 52. Chinese Cymbal |
| 53. Ride Bell |
| 54. Tambourine |
| 55. Splash Cymbal |
| 56. Cowbell |
| 57. Crash Cymabl 2 |
| 58. Vibraslap |
| 59. Ride Cymbal 2 |
| 60. Hi Bongo |
| 61. Low Bongo |
| 62. Mute Hi Conga |
| 63. Open Hi Conga |
| 64. Low Conga |
| 65. High Timbale |
| 66. Low Timbale |
| 67. High Agogo |
| 68. Low Agogo |
| 69. Cabasa |
| 70. Maracas |
| 71. Short Whistle |
| 72. Long Whistle |
| 73. Short Guiro |
| 74. Long Guiro |
| 75. Claves |
| 76. Hi Wood Block |
| 77. Low Wood Block |
| 78. Mute Cuica |
| 79. Open Cuica |
| 80. Mute Triangle |
| 81. Open Triangle |

### Section 3—MIDI Implementation Chart

### MIDI IMPLEMENTATION CHART V2 INSTRUCTIONS

# Introduction

IMPORTANT: MMA recommends manufacturers of MIDI devices and software ship a MIDI Implementation Chart with the device, or make the chart available online. The Version 2 format described in this RP has three pages and is the preferred format. Manufacturers who prefer a one-page chart may continue to use the original format described in the MIDI 1.0 Specification.

This revised version of the standard MIDI Implementation Chart is designed as a quick reference guide that allows users to identify at a glance which MIDI messages and functions are implemented by the device. In this document, the term "device" is defined as a hardware device or software program that (a) transmits and/or receives MIDI messages, and/or (b) reads and/or writes MMA-defined file formats. Use of the V2 MIDI Implementation Chart is optional. The standardization of this chart enables a user to judge the compatibility between two devices to be connected, simply by comparing the "Transmit/Export" column of one device with the "Recognize/Import" column of the other. For this reason, each chart should be the same size and should have the same number of lines if at all possible. This chart has been designed to fit both standard A4 and 8½ inch x 11 inch paper. If a smaller page size is required for a particular product, page breaks may be inserted as necessary, but it is strongly recommended to maintain the row height of the original chart, in order to facilitate comparisons.

IMPORTANT: The MMA Technical Standard Board will review the MIDI Implementation Chart annually, and will update the chart template and these instructions as necessary to reflect newly standardized MIDI features.

## All Pages

- Use the header at the top of each page of the chart to enter the manufacturer's name, model name/number of the device, version number, and date of chart preparation.
- On all pages, if the manufacturer wishes to present additional information that will not physically fit in the "Remarks" column, this must be done by inserting a reference to the appropriate page or section number in the user manual where the information can be found. If the number of banks the device supports does not fit in the "Comments" section, the manufacturer should continue the list on a separate sheet of paper.

## Page 1: Basic Information, MIDI Timing and Synchronization, and Extensions Compatibility?

### General?

The body of page 1 of the chart is divided into four columns. The first column lists the specific function or item, the next two columns give information about whether the specified function is transmitted or exported and/or received or imported (and, if so, may contain information about the range of data)/. The fourth column is used for remarks about anything unique to this implementation. For functions involving files, the 2nd and 3rd columns give information on whether the files can be saved (exported) or opened (imported), and, if so, what degree of compatibility is provided.

### Functions Description

MIDI channels — The range of MIDI channels that the device transmits, exports, responds to, and/or imports. Devices using extended channel systems via multiple cables or input/output ports should list the total number of channels in the appropriate "Transmitted" or "Recognized"

| | columns and should use the "Remarks" column to indicate the terminology used by the device to identify the extra channels (i.e., "A1–A16, B1–B16"). |

Note numbers
The total range of transmitted or recognized notes.

Program Change
Indicate the range of Program Change numbers that are transmitted and/or recognized. If not implemented, enter a "No" in the appropriate column.

Bank Select response
Use a "Yes" or "No" to indicate whether or not the device correctly responds to Bank Select messages as per the MIDI 1.0 Specification. Devices that respond only to Bank Select MSB (cc #0) but not to the LSB (cc #32) should place a "No" in the "Recognized" column and should indicate this in the "Remarks" column. If the device does correctly respond to Bank Select messages, use the "Remarks" column to indicate what banks or ranges of banks are available in the device. If certain banks are accessible only by MIDI (and not by front panel user control), these should be listed in the "Remarks" column.

Modes supported
Use a "Yes" or "No" to indicate whether or not the device supports each of the five listed modes of reception.

Note-On Velocity
Use a "Yes" or "No" to indicate whether or not the device transmits, exports, responds to, and/or imports Note-On Velocity.

| | |
|---|---|
| Note-Off Velocity | Use a "Yes" or "No" to indicate whether or not the device transmits, exports, responds to, and/or imports Note-Off Velocity. |
| Channel Aftertouch | Use a "Yes" or "No" to indicate whether or not the device transmits, exports, responds to, and/or imports Channel Aftertouch. |
| Poly (Key) Aftertouch | Use a "Yes" or "No" to indicate whether or not the device transmits, exports, responds to, and/or imports Poly (Key) Aftertouch. |
| Pitch Bend | Use a "Yes" or "No" to indicate whether or not the device transmits, exports, responds to, and/or imports Pitch Bend. |
| Active Sensing? | Use a "Yes" or "No" to indicate whether or not the device transmits, exports, responds to, and/or imports Active Sensing. |
| System Reset? | Use a "Yes" or "No" to indicate whether or not the device transmits, exports, responds to, and/or imports System Reset. |
| Tune Request? | Use a "Yes" or "No" to indicate whether or not the device transmits, exports, responds to, and/or imports Tune Request. |
| Universal System Exclusive | Use a "Yes" or "No" to indicate whether or not the device transmits, exports, responds to, and/or imports the various Universal System Exclusive messages described. If the device supports additional Universal System Exclusive messages that are not listed, for example, the SP-MIDI MIP message or |

| | Global Parameter Control, use the "Other" category and, in the Remarks column, enter the name(s) of the message(s) supported. |
|---|---|
| Manufacturer or Non-Commercial System Exclusive | Use a "Yes" or "No" to indicate whether or not the device transmits, exports, responds to, and/or imports any Manufacturer System Exclusive messages or Non-Commercial System Exclusive messages. In the Remarks column, enter the name(s) of the message(s) supported, and either the words "Non-Commercial" or the manufacturer name(s) and MMA Manufacturer ID(s) for the message(s) supported. |
| NRPNs | Use a "Yes" or "No" to indicate whether or not the device transmits, exports, responds to, and/or imports NRPNs. Manufacturers may wish to list the NRPNs the device uses in the "Remarks" column (if this information will not physically fit in the "Remarks" column, provide a reference to the page or section number in the user manual where the information can be found). |
| RPNs | Use a "Yes" or "No" to indicate whether or not the device transmits, exports, responds to, and/or imports each of the specified RPNs. |

*MIDI Timing and Synchronization*

| MIDI Clock? | Use a "Yes" or "No" to indicate whether or not the device transmits, exports, responds to, and/or imports MIDI Time Code (MTC). |
|---|---|

| | |
|---|---|
| Song Position Pointer | Use a "Yes" or "No" to indicate whether or not the device transmits, exports, responds to, and/or imports MIDI Machine Control (MMC). If yes, indicate in the Remarks column whether the device transmits and/or responds in Open or Closed Loop mode. Manufacturers of devices utilizing MIDI Machine Control may wish to attach a separate chart indicating the specific MMC messages transmitted and/or recognized by the device. If so, indicate the presence of this "sub-chart" in the Remarks column. |
| Song Select | Indicate whether or not the device transmits, exports, responds to, and/or imports MIDI Show Control (MSC). If not, indicate "No". If yes, indicate the Level of MIDI Show Control supported. Manufacturers of devices utilizing MIDI Show Control may wish to attach a separate chart indicating the specific MSC messages transmitted and/or recognized by the device. If so, indicate the presence of this "sub-chart" in the Remarks column. |
| Start/ Continue/ Stop | Indicate whether or not the device has a mode of operation that complies with any of the General MIDI specifications: General MIDI System Level 1 (GM), General MIDI System Level 2 (GM2), and/or General MIDI Lite (GM Lite). If not, indicate "No." If yes, indicate the GM Level(s) supported. Also, if GM is the default power-up mode, indicate GM Lite, GM Level 1 or GM Level 2. If not, indicate "No." |

| MIDI Time Code | Indicate whether or not the device has a mode of operation that complies with any of the Downloadable Sounds specifications: DLS Level 1 (DLS), DLS Level 2 (DLS2, including DLS 2.1 and DLS 2.2), and/or Mobile DLS. If not, indicate "No." If yes, indicate the DLS Level(s) supported. Also, indicate whether or not the device can import and/or export DLS files. If not, indicate "No." If yes, indicate what types. It is recommended that manufacturers indicate in the Remarks column the means of receiving DLS data (i.e., specific physical format, device interface, or transport protocol, etc.) and, if a file system media is used, indicate in the Remarks column the exact format(s) supported (i.e., Windows, Mac OS, or Linux file system version, etc.). |
| MIDI Machine Control | Use a "Yes" or "No" to indicate whether or not the device has a mode of operation that can play, import, and/or export any of the Standard MIDI File formats, and, if so, the formats(s) supported: format 0 (single track), format 1 (multi-track), and/or format 2 (multiple independent single-track patterns). If yes, it is also recommended that manufacturers indicate in the Remarks column the means of receiving SMF data (i.e., specific physical format, device interface, or transport protocol, etc.) and, if a file system media is used, indicate in the Remarks column the exact format(s) supported (i.e., Windows, Mac OS, or Linux file system version, etc.). |

| | |
|---|---|
| MIDI Show Control | Use a "Yes" or "No" to indicate whether or not the device transmits, exports, responds to, and/or imports MIDI Time Code (MTC). |

### Extensions Compatibility

| | |
|---|---|
| General MIDI | Indicate whether or not the device transmits, exports, responds to, and/or imports MIDI Show Control (MSC). If not, indicate "No." If yes, indicate the Level of MIDI Show Control supported. Manufacturers of devices utilizing MIDI Show Control may wish to attach a separate chart indicating the specific MSC messages transmitted and/or recognized by the device. If so, indicate the presence of this "sub-chart" in the Remarks column. |
| DLS | Indicate whether or not the device has a mode of operation that complies with any of the General MIDI specifications: General MIDI System Level 1 (GM), General MIDI System Level 2 (GM2) and/or General MIDI Lite (GM Lite). If not, indicate "No." If yes, indicate the GM Level(s) supported. Also, if GM is the default power-up mode, indicate GM Lite, GM Level 1 or GM Level 2. If not, indicate "No." |
| Standard MIDI Files | Indicate whether or not the device has a mode of operation that complies with any of the Downloadable Sounds specifications: DLS Level 1 (DLS), DLS Level 2 (DLS2, including DLS 2.1 and DLS 2.2), and/or Mobile DLS. If not, indicate |

|  |  |
|---|---|
|  | "No." If yes, indicate the DLS Level(s) supported. Also, indicate whether or not the device can import and/or export DLS files. If not, indicate "No." If yes, indicate what types. It is recommended that manufacturers indicate in the Remarks column the means of receiving DLS data (i.e., specific physical format, device interface, or transport protocol, etc.) and, if a file system media is used, indicate in the Remarks column the exact format(s) supported (i.e., Windows, Mac OS, or Linux file system version, etc.). |
| XMF | Indicate whether or not the device has a mode of operation that can play, import, and/or export any of the officially defined XMF File Types: XMF Type 0, XMF Type 1, or Mobile XMF |
| (XMF Type 2). | If the device uses the XMF Meta File Format in a manner that does not conform to any of the XMF File Type specifications, indicate this in the Remarks column. |
| SP-MIDI | Indicate whether or not the device has a mode of operation that can play, import, and/or export Scalable Polyphony MIDI (SP-MIDI) data. If yes, indicate which SP-MIDI profile specification(s) that the device conforms to, for example, SP-MIDI 5-24 Voice Profile for 3GPP. |

## Pages 2 and 3: Control Number Information

### General

Pages 2 and 3 of the chart are used to describe how the device implements the 128 MIDI Control Change messages (including those reserved for Channel Mode messages). IMPORTANT: The use of pages 2 and 3 is optional for devices that do not transmit, export, respond to, and/or import any Control Change messages. The first 120 Control Change messages are controller numbers, and the last 8 (cc# 120–127) reserved for Channel Mode messages. These pages are divided into five columns, with the first column listing the control number in decimal. The second column lists the defined function from the MIDI 1.0 Specification for that control number if one exists, or is blank if undefined in the MIDI 1.0 Specification. Manufacturers using these undefined controller numbers should enter in the title of the assigned function in this column and should make an entry in the fifth, "Remarks" column noting this proprietary usage. The third and fourth columns are used to indicate whether the specified controller number is transmitted, exported, responded to, and/or imported.

### Functions Description

The inclusion of these two pages in a MIDI device's owner's manual is optional. Use a "Yes" or "No" to indicate whether or not the device transmits and/or responds to each of the listed control numbers. Use the "Remarks" column to indicate whether a particular controller number is assignable or if the controller is being used in a non-standard way (i.e., if the device is capable of receiving the controller message but routes it in an unusual way). If using any undefined controller number, enter the title of the assigned function in the second, "Function" column and make an entry in the fifth, "Remarks" column noting this proprietary usage.

| MIDI Implementation Chart v. 2.0 (Page 1 of 3) | | | |
|---|---|---|---|
| Manufacturer:       Model:       Version:   Date: | | | |
| | **Transmit/Export** | **Recognize/Import** | **Remarks** |
| *1. Basic Information* | | | |
| MIDI channels | | | |
| Note numbers | | | |
| Program change | | | |
| Bank Select response? (Yes/No) | | | |
|   If yes, list banks utilized in remarks column | | | |
| Modes supported :    Mode 1: Omni-On, Poly (Yes/No) | | | |
|                Mode 2: Omni-On, Mono (Yes/No) | | | |
|                Mode 3: Omni-Off, Poly (Yes/No) | | | |
|                Mode 4: Omni-Off, Mono (Yes/No) | | | |
|                Multi Mode (Yes/No) | | | |
| Note-On Velocity (Yes/No) | | | |
| Note-Off Velocity (Yes/No) | | | |
| Channel Aftertouch (Yes/No) | | | |
| Poly (Key) Aftertouch (Yes/No) | | | |
| Pitch Bend (Yes/No) | | | |
| Active Sensing (Yes/No) | | | |
| System Reset (Yes/No) | | | |
| Tune Request (Yes/No) | | | |
| Universal System Exclusive: Sample Dump Standard (Yes/No) | | | |
|                Device Inquiry (Yes/No) | | | |
|                File Dump (Yes/No) | | | |
|                MIDI Tuning (Yes/No) | | | |
|                Master Volume (Yes/No) | | | |
|                Master Balance (Yes/No) | | | |
|                Notation Information (Yes/No) | | | |
|                Turn GM1 System On (Yes/No) | | | |
|                Turn GM2 System On (Yes/No) | | | |
|                Turn GM System Off (Yes/No) | | | |
|                DLS-1 (Yes/No) | | | |
|                File Reference (Yes/No) | | | |
|                Controller Destination (Yes/No) | | | |
|                Key-based Instrument Ctrl (Yes/No) | | | |
|                Master Fine/Coarse Tune (Yes/No) | | | |
|                Other Universal System Exclusive | | | |
| Manufacturer or Non-Commercial System Exclusive | | | |
| NRPNs (Yes/No) | | | |
| RPN 00 (Pitch Bend Sensitivity) (Yes/No) | | | |
| RPN 01 (Channel Fine Tune) (Yes/No) | | | |
| RPN 02 (Channel Coarse Tune) (Yes/No) | | | |
| RPN 03 (Tuning Program Select) (Yes/No) | | | |
| RPN 04 (Tuning Bank Select) (Yes/No) | | | |
| RPN 05 (Modulation Depth Range) (Yes/No) | | | |
| *2. MIDI Timing and Synchronization* | | | |
| MIDI Clock (Yes/No) | | | |
| Song Position Pointer (Yes/No) | | | |
| Song Select (Yes/No) | | | |
| Start (Yes/No) | | | |
| Continue (Yes/No) | | | |
| Stop (Yes/No) | | | |
| MIDI Time Code (Yes/No) | | | |
| MIDI Machine Control (Yes/No) | | | |
| MIDI Show Control (Yes/No) | | | |
|   If yes, MSC Level supported | | | |
| *3. Extensions Compatibility* | | | |
| General MIDI compatible? (Level(s)/No) | | | |
|   Is GM default power-up mode? (Level/No) | | | |
| DLS compatible? (Levels(s)/No) | | | |
| (DLS File Type(s)/No) | | | |
| Standard MIDI Files (Type(s)/No) | | | |
| XMF Files (Type(s)/No) | | | |
| SP-MIDI compatible? (Yes/No) | | | |

**MIDI Implementation Chart v 2.0 Control Number Information (Page 2 of 3)**

Manufacturer:        Model:        Version:        Date:

| Control # | Function | Transmitted (Y/N) | Recognized (Y/N) | Remarks |
|---|---|---|---|---|
| 0 | Bank Select (MSB) | | | |
| 1 | Modulation Wheel (MSB) | | | |
| 2 | Breath Controller (MSB) | | | |
| 3 | | | | |
| 4 | Foot Controller (MSB) | | | |
| 5 | Portamento Time (MSB) | | | |
| 6 | Data Entry (MSB) | | | |
| 7 | Channel Volume (MSB) | | | |
| 8 | Balance (MSB) | | | |
| 9 | | | | |
| 10 | Pan (MSB) | | | |
| 11 | Expression (MSB) | | | |
| 12 | Effect Control 1 (MSB) | | | |
| 13 | Effect Control 2 (MSB) | | | |
| 14 | | | | |
| 15 | | | | |
| 16 | General Purpose Controller 1 (MSB) | | | |
| 17 | General Purpose Controller 2 (MSB) | | | |
| 18 | General Purpose Controller 3 (MSB) | | | |
| 19 | General Purpose Controller 4 (MSB) | | | |
| 20 | | | | |
| 21 | | | | |
| 22 | | | | |
| 23 | | | | |
| 24 | | | | |
| 25 | | | | |
| 26 | | | | |
| 27 | | | | |
| 28 | | | | |
| 29 | | | | |
| 30 | | | | |
| 31 | | | | |
| 32 | Bank Select (LSB) | | | |
| 33 | Modulation Wheel (LSB) | | | |
| 34 | Breath Controller (LSB) | | | |
| 35 | | | | |
| 36 | Foot Controller (LSB) | | | |
| 37 | Portamento Time (LSB) | | | |
| 38 | Data Entry (LSB) | | | |
| 39 | Channel Volume (LSB) | | | |
| 40 | Balance (LSB) | | | |
| 41 | | | | |
| 42 | Pan (LSB) | | | |
| 43 | Expression (LSB) | | | |
| 44 | Effect Control 1 (LSB) | | | |
| 45 | Effect Control 2 (LSB) | | | |
| 46 | | | | |
| 47 | | | | |
| 48 | General Purpose Controller 1 (LSB) | | | |
| 49 | General Purpose Controller 2 (LSB) | | | |
| 50 | General Purpose Controller 3 (LSB) | | | |
| 51 | General Purpose Controller 4 (LSB) | | | |
| 52 | | | | |
| 53 | | | | |
| 54 | | | | |
| 55 | | | | |
| 56 | | | | |
| 57 | | | | |
| 58 | | | | |
| 59 | | | | |
| 60 | | | | |
| 61 | | | | |
| 62 | | | | |
| 63 | | | | |

| MIDI Implementation Chart v 2.0 Control Number Information (Page 3 of 3) | | | | |
|---|---|---|---|---|
| Manufacturer: | Model: | Version: | Date: | |
| Control # | Function | Transmitted (Y/N) | Recognized (Y/N) | Remarks |
| 64 | Sustain Pedal | | | |
| 65 | Portamento On/Off | | | |
| 66 | Sostenuto | | | |
| 67 | Soft Pedal | | | |
| 68 | Legato Footswitch | | | |
| 69 | Hold 2 | | | |
| 70 | Sound Controller 1 (default: Sound Variation) | | | |
| 71 | Sound Controller 2 (default: Timbre / Harmonic Quality) | | | |
| 72 | Sound Controller 3 (default: Release Time) | | | |
| 73 | Sound Controller 4 (default: Attack Time) | | | |
| 74 | Sound Controller 5 (default: Brightness) | | | |
| 75 | Sound Controller 6 (GM2 default: Decay Time) | | | |
| 76 | Sound Controller 7 (GM2 default: Vibrato Rate) | | | |
| 77 | Sound Controller 8 (GM2 default: Vibrato Depth) | | | |
| 78 | Sound Controller 9 (GM2 default: Vibrato Delay) | | | |
| 79 | Sound Controller 10 (GM2 default: Undefined) | | | |
| 80 | General Purpose Controller 5 | | | |
| 81 | General Purpose Controller 6 | | | |
| 82 | General Purpose Controller 7 | | | |
| 83 | General Purpose Controller 8 | | | |
| 84 | Portamento Control | | | |
| 85 | | | | |
| 86 | | | | |
| 87 | | | | |
| 88 | | | | |
| 89 | | | | |
| 90 | | | | |
| 91 | Effects 1 Depth (default: Reverb Send) | | | |
| 92 | Effects 2 Depth (default: Tremolo Depth) | | | |
| 93 | Effects 3 Depth (default: Chorus Send) | | | |
| 94 | Effects 4 Depth (default: Celeste [Detune] Depth) | | | |
| 95 | Effects 5 Depth (default: Phaser Depth) | | | |
| 96 | Data Increment | | | |
| 97 | Data Decrement | | | |
| 98 | Non-Registered Parameter Number (LSB) | | | |
| 99 | Non-Registered Parameter Number(MSB) | | | |
| 100 | Registered Parameter Number (LSB) | | | |
| 101 | Registered Parameter Number(MSB) | | | |
| 102 | | | | |
| 103 | | | | |
| 104 | | | | |
| 105 | | | | |
| 106 | | | | |
| 107 | | | | |
| 108 | | | | |
| 109 | | | | |
| 110 | | | | |
| 111 | | | | |
| 112 | | | | |
| 113 | | | | |
| 114 | | | | |
| 115 | | | | |
| 116 | | | | |
| 117 | | | | |
| 118 | | | | |
| 119 | | | | |
| 120 | All Sound Off | | | |
| 121 | Reset All Controllers | | | |
| 122 | Local Control On/Off | | | |
| 123 | All Notes Off | | | |
| 124 | Omni Mode Off | | | |
| 125 | Omni Mode On | | | |
| 126 | Poly Mode Off | | | |
| 127 | Poly Mode On | | | |

Section 4—MIDI Messages

# MIDI Messages
## *Table 1—Summary of MIDI Messages*

The following table lists many of the major MIDI messages in numerical (binary) order. This table is intended as an overview of MIDI, and is by no means complete. Additional messages are listed in the printed documentation available from the MMA.

**WARNING! Details about implementing these messages can dramatically impact compatibility with other products. We strongly recommend consulting the official** *MMA Detailed MIDI Specification* (http://www.midi.org/techspecs/midispec.php) **for additional information.**

## *Table 12.1   MIDI 1.0 Specification Message Summary*

| Status D7–D0 | Data Byte(s) D7–D0 | Description |
|---|---|---|
| **Channel Voice Messages [nnnn = 0–15 (MIDI Channel Number 1–16)]** | | |
| 1000nnnn | 0kkkkkkk<br>0vvvvvvv | Note Off event.<br>This message is sent when a note is released (ended). (kkkkkkk) is the key (note) number. (vvvvvvv) is the velocity. |
| 1001nnnn | 0kkkkkkk<br>0vvvvvvv | Note On event.<br>This message is sent when a note is depressed (start). (kkkkkkk) is the key (note) number. (vvvvvvv) is the velocity. |
| 1010nnnn | 0kkkkkkk<br>0vvvvvvv | Polyphonic Key Pressure (Aftertouch).<br>This message is most often sent by pressing down on the key after it "bottoms out". (kkkkkkk) is the key (note) number. (vvvvvvv) is the pressure value. |
| 1011nnnn | 0ccccccc<br>0vvvvvvv | Control Change.<br>This message is sent when a controller value changes. Controllers include devices such as pedals and levers. Controller numbers 120–127 are reserved as "Channel Mode Messages" (below). (ccccccc) is the controller number (0–119). (vvvvvvv) is the controller value (0–127). |

| 1100nnnn | 0ppppppp | Program Change. This message sent when the patch number changes. (ppppppp) is the new program number. |
| 1101nnnn | 0vvvvvvv | Channel Pressure (After-touch). This message is most often sent by pressing down on the key after it "bottoms out". This message is different from polyphonic after-touch. Use this message to send the single greatest pressure value (of all the current depressed keys). (vvvvvvv) is the pressure value. |
| 1110nnnn | 0lllllll 0mmmmmmm | Pitch Wheel Change. This message is sent to indicate a change in the pitch wheel. The pitch wheel is measured by a fourteen bit value. Center (no pitch change) is 2000H. Sensitivity is a function of the transmitter. (lllllll) are the least significant 7 bits. (mmmmmm) are the most significant 7 bits. |

## Channel Mode Messages (See also Control Change, above)

| 1011nnnn | 0ccccccc 0vvvvvvv | Channel Mode Messages. This the same code as the Control Change (above), but implements Mode control and special message by using reserved controller numbers 120–127. The commands are: |
| | | All Sound Off. When All Sound Off is received all oscillators will turn off, and their volume envelopes are set to zero as soon as possible. c = 120, v = 0: All Sound Off |
| | | Reset All Controllers. When Reset All Controllers is received, all controller values are reset to their default values. (See specific Recommended Practices for defaults). c = 121, v = x: Value must only be zero unless otherwise allowed in a specific Recommended Practice. |
| | | Local Control. When Local Control is Off, all devices on a given channel will respond only to data received over MIDI. Played data, etc. will be ignored. Local Control On restores the functions of the normal controllers. c = 122, v = 0: Local Control Off c = 122, v = 127: Local Control On |
| | | All Notes Off. When an All Notes Off is received, all oscillators will turn off. c = 123, v = 0: All Notes Off (See text for description of actual mode commands.) c = 124, v = 0: Omni Mode Off c = 125, v = 0: Omni Mode On c = 126, v = M: Mono Mode On (Poly Off) where M is the number of channels (Omni Off) or 0 (Omni On) c = 127, v = 0: Poly Mode On (Mono Off) (Note: These four messages also cause All Notes Off) |

*(Continued)*

**375**

## Table 12.1 (Continued)

| Status<br>D7—D0 | Data Byte(s)<br>D7—D0 | Description |
|---|---|---|

### System Common Messages

| Status<br>D7—D0 | Data Byte(s)<br>D7—D0 | Description |
|---|---|---|
| 11110000 | 0iiiiiii<br>[0iiiiiii<br>0iiiiiii]<br>0ddddddd<br>—<br>—<br>0ddddddd<br>11110111 | System Exclusive.<br>This message type allows manufacturers to create their own messages (such as bulk dumps, patch parameters, and other non-spec data) and provides a mechanism for creating additional MIDI Specification messages. The Manufacturer's ID code (assigned by MMA or AMEI) is either 1 byte (0iiiiiii) or 3 bytes (0iiiiiii 0iiiiiii 0iiiiiii). Two of the 1 Byte IDs are reserved for extensions called Universal Exclusive Messages, which are not manufacturer-specific. If a device recognizes the ID code as its own (or as a supported Universal message) it will listen to the rest of the message (0ddddddd). Otherwise, the message will be ignored. (Note: Real-Time messages ONLY may be interleaved with a System Exclusive.) |
| 11110001 | 0nnndddd | MIDI Time Code Quarter Frame.<br>nnn = Message Type<br>dddd = Values |
| 11110010 | 0lllllll<br>0mmmmmmm | Song Position Pointer.<br>This is an internal 14 bit register that holds the number of MIDI beats (1 beat = six MIDI clocks) since the start of the song. l is the LSB, m the MSB. |
| 11110011 | 0sssssss | Song Select.<br>The Song Select specifies which sequence or song is to be played. |
| 11110100 | | Undefined. (Reserved) |
| 11110101 | | Undefined. (Reserved) |
| 11110110 | | Tune Request. Upon receiving a Tune Request, all analog synthesizers should tune their oscillators. |
| 11110111 | | End of Exclusive. Used to terminate a System Exclusive dump (see above). |

### System Real-Time Messages

| Status<br>D7—D0 | Data Byte(s)<br>D7—D0 | Description |
|---|---|---|
| 11111000 | | Timing Clock. Sent 24 times per quarter note when synchronization is required (see text). |
| 11111001 | | Undefined. (Reserved) |
| 11111010 | | Start. Start the current sequence playing. (This message will be followed with Timing Clocks). |
| 11111011 | | Continue. Continue at the point the sequence was Stopped. |
| 11111100 | | Stop. Stop the current sequence. |
| 11111101 | | Undefined. (Reserved) |

| 11111110 | Active Sensing. This message is intended to be sent repeatedly to tell the receiver that a connection is alive. Use of this message is optional. When initially received, the receiver will expect to receive another Active Sensing message each 300ms (max), and if it does not then it will assume that the connection has been terminated. At termination, the receiver will turn off all voices and return to normal (non- active sensing) operation. |
| 11111111 | Reset. Reset all receivers in the system to power-up status. This should be used sparingly, preferably under manual control. In particular, it should not be sent on power-up. |

## Table 12.2  Expanded Status Bytes List

| Status Byte | | Data Bytes | |
| --- | --- | --- | --- |
| 1st Byte Value<br>Binary \|Hex\| Dec | Function | 2nd Byte | 3rd Byte |
| 10000000 = 80 = 128 | Chan 1 Note off | Note Number (0–127) | Note Velocity (0–127) |
| 10000001 = 81 = 129 | Chan 2 Note off | Note Number (0–127) | Note Velocity (0–127) |
| 10000010 = 82 = 130 | Chan 3 Note off | Note Number (0–127) | Note Velocity (0–127) |
| 10000011 = 83 = 131 | Chan 4 Note off | Note Number (0–127) | Note Velocity (0–127) |
| 10000100 = 84 = 132 | Chan 5 Note off | Note Number (0–127) | Note Velocity (0–127) |
| 10000101 = 85 = 133 | Chan 6 Note off | Note Number (0–127) | Note Velocity (0–127) |
| 10000110 = 86 = 134 | Chan 7 Note off | Note Number (0–127) | Note Velocity (0–127) |
| 10000111 = 87 = 135 | Chan 8 Note off | Note Number (0–127) | Note Velocity (0–127) |
| 10001000 = 88 = 136 | Chan 9 Note off | Note Number (0–127) | Note Velocity (0–127) |
| 10001001 = 89 = 137 | Chan 10 Note off | Note Number (0–127) | Note Velocity (0–127) |
| 10001010 = 8A = 138 | Chan 11 Note off | Note Number (0–127) | Note Velocity (0–127) |
| 10001011 = 8B = 139 | Chan 12 Note off | Note Number (0–127) | Note Velocity (0–127) |
| 10001100 = 8C = 140 | Chan 13 Note off | Note Number (0–127) | Note Velocity (0–127) |
| 10001101 = 8D = 141 | Chan 14 Note off | Note Number (0–127) | Note Velocity (0–127) |
| 10001110 = 8E = 142 | Chan 15 Note off | Note Number (0–127) | Note Velocity (0–127) |
| 10001111 = 8F = 143 | Chan 16 Note off | Note Number (0–127) | Note Velocity (0–127) |
| 10010000 = 90 = 144 | Chan 1 Note on | Note Number (0–127) | Note Velocity (0–127) |
| 10010001 = 91 = 145 | Chan 2 Note on | Note Number (0–127) | Note Velocity (0–127) |

*(Continued)*

## *Table 12.2* (Continued)

| Status Byte | | Data Bytes | |
|---|---|---|---|
| 1st Byte Value<br>Binary \|Hex\| Dec | Function | 2nd Byte | 3rd Byte |
| 10010010 = 92 = 146 | Chan 3 Note on | Note Number (0–127) | Note Velocity (0–127) |
| 10010011 = 93 = 147 | Chan 4 Note on | Note Number (0–127) | Note Velocity (0–127) |
| 10010100 = 94 = 148 | Chan 5 Note on | Note Number (0–127) | Note Velocity (0–127) |
| 10010101 = 95 = 149 | Chan 6 Note on | Note Number (0–127) | Note Velocity (0–127) |
| 10010110 = 96 = 150 | Chan 7 Note on | Note Number (0–127) | Note Velocity (0–127) |
| 10010111 = 97 = 151 | Chan 8 Note on | Note Number (0–127) | Note Velocity (0–127) |
| 10011000 = 98 = 152 | Chan 9 Note on | Note Number (0–127) | Note Velocity (0–127) |
| 10011001 = 99 = 153 | Chan 10 Note on | Note Number (0–127) | Note Velocity (0–127) |
| 10011010 = 9A = 154 | Chan 11 Note on | Note Number (0–127) | Note Velocity (0–127) |
| 10011011 = 9B = 155 | Chan 12 Note on | Note Number (0–127) | Note Velocity (0–127) |
| 10011100 = 9C = 156 | Chan 13 Note on | Note Number (0–127) | Note Velocity (0–127) |
| 10011101 = 9D = 157 | Chan 14 Note on | Note Number (0–127) | Note Velocity (0–127) |
| 10011110 = 9E = 158 | Chan 15 Note on | Note Number (0–127) | Note Velocity (0–127) |
| 10011111 = 9F = 159 | Chan 16 Note on | Note Number (0–127) | Note Velocity (0–127) |
| 10100000 = A0 = 160 | Chan 1 Polyphonic Aftertouch | Note Number (0–127) | Pressure (0–127) |
| 10100001 = A1 = 161 | Chan 2 Polyphonic Aftertouch | Note Number (0–127 | Pressure (0–127) |
| 10100010 = A2 = 162 | Chan 3 Polyphonic Aftertouch | Note Number (0–127 | Pressure (0–127) |
| 10100011 = A3 = 163 | Chan 4 Polyphonic Aftertouch | Note Number (0–127 | Pressure (0–127) |
| 10100100 = A4 = 164 | Chan 5 Polyphonic Aftertouch | Note Number (0–127 | Pressure (0–127) |
| 10100101 = A5 = 165 | Chan 6 Polyphonic Aftertouch | Note Number (0–127 | Pressure (0–127) |
| 10100110 = A6 = 166 | Chan 7 Polyphonic Aftertouch | Note Number (0–127 | Pressure (0–127) |
| 10100111 = A7 = 167 | Chan 8 Polyphonic Aftertouch | Note Number (0–127 | Pressure (0–127) |
| 10101000 = A8 = 168 | Chan 9 Polyphonic Aftertouch | Note Number (0–127 | Pressure (0–127) |
| 10101001 = A9 = 169 | Chan 10 Polyphonic Aftertouch | Note Number (0–127 | Pressure (0–127) |
| 10101010 = AA = 170 | Chan 11 Polyphonic Aftertouch | Note Number (0–127 | Pressure (0–127) |
| 10101011 = AB = 171 | Chan 12 Polyphonic Aftertouch | Note Number (0–127 | Pressure (0–127) |
| 10101100 = AC = 172 | Chan 13 Polyphonic Aftertouch | Note Number (0–127 | Pressure (0–127) |
| 10101101 = AD = 173 | Chan 14 Polyphonic Aftertouch | Note Number (0–127 | Pressure (0–127) |
| 10101110 = AE = 174 | Chan 15 Polyphonic Aftertouch | Note Number (0–127 | Pressure (0–127) |

| | | | |
|---|---|---|---|
| 10101111 = AF = 175 | Chan 16 Polyphonic Aftertouch | Note Number (0–127 | Pressure (0–127) |
| 10110000 = B0 = 176 | Chan 1 Control/Mode Change | see Table 3 | see Table 3 |
| 10110001 = B1 = 177 | Chan 2 Control/Mode Change | see Table 3 | see Table 3 |
| 10110010 = B2 = 178 | Chan 3 Control/Mode Change | see Table 3 | see Table 3 |
| 10110011 = B3 = 179 | Chan 4 Control/Mode Change | see Table 3 | see Table 3 |
| 10110100 = B4 = 180 | Chan 5 Control/Mode Change | see Table 3 | see Table 3 |
| 10110101 = B5 = 181 | Chan 6 Control/Mode Change | see Table 3 | see Table 3 |
| 10110110 = B6 = 182 | Chan 7 Control/Mode Change | see Table 3 | see Table 3 |
| 10110111 = B7 = 183 | Chan 8 Control/Mode Change | see Table 3 | see Table 3 |
| 10111000 = B8 = 184 | Chan 9 Control/Mode Change | see Table 3 | see Table 3 |
| 10111001 = B9 = 185 | Chan 10 Control/Mode Change | see Table 3 | see Table 3 |
| 10111010 = BA = 186 | Chan 11 Control/Mode Change | see Table 3 | see Table 3 |
| 10111011 = BB = 187 | Chan 12 Control/Mode Change | see Table 3 | see Table 3 |
| 10111100 = BC = 188 | Chan 13 Control/Mode Change | see Table 3 | see Table 3 |
| 10111101 = BD = 189 | Chan 14 Control/Mode Change | see Table 3 | see Table 3 |
| 10111110 = BE = 190 | Chan 15 Control/Mode Change | see Table 3 | see Table 3 |
| 10111111 = BF = 191 | Chan 16 Control/Mode Change | see Table 3 | see Table 3 |
| 11000000 = C0 = 192 | Chan 1 Program Change | Program # (0–127) | none |
| 11000001 = C1 = 193 | Chan 2 Program Change | Program # (0–127) | none |
| 11000010 = C2 = 194 | Chan 3 Program Change | Program # (0–127) | none |
| 11000011 = C3 = 195 | Chan 4 Program Change | Program # (0–127) | none |
| 11000100 = C4 = 196 | Chan 5 Program Change | Program # (0–127) | none |
| 11000101 = C5 = 197 | Chan 6 Program Change | Program # (0–127) | none |
| 11000110 = C6 = 198 | Chan 7 Program Change | Program # (0–127) | none |
| 11000111 = C7 = 199 | Chan 8 Program Change | Program # (0–127) | none |
| 11001000 = C8 = 200 | Chan 9 Program Change | Program # (0–127) | none |
| 11001001 = C9 = 201 | Chan 10 Program Change | Program # (0–127) | none |
| 11001010 = CA = 202 | Chan 11 Program Change | Program # (0–127) | none |
| 11001011 = CB = 203 | Chan 12 Program Change | Program # (0–127) | none |
| 11001100 = CC = 204 | Chan 13 Program Change | Program # (0–127) | none |
| 11001101 = CD = 205 | Chan 14 Program Change | Program # (0–127) | none |
| 11001110 = CE = 206 | Chan 15 Program Change | Program # (0–127) | none |
| 11001111 = CF = 207 | Chan 16 Program Change | Program # (0–127) | none |

*(Continued)*

**Table 12.2** (Continued)

| Status Byte | | Data Bytes | |
|---|---|---|---|
| *1st Byte Value Binary \|Hex\| Dec* | *Function* | *2nd Byte* | *3rd Byte* |
| 11010000 = D0 = 208 | Chan 1 Channel Aftertouch | Pressure (0–127) | none |
| 11010001 = D1 = 209 | Chan 2 Channel Aftertouch | Pressure (0–127) | none |
| 11010010 = D2 = 210 | Chan 3 Channel Aftertouch | Pressure (0–127) | none |
| 11010011 = D3 = 211 | Chan 4 Channel Aftertouch | Pressure (0–127) | none |
| 11010100 = D4 = 212 | Chan 5 Channel Aftertouch | Pressure (0–127) | none |
| 11010101 = D5 = 213 | Chan 6 Channel Aftertouch | Pressure (0–127) | none |
| 11010110 = D6 = 214 | Chan 7 Channel Aftertouch | Pressure (0–127) | none |
| 11010111 = D7 = 215 | Chan 8 Channel Aftertouch | Pressure (0–127) | none |
| 11011000 = D8 = 216 | Chan 9 Channel Aftertouch | Pressure (0–127) | none |
| 11011001 = D9 = 217 | Chan 10 Channel Aftertouch | Pressure (0–127) | none |
| 11011010 = DA = 218 | Chan 11 Channel Aftertouch | Pressure (0–127) | none |
| 11011011 = DB = 219 | Chan 12 Channel Aftertouch | Pressure (0–127) | none |
| 11011100 = DC = 220 | Chan 13 Channel Aftertouch | Pressure (0–127) | none |
| 11011101 = DD = 221 | Chan 14 Channel Aftertouch | Pressure (0–127) | none |
| 11011110 = DE = 222 | Chan 15 Channel Aftertouch | Pressure (0–127) | none |
| 11011111 = DF = 223 | Chan 16 Channel Aftertouch | Pressure (0–127) | none |
| 11100000 = E0 = 224 | Chan 1 Pitch Wheel Control | Pitch Wheel LSB (0–127) | Pitch Wheel MSB (0–127) |
| 11100001 = E1 = 225 | Chan 2 Pitch Wheel Control | Pitch Wheel LSB (0–127) | Pitch Wheel MSB (0–127) |
| 11100010 = E2 = 226 | Chan 3 Pitch Wheel Control | Pitch Wheel LSB (0–127) | Pitch Wheel MSB (0–127) |
| 11100011 = E3 = 227 | Chan 4 Pitch Wheel Control | Pitch Wheel LSB (0–127) | Pitch Wheel MSB (0–127) |
| 11100100 = E4 = 228 | Chan 5 Pitch Wheel Control | Pitch Wheel LSB (0–127) | Pitch Wheel MSB (0–127) |
| 11100101 = E5 = 229 | Chan 6 Pitch Wheel Control | Pitch Wheel LSB (0–127) | Pitch Wheel MSB (0–127) |
| 11100110 = E6 = 230 | Chan 7 Pitch Wheel Control | Pitch Wheel LSB (0–127) | Pitch Wheel MSB (0–127) |
| 11100111 = E7 = 231 | Chan 8 Pitch Wheel Control | Pitch Wheel LSB (0–127) | Pitch Wheel MSB (0–127) |
| 11101000 = E8 = 232 | Chan 9 Pitch Wheel Control | Pitch Wheel LSB (0–127) | Pitch Wheel MSB (0–127) |
| 11101001 = E9 = 233 | Chan 10 Pitch Wheel Control | Pitch Wheel LSB (0–127) | Pitch Wheel MSB (0–127) |
| 11101010 = EA = 234 | Chan 11 Pitch Wheel Control | Pitch Wheel LSB (0–127) | Pitch Wheel MSB (0–127) |
| 11101011 = EB = 235 | Chan 12 Pitch Wheel Control | Pitch Wheel LSB (0–127) | Pitch Wheel MSB (0–127) |
| 11101100 = EC = 236 | Chan 13 Pitch Wheel Control | Pitch Wheel LSB (0–127) | Pitch Wheel MSB (0–127) |

| | | | |
|---|---|---|---|
| 11101101 = ED = 237 | Chan 14 Pitch Wheel Control | Pitch Wheel LSB (0–127) | Pitch Wheel MSB (0–127) |
| 11101110 = EE = 238 | Chan 15 Pitch Wheel Control | Pitch Wheel LSB (0–127) | Pitch Wheel MSB (0–127) |
| 11101111 = EF = 239 | Chan 16 Pitch Wheel Control | Pitch Wheel LSB (0–127) | Pitch Wheel MSB (0–127) |
| 11110000 = F0 = 240 | System Exclusive | ** | ** |
| 11110001 = F1 = 241 | MIDI Time Code Qtr. Frame | –see spec– | –see spec– |
| 11110010 = F2 = 242 | Song Position Pointer | LSB | MSB |
| 11110011 = F3 = 243 | Song Select (Song #) | (0–127) | none |
| 11110100 = F4 = 244 | Undefined (Reserved) | — | — |
| 11110101 = F5 = 245 | Undefined (Reserved) | — | — |
| 11110110 = F6 = 246 | Tune request | none | none |
| 11110111 = F7 = 247 | End of SysEx (EOX) | none | none |
| 11111000 = F8 = 248 | Timing clock | none | none |
| 11111001 = F9 = 249 | Undefined (Reserved) | — | — |
| 11111010 = FA = 250 | Start | none | none |
| 11111011 = FB = 251 | Continue | none | none |
| 11111100 = FC = 252 | Stop | none | none |
| 11111101 = FD = 253 | Undefined (Reserved) | — | — |
| 11111110 = FE = 254 | Active Sensing | none | none |
| 11111111 = FF = 255 | System Reset | none | none |

** Note: System Exclusive (data dump) 2nd byte = Vendor ID (or Universal Exclusive) followed by more data bytes and ending with EOX.

## Table 12.3  Control Changes and Mode Changes
### (Status Bytes 176–191)

| Control Number 2nd Byte Value | | | Control Function | 3rd Byte Value | |
|---|---|---|---|---|---|
| Decimal | Binary | Hex | | Value | Used As |
| 0 | 00000000 | 00 | Bank Select | 0–127 | MSB |
| 1 | 00000001 | 01 | Modulation Wheel or Lever | 0–127 | MSB |
| 2 | 00000010 | 02 | Breath Controller | 0–127 | MSB |
| 3 | 00000011 | 03 | Undefined | 0–127 | MSB |

*(Continued)*

## **Table 12.3** (Continued)

| Control Number 2nd Byte Value | | | Control Function | 3rd Byte Value | |
| --- | --- | --- | --- | --- | --- |
| Decimal | Binary | Hex | | Value | Used As |
| 4 | 00000100 | 04 | Foot Controller | 0–127 | MSB |
| 5 | 00000101 | 05 | Portamento Time | 0–127 | MSB |
| 6 | 00000110 | 06 | Data Entry MSB | 0–127 | MSB |
| 7 | 00000111 | 07 | Channel Volume (formerly Main Volume) | 0–127 | MSB |
| 8 | 00001000 | 08 | Balance | 0–127 | MSB |
| 9 | 00001001 | 09 | Undefined | 0–127 | MSB |
| 10 | 00001010 | 0A | Pan | 0–127 | MSB |
| 11 | 00001011 | 0B | Expression Controller | 0–127 | MSB |
| 12 | 00001100 | 0C | Effect Control 1 | 0–127 | MSB |
| 13 | 00001101 | 0D | Effect Control 2 | 0–127 | MSB |
| 14 | 00001110 | 0E | Undefined | 0–127 | MSB |
| 15 | 00001111 | 0F | Undefined | 0–127 | MSB |
| 16 | 00010000 | 10 | General Purpose Controller 1 | 0–127 | MSB |
| 17 | 00010001 | 11 | General Purpose Controller 2 | 0–127 | MSB |
| 18 | 00010010 | 12 | General Purpose Controller 3 | 0–127 | MSB |
| 19 | 00010011 | 13 | General Purpose Controller 4 | 0–127 | MSB |
| 20 | 00010100 | 14 | Undefined | 0–127 | MSB |
| 21 | 00010101 | 15 | Undefined | 0–127 | MSB |
| 22 | 00010110 | 16 | Undefined | 0–127 | MSB |
| 23 | 00010111 | 17 | Undefined | 0–127 | MSB |
| 24 | 00011000 | 18 | Undefined | 0–127 | MSB |
| 25 | 00011001 | 19 | Undefined | 0–127 | MSB |
| 26 | 00011010 | 1A | Undefined | 0–127 | MSB |
| 27 | 00011011 | 1B | Undefined | 0–127 | MSB |
| 28 | 00011100 | 1C | Undefined | 0–127 | MSB |
| 29 | 00011101 | 1D | Undefined | 0–127 | MSB |
| 30 | 00011110 | 1E | Undefined | 0–127 | MSB |
| 31 | 00011111 | 1F | Undefined | 0–127 | MSB |

| 32 | 00100000 | 20 | LSB for Control 0 (Bank Select) | 0–127 | LSB |
|----|----------|----|--------------------------------|-------|-----|
| 33 | 00100001 | 21 | LSB for Control 1 (Modulation Wheel or Lever) | 0–127 | LSB |
| 34 | 00100010 | 22 | LSB for Control 2 (Breath Controller) | 0–127 | LSB |
| 35 | 00100011 | 23 | LSB for Control 3 (Undefined) | 0–127 | LSB |
| 36 | 00100100 | 24 | LSB for Control 4 (Foot Controller) | 0–127 | LSB |
| 37 | 00100101 | 25 | LSB for Control 5 (Portamento Time) | 0–127 | LSB |
| 38 | 00100110 | 26 | LSB for Control 6 (Data Entry) | 0–127 | LSB |
| 39 | 00100111 | 27 | LSB for Control 7 (Channel Volume, formerly Main Volume) | 0–127 | LSB |
| 40 | 00101000 | 28 | LSB for Control 8 (Balance) | 0–127 | LSB |
| 41 | 00101001 | 29 | LSB for Control 9 (Undefined) | 0–127 | LSB |
| 42 | 00101010 | 2A | LSB for Control 10 (Pan) | 0–127 | LSB |
| 43 | 00101011 | 2B | LSB for Control 11 (Expression Controller) | 0–127 | LSB |
| 44 | 00101100 | 2C | LSB for Control 12 (Effect control 1) | 0–127 | LSB |
| 45 | 00101101 | 2D | LSB for Control 13 (Effect control 2) | 0–127 | LSB |
| 46 | 00101110 | 2E | LSB for Control 14 (Undefined) | 0–127 | LSB |
| 47 | 00101111 | 2F | LSB for Control 15 (Undefined) | 0–127 | LSB |
| 48 | 00110000 | 30 | LSB for Control 16 (General Purpose Controller 1) | 0–127 | LSB |
| 49 | 00110001 | 31 | LSB for Control 17 (General Purpose Controller 2) | 0–127 | LSB |
| 50 | 00110010 | 32 | LSB for Control 18 (General Purpose Controller 3) | 0–127 | LSB |
| 51 | 00110011 | 33 | LSB for Control 19 (General Purpose Controller 4) | 0–127 | LSB |
| 52 | 00110100 | 34 | LSB for Control 20 (Undefined) | 0–127 | LSB |
| 53 | 00110101 | 35 | LSB for Control 21 (Undefined) | 0–127 | LSB |
| 54 | 00110110 | 36 | LSB for Control 22 (Undefined) | 0–127 | LSB |
| 55 | 00110111 | 37 | LSB for Control 23 (Undefined) | 0–127 | LSB |
| 56 | 00111000 | 38 | LSB for Control 24 (Undefined) | 0–127 | LSB |
| 57 | 00111001 | 39 | LSB for Control 25 (Undefined) | 0–127 | LSB |
| 58 | 00111010 | 3A | LSB for Control 26 (Undefined) | 0–127 | LSB |
| 59 | 00111011 | 3B | LSB for Control 27 (Undefined) | 0–127 | LSB |
| 60 | 00111100 | 3C | LSB for Control 28 (Undefined) | 0–127 | LSB |
| 61 | 00111101 | 3D | LSB for Control 29 (Undefined) | 0–127 | LSB |
| 62 | 00111110 | 3E | LSB for Control 30 (Undefined) | 0–127 | LSB |
| 63 | 00111111 | 3F | LSB for Control 31 (Undefined) | 0–127 | LSB |

(*Continued*)

## **Table 12.3** (Continued)

| Control Number 2nd Byte Value | | | Control Function | 3rd Byte Value | |
|---|---|---|---|---|---|
| Decimal | Binary | Hex | | Value | Used As |
| 64 | 01000000 | 40 | Damper Pedal on/off (Sustain) | ≤63 off, ≥64 on | — |
| 65 | 01000001 | 41 | Portamento On/Off | ≤63 off, ≥64 on | — |
| 66 | 01000010 | 42 | Sostenuto On/Off | ≤63 off, ≥64 on | — |
| 67 | 01000011 | 43 | Soft Pedal On/Off | ≤63 off, ≥64 on | — |
| 68 | 01000100 | 44 | Legato Footswitch | ≤63 Normal, ≥64 Legato | — |
| 69 | 01000101 | 45 | Hold 2 | ≤63 off, ≥64 on | — |
| 70 | 01000110 | 46 | Sound Controller 1 (default: Sound Variation) | 0–127 | LSB |
| 71 | 01000111 | 47 | Sound Controller 2 (default: Timbre/Harmonic Intens.) | 0–127 | LSB |
| 72 | 01001000 | 48 | Sound Controller 3 (default: Release Time) | 0–127 | LSB |
| 73 | 01001001 | 49 | Sound Controller 4 (default: Attack Time) | 0–127 | LSB |
| 74 | 01001010 | 4A | Sound Controller 5 (default: Brightness) | 0–127 | LSB |
| 75 | 01001011 | 4B | Sound Controller 6 (default: Decay Time—see MMA RP-021) | 0–127 | LSB |
| 76 | 01001100 | 4C | Sound Controller 7 (default: Vibrato Rate—see MMA RP-021) | 0–127 | LSB |
| 77 | 01001101 | 4D | Sound Controller 8 (default: Vibrato Depth—see MMA RP-021) | 0–127 | LSB |
| 78 | 01001110 | 4E | Sound Controller 9 (default: Vibrato Delay—see MMA RP-021) | 0–127 | LSB |
| 79 | 01001111 | 4F | Sound Controller 10 (default undefined—see MMA RP-021) | 0–127 | LSB |
| 80 | 01010000 | 50 | General Purpose Controller 5 | 0–127 | LSB |
| 81 | 01010001 | 51 | General Purpose Controller 6 | 0–127 | LSB |
| 82 | 01010010 | 52 | General Purpose Controller 7 | 0–127 | LSB |
| 83 | 01010011 | 53 | General Purpose Controller 8 | 0–127 | LSB |
| 84 | 01010100 | 54 | Portamento Control | 0–127 | LSB |
| 85 | 01010101 | 55 | Undefined | — | — |
| 86 | 01010110 | 56 | Undefined | — | — |
| 87 | 01010111 | 57 | Undefined | — | — |

| 88 | 01011000 | 58 | High Resolution Velocity Prefix | 0–127 | LSB |
| 89 | 01011001 | 59 | Undefined | — | — |
| 90 | 01011010 | 5A | Undefined | — | — |
| 91 | 01011011 | 5B | Effects 1 Depth | 0–127 | — |
| | | | (default: Reverb Send Level—see MMA RP-023) (formerly External Effects Depth) | | |
| 92 | 01011100 | 5C | Effects 2 Depth (formerly Tremolo Depth) | 0–127 | — |
| 93 | 01011101 | 5D | Effects 3 Depth | 0–127 | — |
| | | | (default: Chorus Send Level—see MMA RP-023) (formerly Chorus Depth) | | |
| 94 | 01011110 | 5E | Effects 4 Depth (formerly Celeste [Detune] Depth) | 0–127 | — |
| 95 | 01011111 | 5F | Effects 5 Depth (formerly Phaser Depth) | 0–127 | — |
| 96 | 01100000 | 60 | Data Increment (Data Entry +1) (see MMA RP-018) | N/A | — |
| 97 | 01100001 | 61 | Data Decrement (Data Entry −1) (see MMA RP-018) | N/A | — |
| 98 | 01100010 | 62 | Non-Registered Parameter Number (NRPN)—LSB | 0–127 | LSB |
| 99 | 01100011 | 63 | Non-Registered Parameter Number (NRPN)—MSB | 0–127 | MSB |
| 100 | 01100100 | 64 | Registered Parameter Number (RPN)—LSB* | 0–127 | LSB |
| 101 | 01100101 | 65 | Registered Parameter Number (RPN)—MSB* | 0–127 | MSB |
| 102 | 01100110 | 66 | Undefined | — | — |
| 103 | 01100111 | 67 | Undefined | — | — |
| 104 | 01101000 | 68 | Undefined | — | — |
| 105 | 01101001 | 69 | Undefined | — | — |
| 106 | 01101010 | 6A | Undefined | — | — |
| 107 | 01101011 | 6B | Undefined | — | — |
| 108 | 01101100 | 6C | Undefined | — | — |
| 109 | 01101101 | 6D | Undefined | — | — |
| 110 | 01101110 | 6E | Undefined | — | — |
| 111 | 01101111 | 6F | Undefined | — | — |

*(Continued)*

**Table 12.3** (Continued)

| Control Number 2nd Byte Value | | | Control Function | 3rd Byte Value | |
|---|---|---|---|---|---|
| Decimal | Binary | Hex | | Value | Used As |
| 112 | 01110000 | 70 | Undefined | — | — |
| 113 | 01110001 | 71 | Undefined | — | — |
| 114 | 01110010 | 72 | Undefined | — | — |
| 115 | 01110011 | 73 | Undefined | — | — |
| 116 | 01110100 | 74 | Undefined | — | — |
| 117 | 01110101 | 75 | Undefined | — | — |
| 118 | 01110110 | 76 | Undefined | — | — |
| 119 | 01110111 | 77 | Undefined | — | — |

**Note:** Controller numbers 120–127 are reserved for Channel Mode Messages, which rather than controlling sound parameters, affect the channel's operating mode. (See also Table 12.1.)

| | | | | | |
|---|---|---|---|---|---|
| 120 | 01111000 | 78 | [Channel Mode Message] All Sound Off | 0 | — |
| 121 | 01111001 | 79 | [Channel Mode Message] Reset All Controllers (See MMA RP-015) | 0 | — |
| 122 | 01111010 | 7A | [Channel Mode Message] Local Control On/Off | 0 off, 127 on | — |
| 123 | 01111011 | 7B | [Channel Mode Message] All Notes Off | 0 | — |
| 124 | 01111100 | 7C | [Channel Mode Message] Omni Mode Off (+ all notes off) | 0 | — |
| 125 | 01111101 | 7D | [Channel Mode Message] Omni Mode On (+ all notes off) | 0 | — |
| 126 | 01111110 | 7E | [Channel Mode Message] Mono Mode On (+ poly off, + all notes off) | 0 | — |

**Note:** This equals the number of channels, or zero if the number of channels equals the number of voices in the receiver.

| | | | | | |
|---|---|---|---|---|---|
| 127 | 01111111 | 7F | [Channel Mode Message] Poly Mode On (+ mono off, + all notes off) | 0 | — |

Content provided by MIDI Manufacturers Association (www.midi.org). Used with Permission.

Table 12.3a: Registered Parameter Numbers

To set or change the value of a Registered Parameter:

1. Send two Control Change messages using Control Numbers 101 (65H) and 100 (64H) to select the desired Registered Parameter Number, as per the following table.

2. To set the selected Registered Parameter to a specific value, send a Control Change messages to the Data Entry MSB controller (Control Number 6). If the selected Registered Parameter requires the LSB to be set, send another Control Change message to the Data Entry LSB controller (Control Number 38).

3. To make a relative adjustment to the selected Registered Parameter's current value, use the Data Increment or Data Decrement controllers (Control Numbers 96 and 97).

| Parameter Number | | Parameter Function | Data Entry Value |
|---|---|---|---|
| *MSB: Control 101 (65H) Value* | *LSB: Control 100 (64H) Value* | | |
| 00H | 00H | Pitch Bend Sensitivity | MSB = +/− semitones<br>LSB = +/− cents |
| | 01H | Channel Fine Tuning<br>(formerly Fine Tuning—see MMA RP-022) | Resolution 100/8192 cents<br>00H 00H = −100 cents<br>40H 00H = A440<br>7FH 7FH = +100 cents |
| | 02H | Channel Coarse Tuning<br>(formerly Coarse Tuning—see MMA RP-022) | Only MSB used<br>Resolution 100 cents<br>00H = −6400 cents<br>40H = A440<br>7FH = +6300 cents |
| | 03H | Tuning Program Change | Tuning Program Number |
| | 04H | Tuning Bank Select | Tuning Bank Number |
| | 05H | Modulation Depth Range<br>(see MMA General MIDI Level 2 Specification) | For GM2, defined in GM2 Specification.<br>For other systems, defined by manufacturer |
| . . . | . . . | All RESERVED for future MMA Definition | . . . |
| | | Three Dimensional Sound Controllers | |
| 3DH (61) | 00H | AZIMUTH ANGLE | See RP-049 |
| | 01H | ELEVATION ANGLE | See RP-049 |
| | 02H | GAIN | See RP-049 |
| | 03H | DISTANCE RATIO | See RP-049 |

*(Continued)*

## Table 12.3 (Continued)

| Parameter Number | | Parameter Function | Data Entry Value |
|---|---|---|---|
| MSB: Control 101 (65H) Value | LSB: Control 100 (64H) Value | | |
| | 04H | MAXIMUM DISTANCE | See RP-049 |
| | 05H | GAIN AT MAXIMUM DISTANCE | See RP-049 |
| | 06H | REFERENCE DISTANCE RATIO | See RP-049 |
| | 07H | PAN SPREAD ANGLE | See RP-049 |
| | 08H | ROLL ANGLE | See RP-049 |
| . . . | . . . | All RESERVED for future MMA Definition | . . . |
| 7FH | 7FH | Null Function Number for RPN/NRPN | Setting RPN to 7FH, 7FH will disable the data entry, data increment, and data decrement controllers until a new RPN or NRPN is selected. |

## Table 12.4  Defined Universal System Exclusive Messages

| Non-Real Time (7EH) | | Description |
|---|---|---|
| Sub-ID #1 | Sub-ID #2 | |
| 00 | | Unused |
| 01 | | Sample Dump Header |
| 02 | | Sample Data Packet |
| 03 | | Sample Dump Request |
| 04 | nn | MIDI Time Code |
| | 00 | Special |
| | 01 | Punch In Points |
| | 02 | Punch Out Points |
| | 03 | Delete Punch In Point |
| | 04 | Delete Punch Out Point |
| | 05 | Event Start Point |
| | 06 | Event Stop Point |
| | 07 | Event Start Points with additional info. |

| | | |
|---|---|---|
| | 08 | Event Stop Points with additional info. |
| | 09 | Delete Event Start Point |
| | 0A | Delete Event Stop Point |
| | 0B | Cue Points |
| | 0C | Cue Points with additional info. |
| | 0D | Delete Cue Point |
| | 0E | Event Name in additional info. |
| 05 | nn | Sample Dump Extensions |
| | 01 | Loop Points Transmission |
| | 02 | Loop Points Request |
| | 03 | Sample Name Transmission |
| | 04 | Sample Name Request |
| | 05 | Extended Dump Header |
| | 06 | Extended Loop Points Transmission |
| | 07 | Extended Loop Points Request |
| 06 | nn | General Information |
| | 01 | Identity Request |
| | 02 | Identity Reply |
| 07 | nn | File Dump |
| | 01 | Header |
| | 02 | Data Packet |
| | 03 | Request |
| 08 | nn | MIDI Tuning Standard (Non-Real Time) |
| | 00 | Bulk Dump Request |
| | 01 | Bulk Dump Reply |
| | 03 | Tuning Dump Request |
| | 04 | Key-Based Tuning Dump |
| | 05 | Scale/Octave Tuning Dump, 1 byte format |
| | 06 | Scale/Octave Tuning Dump, 2 byte format |
| | 07 | Single Note Tuning Change with Bank Select |
| | 08 | Scale/Octave Tuning, 1 byte format |
| | 09 | Scale/Octave Tuning, 2 byte format |
| 09 | nn | General MIDI |
| | 01 | General MIDI 1 System On |
| | 02 | General MIDI System Off |
| | 03 | General MIDI 2 System On |

*(Continued)*

## *Table 12.4* (Continued)

| Non-Real Time (7EH) | | Description |
|---|---|---|
| Sub-ID #1 | Sub-ID #2 | |
| 0A | nn | Downloadable Sounds |
| | 01 | Turn DLS On |
| | 02 | Turn DLS Off |
| | 03 | Turn DLS Voice Allocation Off |
| | 04 | Turn DLS Voice Allocation On |
| 0B | nn | File Reference Message |
| | 00 | reserved (do not use) |
| | 01 | Open File |
| | 02 | Select or Reselect Contents |
| | 03 | Open File and Select Contents |
| | 04 | Close File |
| | 05-7F | reserved (do not use) |
| 0C | nn | MIDI Visual Control |
| | 00-7F | MVC Commands (*See MVC Documentation*) |
| 7B | — | End of File |
| 7C | — | Wait |
| 7D | — | Cancel |
| 7E | — | NAK |
| 7F | — | ACK |

| Real Time (7FH) | | Description |
|---|---|---|
| Sub-ID #1 | Sub-ID #2 | |
| 00 | — | Unused |
| 01 | nn | MIDI Time Code |
| | 01 | Full Message |
| | 02 | User Bits |
| 02 | nn | MIDI Show Control |
| | 00 | MSC Extensions |
| | 01-7F | MSC Commands (*see MSC Documentation*) |

| | | |
|---|---|---|
| 03 | nn | Notation Information |
| | 01 | Bar Number |
| | 02 | Time Signature (Immediate) |
| | 42 | Time Signature (Delayed) |
| 04 | nn | Device Control |
| | 01 | Master Volume |
| | 02 | Master Balance |
| | 03 | Master Fine Tuning |
| | 04 | Master Course Tuning |
| | 05 | Global Parameter Control |
| 05 | nn | Real Time MTC Cueing |
| | 00 | Special |
| | 01 | Punch In Points |
| | 02 | Punch Out Points |
| | 03 | (Reserved) |
| | 04 | (Reserved) |
| | 05 | Event Start points |
| | 06 | Event Stop points |
| | 07 | Event Start points with additional info. |
| | 08 | Event Stop points with additional info. |
| | 09 | (Reserved) |
| | 0A | (Reserved) |
| | 0B | Cue points |
| | 0C | Cue points with additional info. |
| | 0D | (Reserved) |
| | 0E | Event Name in additional info. |
| 06 | nn | MIDI Machine Control Commands |
| | 00-7F | MMC Commands (*See MMC Documentation*) |
| 07 | nn | MIDI Machine Control Responses |
| | 00-7F | MMC Responses (*See MMC Documentation*) |
| 08 | nn | MIDI Tuning Standard (Real Time) |
| | 02 | Single Note Tuning Change |
| | 07 | Single Note Tuning Change with Bank Select |
| | 08 | Scale/Octave Tuning, 1 byte format |
| | 09 | Scale/Octave Tuning, 2 byte format |

(*Continued*)

**Table 12.4**  (Continued)

| Real Time (7FH) | | Description |
|---|---|---|
| Sub-ID #1 | Sub-ID #2 | |
| 09 | nn | Controller Destination Setting (*See GM2 Documentation*) |
| | 01 | Channel Pressure (Aftertouch) |
| | 02 | Polyphonic Key Pressure (Aftertouch) |
| | 03 | Controller (Control Change) |
| 0A | 01 | Key-based Instrument Control |
| 0B | 01 | Scalable Polyphony MIDI MIP Message |
| 0C | 00 | Mobile Phone Control Message |

Section 5—MIDI Specification Summaries

# General MIDI 1, 2, and Lite Specifications
## *General MIDI (GM1)*

"General MIDI" is not the same as MIDI. Where MIDI is a language, a file format, and a connector specification, the "General MIDI System Level 1" specification—also known as "GM," "General MIDI 1" and "GM1"—defines specific features of a MIDI instrument. Without General MIDI, playback of MIDI files created on one MIDI instrument might sound totally different on a different MIDI instrument, because the only sound definition in MIDI is a sound number (Program Number), not the actual characteristics of the sound. GM helped establish a consistent level of performance compatibility among MIDI instruments by establishing that specific sounds should be selected by certain Program Numbers, paving the way for MIDI data to be used in computer games and cell phones.

Note: The General MIDI (GM1) specification was superceded in 1999 by General MIDI 2, which supports additional features and capabilities commonly available. However, GM1 remains a popular format for lower-cost synthesizers and is commonly used for music distributed as Standard MIDI Files. General MIDI Lite is an even lower-cost version of GM developed specifically for use in low-power portable devices such as cell phones.

### *GM1 Features*

To be GM1 compatible, a GM1 sound-generating device (keyboard, sound module, sound card, IC, software program, or other product) must meet the General MIDI System Level 1 performance requirements outlined below, instantaneously upon demand, and without additional modification or adjustment/configuration by the user.

- Voices: A minimum of either 24 fully dynamically allocated voices are available simultaneously for both melodic and percussive sounds, or 16 dynamically allocated voices are available for melody plus 8 for percussion. All voices respond to velocity.

- Channels: All 16 MIDI Channels are supported. Each Channel can play a variable number of voices (polyphony). Each Channel can play a different instrument (sound/patch/ timbre). Key-based percussion is always on MIDI Channel 10.
- Instruments: A minimum of 16 simultaneous and different timbres playing various instruments. A minimum of 128 preset instruments (MIDI program numbers) conforming to the GM1 Instrument Patch Map and 47 percussion sounds which conform to the GM1 Percussion Key Map.
- Channel Messages: Support for continuous controllers 1, 7, 10, 11, 64, 121, and 123; RPN #s 0, 1, 2; Channel Pressure, Pitch Bend.
- Other Messages: Respond to the data entry controller and the RPNs for fine and course tuning and Pitch Bend range, as well as all General MIDI Level 1 System Messages.

### GM1 Developer Information

The MMA's GM Developer Guidelines document describes additional recommendations and clarifications of the GM Specification for content producers and device makers, to ensure improved compatibility among GM products.

The GM1 Logo was created to ensure consumer recognition for products that meet the General MIDI Level 1 Specification. The GM Logo is the property of the MMA and AMEI and must be used in accordance with guidelines established to ensure the value of the GM Logo for our members and for the consumer.

## General MIDI 2 (GM2)

General MIDI 1 made great strides in the music industry by providing a platform for compatibility between device manufacturers and content providers. Still, by 1999 many manufacturers felt there needed to be additional functionality. General MIDI 2 (GM2) is a group of extensions made to General MIDI 1, which increases both the number of available sounds and the amount of control available for sound editing and musical performance. All GM2 devices are also fully compatible with General MIDI 1.

### New MIDI Messages

To support new features in GM2 devices, the MIDI specification was also extended with numerous new control messages, include MIDI Tuning, Controllers, RPNs, and Universal System Exclusive Messages. Of particular significance are the new Universal System Exclusive Messages, including Controller Destination Setting, Key-Based Instrument Controllers, Global Parameter Control, and Master Fine/Coarse Tuning.

- Controller Destination SysEx Message (.pdf)
- Key-Based Instrument Controller SysEx Message (.pdf)
- Global Parameter Control SysEx Message (.pdf)
- Master Fine/Course Tuning SysEx Message (.pdf)
- Redefinition of RPN01 and RPN02 (Channel Fine/Course Tuning)
- RPN05 Modulation Depth Range (.pdf)

## GM2 Specification Update 1.1

In September 2003 a new version of the General MIDI 2 Specification document was made available, reflecting changes to the specification mandated by two new Recommended Practices:

- RP-036: Sets a default Pan Curve for future AMEI/MMA specifications (equivalent to the Pan Curve defined in GML and DLS) and amends GM2 to include this curve.
- RP-037: Adds a recommendation that GM 2 devices support the MIDI Tuning

Extension "Scale/Octave Tuning Real Time One-Byte form" message.

## GM2 Specification Update 1.2

In 2007 Recommend Practice RP-044 was adopted for implementing the Mod Depth Range RPN message on GM2 devices. This recommendation does not apply to other device specifications (i.e. SP-MIDI) that refer to GM 2. For those devices, the recommended response to Mod Depth Range RPN is either undefined or should be defined in those specifications.

## GM2 Features

- Requirements
- Number of Notes: 32 simultaneous notes
- MIDI Channels: 16
    - Simultaneous Melodic Instruments = up to 16 (all Channels)
    - Simultaneous Percussion Kits = up to 2 (Channel 10/11)
- Control Change Messages (Some Optional)
    - Bank Select (cc#0/32)
    - Modulation Depth (cc#1)
    - Portamento Time (cc#5)
    - Channel Volume (cc#7)
    - Pan (cc#10)
    - Expression (cc#11)
    - Hold1 (Damper) (cc#64)
    - Portamento ON/OFF (cc#65)
    - Sostenuto (cc#66)
    - Soft (cc#67)
    - Filter Resonance (Timbre/Harmonic Intensity) (cc#71)
    - Release Time (cc#72)
    - Attack time (cc#73)
    - Brightness (cc#74)
    - Decay Time (cc#75) (new message)
    - Vibrato Rate (cc#76) (new message)
    - Vibrato Depth (cc#77) (new message)
    - Vibrato Delay (cc#78) (new message)
    - Reverb Send Level (cc#91)
    - Chorus Send Level (cc#93)
    - Data Entry (cc#6/38)
    - RPN LSB/MSB (cc#100/101)
- Registered Parameter Numbers
    - Pitch Bend Sensitivity
    - Channel Fine Tune
    - Channel Coarse Tune

- Modulation Depth Range (Vibrato Depth Range)
- RPN NULL
- Universal System Exclusive Messages
  - Master Volume
  - Master Fine Tuning
  - Master Coarse Tuning
  - Reverb Type
  - Reverb Time
  - Chorus Type
  - Chorus Mod Rate
  - Chorus Mod Depth
  - Chorus Feedback
  - Chorus Send to Reverb
  - Controller Destination Setting
  - Scale/Octave Tuning Adjust
  - Key-Based Instrument Controllers
  - GM2 System On
- GM2 Instrument Sound Set
- GM2 Percussion Sound Set

## GM2 Developer Information

Developers of GM2 compatible devices or content are urged to consult the GM1 Developer Guidelines (included in the Complete MIDI 1.0 Specification) that describe recommendations for content producers and device makers to ensure improved compatibility among GM products.

The GM2 Logo was created to ensure consumer recognition for products that meet the General MIDI 2 Specification. The GM Logos are the property of the MMA and AMEI and must be used in accordance with guidelines established to ensure the value of the GM Logos for our members and for the consumer.

## General MIDI "Lite" (GML)
### *plus Guidelines for Mobile Applications*

The General MIDI Lite Specification describes one of two platforms for mobile MIDI communication that have been approved and adopted as a standard by the MIDI industry. This document has three primary components:

- A specification called General MIDI Lite (GM Lite), which defines a new level of tone generation (sound module) device;
- Authoring guidelines for music data in SMF (Standard MIDI File) format that is intended for playback on GM Lite devices;
- Implementation guidelines for GM Lite file players.

## GM Lite vs. SP-MIDI

The General MIDI Lite Specification defines a fixed-polyphony MIDI device, intended to meet a particular set of current and future market needs. The Scalable Polyphony MIDI (SP-MIDI) Specification complements GML by defining flexible polyphony MIDI devices and content. Developers of GM Lite players are strongly advised to keep as much flexibility as possible in how their players handle channel priorities, drum channels, and other System messages. This will make it far easier for their products to be compatible with song data authored for the Scalable Polyphony MIDI specification.

## GM Lite vs. GM1

The General MIDI Lite device specification is intended for equipment that does not have the capability to support the full feature set defined in General MIDI 1.0, on the assumption that the reduced performance may be acceptable (and even required) in some mobile applications. GM Lite represents just one standardized set of performance capabilities for portable applications—other performance levels are likely to be standardized in the future.

## GM Lite Features

- Requirements
- Number of Notes: 16 simultaneous notes
- MIDI Channels: 16
  - Simultaneous Melodic Instruments = up to 15
  - Simultaneous Percussion Kits = 1 (Channel 10)

- Control Change Messages
  - Modulation Depth (cc#1)
  - Channel Volume (cc#7)
  - Pan (cc#10)
  - Expression (cc#11)
  - Data Entry (cc#6/38)
  - Hold1 (Damper) (cc#64)
  - RPN LSB/MSB (cc#100/101)
  - Pitch Bend
  - All Sound Off, All Notes Off, Reset All Controllers
- Registered Parameter Numbers
  - Pitch Bend Sensitivity
- Universal System Exclusive Messages
  - GM1 System On
- GM Lite Instrument Sound Set
- GM Lite Percussion Sound Set

For complete details on GML features and MIDI message syntax, please consult the General MIDI Lite Specification (see below to order).

## GM Lite Developer Information

Recommended guidelines for Using GM Lite in Mobile Applications are included in the GM Lite Specification document. Developers are also urged to consult the GM1 Developer Guidelines (included in the Complete MIDI 1.0 Specification).

The GML Logo was created to ensure consumer recognition for products that meet the General MIDI Lite Specification. The GM Logos are the property of the MMA and AMEI and must be used in accordance with guidelines established to ensure the value of the GM Logos for our members and for the consumer.

Section 6—Interesting MIDI Articles

## Computer Audio Comes of Age

May 1996
Editorial by Tom White, President & CEO, MMA

Even in the era of "moving pictures" the pioneers of modern entertainment recognized the importance of providing high-quality audio to enhance the video experience. Before the "talking pictures," the theater organist provided musical accompaniment. With talkies came dialogue and sound effects. Today, movie sound tracks are the state of the art for the entertainment business, demanding the best composers and using innovative technologies such as "surround sound" and multi-channel all-digital playback.

In sharp contrast, computer-based entertainment is just now coming out of the dark ages as far as sound is concerned. The majority of today's "multimedia" computing systems do not offer state-of-the-art audio performance, relying instead on commonly available but inferior technologies for generating sound. The result is that content developers are unable to produce compelling and realistic sound tracks for their titles.

Part of the problem lies with a technology called "FM synthesis." In playback of music, synthesis allows for creation of many different sounds that are not otherwise available. For example, with a synthesizer it is possible to imitate the sound of a Grand Piano without ever having the piano at your touch. But FM synthesis is only one method of generating sounds, and is not a particularly realistic method. In fact, though developed for professional musical instruments, FM synthesis is largely obsolete in that market today.

The best quality commonly available today happens to be the most obvious: recording the actual instruments and storing them for playback. This technique is typically called "wavetable synthesis," and requires both a wavetable synthesizer and a library of sound "samples" from which to create required sounds. Data compression schemes and advances in silicon design have dramatically reduced the cost of wavetable synthesizers, making them viable for the PC market.

Though the quality of realism and clarity will vary among manufacturers, a good wavetable synthesizer can produce music that is indistinguishable from a music recording made using real instruments. Wavetable synthesis also provides an opportunity for a larger variety of sounds, since any sound can be made available simply by providing "samples," unlike FM, which can only create certain types of sounds based on the physical acoustics of FM sound modeling. As a testament to the superiority of wavetable, virtually all game music composers create their sound tracks on a wavetable synthesizer to realize the fullest sound, and subsequently edit them for playback on lesser FM synthesizers.

Oddly, while the PC market rapidly consumes all increases in CPU and graphics performance, FM synthesis continues to be sold despite the availability of better, cost effective, solutions. The reason FM has been able to hang on so long has little to do with technology (or sound) and everything to do with market conditions. For a long time FM was the only synthesis technology available at the right price point for PC audio, making FM a de facto standard for developers.

Then, in 1991, the MMA (MIDI Manufacturers Association) created "General MIDI", a specification which provides a standardized design for music synthesizers and opened up the PC to better synthesis technology. With General MIDI there is no dependence on FM synthesis, and developers are now able to create music that actually sounds as it was intended.

As the market for multimedia computers matures, consumers will look for even more rewarding applications and better ways to make use of their investment. Thanks to wavetable synthesis, they have an entire orchestra at their fingertips, and are able to embark on adventures in learning or creating music, as well as hear full cinematic scores with their favorite games. Better sound, more variety, and better applications have made wavetable a necessity in multimedia PCs, ending the reign of FM.

—Tom White

Tom White is President & CEO of the MIDI Manufacturers Association (MMA) and a consultant on multimedia technology and marketing, specializing on the convergence of the computer and music industries. Tom also sits on the Steering Committee of the Interactive Audio Special Interest Group, which is developing recommended practices for new audio technologies in multimedia.

## MIDI: Let's Share the 'Secret'

November 2005
Editorial by Tom White, President & CEO, MMA

Consider this: MIDI technology is 20 years old, yet still as useful and popular as ever. MIDI is so much a part of the music products industry that many manufacturers and retailers take it for granted. And yet most people in the world have never heard of MIDI, so they have no idea what opportunities for music making MIDI can provide.

Thanks largely to NAMM , more people than ever before are hearing positive messages about the benefits of music making. But turning those people into music makers will also require helping to remove the various obstacles to playing an instrument, such as time, difficulty, accessibility, and more. Fortunately, the music products industry has technology that can address those obstacles, and it's called MIDI. My suggestion for how to create some more new music makers is to promote MIDI and all the unique ways it can help people to experience and enjoy making music. Here are some examples:

Computer users want to make music.

Computers are not a future trend anymore. Children are using them at very early ages, parents are using them at work and at home, and grandparents are buying them to keep in touch with friends and family. About 10 years ago NAMM commissioned a study that concluded home computer users have significant potential to become computer music makers. In response, the music products industry has done . . . well, not much. Only a handful of companies produce products specifically to encourage music making at home, and few retailers market to computer owners. As a result, computer owners might want to make music, but the majority don't yet know they can even do it. What are needed are market development programs to generate demand from people of all ages that own computers and want to make music. The technology (MIDI) is already built in to the major computer operating systems, and allows the integration of computers with musical instruments of all kinds (even Band & Orchestra instruments!). All that's needed is to get the message to the desired audience.

Making music is hard, but technology can make it easier.

About 10 years ago my son was in high school band, learning to play the trumpet. At some point he had the opportunity to talk with his teacher about what is father did for a living. My son explained that I work with companies that develop technology used for making music. A while later I happened to run into that teacher and after a brief introduction he said to me "oh, I don't like technology, it puts people like me out of business."

"Actually," I replied, "technology could help you. Your goal is to get a group of children to read properly, play properly, and then play together. Your problem is you have to work with all of them at once for one hour. And when they go home to practice, you can't be there to tell them what they are doing right and what they are doing wrong, so when they come to class again, their progress is probably minimal. Now imagine this: your entire repertoire is on a CD-ROM, both the printed sheet music and an audio performance. Your students can display and hear any parts they chose. Now imagine a program that listens to what the student plays, and indicates when the student is flat or sharp or late or early. The music can be played slowly—yet still in pitch—so that the student can develop the necessary skills. And the student's progress can be recorded and viewed by the teacher so that you can provide your personal feedback."

The teacher, wide eyed, responded, "Is that possible?"

The answer, of course, is yes, via MIDI. There are one or two companies that offer products with some of these features, and the industry-sponsored TI:ME organization is reaching out to educators to explain how to use MIDI to teach music. It's a start, but more needs to be done.

Making music can be just for fun

Not everyone wants to work hard at making music. For people who just want to have some fun, a major keyboard manufacturer has developed a program that encourages music making using a simple principal: that technology can help ease the process of learning while making the result more immediately rewarding. Rather than learning to play piano solo, the student plays along with pre-arranged compositions that provide familiar arrangements and a greater sense of accomplishment. Moreover, the lessons can be played at any comfortable speed, and in any key, using whatever instrument sound the student finds most encouraging. This approach has been shown to be particularly useful for encouraging seniors to start playing, and MIDI is the technology that makes it all work. Because MIDI is an open standard, there's no reason more companies couldn't be using it to encourage "recreational music making".

Playing music by yourself is not all that bad.

Industry market development programs like VH1's Save the Music and NAMM's Weekend Warriors promote music making as a social event. But what programs do we have to promote making music in the privacy of your own home? My neighbor, Jerry, is in his 70s, and he makes music on his home computer. Jerry was a sewing machine repairman, and when he retired he decided to start playing the saxophone again, something he hadn't done in 30 years. He found he wasn't very good anymore, but someone turned him on to "Band in a Box" and MIDI files on the Internet, and he got just what he needed: a band that would let him practice without complaint. They played any time he wanted, day or night, any song, in any key, and at any tempo. They'd play the same section over and over again without ever getting tired or angry. Eventually Jerry got good enough to start playing with other people again. His band now plays 40s dance music every week at the local senior center and for private parties. What got Jerry playing again was MIDI.

Making music with MIDI

In each of the above examples there are already companies that understand how MIDI technology can encourage people to make music, and they are taking steps to capitalize on MIDI. But there is no industry-wide effort to inform the public about the benefits received by applying technology to the process of music making—benefits that would certainly encourage more people to consider taking up a musical instrument.

Current industry initiatives to increase music makers all seem positive and successful. But we should do more. Let's develop an industry-wide program that markets MIDI to kids who aren't interested in school band. Let's have a program that markets music making to seniors who already have a home computer. Let's tell moms and dads who spend leisure time playing solitaire on their computer, that they can plug a musical instrument into the computer and jam, or practice, or study, or compose.

Everyone in the music products industry should cooperate to make it known that we can make playing music easier and more rewarding. It doesn't matter what age you are, what instrument you like, what kind of music you like, whether you want to play alone or with others, whether you want to compose original music, arrange music, learn about music, just play for fun or play to become proficient, we have technology to help.

People like technology, and people like music. In MIDI, the music products industry has a proven technology that makes music making easier, more rewarding, and more practical for millions of people. I think we should share that secret with the rest of the world.

## White Paper: Comparison of MIDI and OSC

Nov. 2008
Abstract:

This paper corrects public misinformation about MIDI and how it compares to OSC.

Background:

Products such as Jazz Mutant's "Lemur" and "Dexter", and Euphonix's "MC Control" and "MC Mix" have brought recent attention to technology from CNMAT called "Open Sound Control" ("OSC"). Articles about these products appearing in publications such as Electronic Musician have contained inaccurate comparisons and potentially misleading statements. The document "Open Sound Control—A Flexible Protocol for sensor networking" (Freed, Schmeder, Zbyszynski) provides a chart comparing OSC to MIDI, which understandably attempts to show OSC's advantages over MIDI, but the comparisons are not entirely accurate.

Facts About MIDI:

While OSC can do many things that MIDI is not designed to do, some of the claimed advantages are only true under specific conditions, such as when using the MIDI DIN transport or using pre-defined messages. The following statements correct specific claims that have been made while the footnotes contain the reference to the claim.

MIDI is a hardware transport independent protocol[1]

Both OSC and MIDI are message protocols that are hardware transport independent. There is a transport specification

(MIDI DIN) part of the MIDI 1.0 Specification, but that transport it is not required for using the MIDI protocol. It is quite common for MIDI protocol to be carried on transports such as USB, FireWire, and Ethernet.

MIDI is as Fast as OSC[2]

When carried on Ethernet, MIDI bits move at the same data rate as OSC bits carried on Ethernet, because the data rate is a factor of the transport, not the protocol. In terms of throughput, MIDI can actually have better throughput than OSC because it takes fewer bytes to make common MIDI messages than it does to make comparable OSC messages.

MIDI supports multiple data formats[3]

The majority of data values for defined messages in MIDI are either 7bits (integers 0–127) or 14 bits (integers 0–16383). One defined message (pitch bend) uses signed integer data values (–8192 to +8191). System Exclusive messages can be defined to use other data formats, including strings, floating point, and more, similar to OSC.

MIDI offers pre-defined and product-specific message structures[4]

To maximize interoperability, MIDI is primarily a language of pre-defined messages. However, any software or hardware manufacture may obtain a unique ID that enables them to create System Exclusive messages which can have any structure and use any data format. For non-commercial developers, there is a reserved ID, so any person can create "user-defined" messages if desired.

MIDI offers greater interoperability than OSC[5]

Interoperability is the primary reason for the existence of MIDI, and is accomplished by having pre-defined messages, a standard transport and a standard file format.

Any two devices with MIDI DIN connectors (of which there are hundreds) will interoperate using MIDI protocol upon connection. In contrast, two devices with Ethernet connectors (of which there are millions) will only interoperate if both happen to support OSC (of which there are only dozens).

And because MIDI's messages are primarily pre-defined, it is very easy to design MIDI product to interoperate, whereas OSC messages are implementation-specific. There are thousands of software and hardware products that support MIDI, compared to dozens that support OSC.

Because there is a standard file format for MIDI data, there are millions of MIDI files available and hundreds of programs and devices that will play them.

MIDI has applications in a wide variety of areas besides music[6]

Application areas for MIDI include music, lighting control, show control (and themed events), machine control (audio and video), robotics, and more. MIDI is often used to operate live shows such as the fountain at the Bellagio Hotel, and the Pirate Battle at Treasure Island (both in Las Vegas). Many acts and performers use MIDI-controlled stage lighting. There are also MIDI messages specifically for video performance and machine control.

"Time-tagging" of MIDI events is possible on all the same transports as OSC[7]

The MIDI protocol and transport do not have time-tagging because they are intended for real-time (immediate) delivery. However, MIDI messages transmitted over Ethernet (like OSC), USB, FireWire or in a PC can be time-stamped by the transport/driver, achieving the exact same result as time-tagged OSC events. Events in Standard MIDI Files are stored in relative time order, and there can be multiple events at the same time point.

MIDI sends clocks at quarter-frame SMPTE accuracy[8]

The Timing Clock message is sent 24 times per quarter note (BPM dependent) to synchronize clocks on devices such as sequencers and drum machines. For sync applications such as video production, MIDI Time Code provides a clock signal about every 8 milliseconds at 30 frames per second. Accurate timing of individual MIDI events is a factor of the chosen transport: in the case of the MIDI DIN transport, events have about 1ms accuracy, and in the case of Ethernet it depends on which timing specifications are used (MIDI can use the same one as OSC and have the same timing accuracy).

Footnotes: See "Open Sound Control—A flexible protocol for sensor networking" (Freed, Schmeder, Zbyszynski, 1).

## Notes

1. Chart 1, Row 5: "Hardware Transport Independent | OSC: Yes | MIDI: No"
2. Chart 1, Row 13: "Data Rate | OSC: Gigabit | MIDI:31250 bps"
3. Chart 1, Row 7: "Data formats | OSC: Integer, [Floating] Point, Strings, More | MIDI: [integers] 0–255"
4. Chart 1, Row 8: "Message Structure | OSC: User-defined | MIDI: Pre-determined"
5. Introductory Paragraph: "Compared to [MIDI] OSC's advantages include interoperability. . . ."
6. Chart 1, Row 11: "Application Areas | OSC: Music, Video, Robotics and more | MIDI: Music"
7. Chart 1, Row 4: "Time-tagging | OSC: via Bundles | MIDI: No"
8. Chart 1, Row 12: "Clock-sync accuracy . . . | OSC: picosecond | MIDI:20msec"

# INDEX

Page numbers in italic format indicate figures and tables.

Ableton Live software 229–33, 235–6, 239–40, 299

AC-7 Core 77–80, 99–100

accidentals 260–2, 272

Active Sensing messages 23

ad hoc network 77, 79

Akai MPC60 346–7

Akai MPK88 50

Akai S900 343

All Notes Off messages 21

All Sound Off messages 20

alternate tunings 59–60

Android platform: apps available on 84–94, 243; MIDI on 82–4

Animoog app 90

Apple 82, 98, 220, 242

apps *see* musical instrument apps

Arduino builder kits 318–19

attack setting 188–9

audio device 122–4

Audio Evolution Mobile app 93–4

audio files 126, 133, 135, 170, 222, 225

Audio MIDI Setup utility 76–7, 81–2

Audiotool Sketch app 91–2

Australian Fairlight Computer Music Instrument (CMI) 344–6

auto-map functions 237

automation: effects and 178; in mixing 208–12; track 175–7

backward repeat 269–70

Bank Select messages 363

bass patches 118, 148, 149

beat clock 23, 352

Bergle, Kenny 308–16

binary numbers 27–30

Bluetooth technology 83, 84, 241

body movement control 248

boutique effects 193, 201

buffer size 123–4

built-in envelopes 175

buses 180–3

Caustic 2 app *90*, 91

Channel Aftertouch messages 17–18

Channel Mode messages 19, 370

channels: AC-7 Core and 99; CC messages and 19; GM standard and 33, 36; Omni Mode Off messages and 21; Program Change messages and 18

chord progressions 285–8

chord symbol protocol 282–4

Chord Trigger 165, 166

circle of fifths 276–7

click track 111, 114–17

C major scale 272, 284

compositions 218, 219, 222–3, 225, 246

compression ratio 188

compressors 186–7

*Computer Audio Comes of Age* (White) 409–12
conductor tracks 111–14, 131, 172, 173
Continuous Controllers (CC) 19, 25–6, 35, 185
Control app 84, 86, 87
Control Change (CC) messages 19, 370
Controllerism 245–8
controllers: accessories 50; Akai MPK88 64–70;
    choosing apps for 99–100; vs. control surfaces
    98–9; drum 47; installation of 50–2; Kawai
    SX-240 64–5; keyboard 47; MIDI files and
    31–2; MIDI messages and 17–25; non-HUI 62;
    percussion 136; purpose of 46–7; for recording
    127–30; wind 137
control surfaces: AC-7 Core 99; choosing apps
    for 99–100; vs. controllers 98–9; hooking-up 62;
    purpose of 61–2
counting beats process 265–6
CS-10 Controller Assignments 25–6
Cubase 134, 289, 291–2, 294–5, 331
Cullinan, Cory 295–7

D.C. (Da Capo) 271
decay time 206
delay effect 207–8
Digital Audio Workstations (DAWs): Ableton
    Live 229–33; automation modes and 210;
    control surfaces and 62; electronic music and
    217–18; FL Studio 226–9; live performance and
    106–7; Logic Pro 64–70; MIDI inputs and 108–9;
    MIDI mapping and 237; reliability of 6–7;
    sequencers and 100–1, 220; Sonar 224–6; *see also*
    Musical Instrument Digital Interface (MIDI);
    recording
digital reverbs 205
diminished triad 281, 283
DLS files 367, 369
dotted notes 266–7
Dr. Noize 295–7
Drummeller, C. J. 298–302
drum machines 51, 91, 92, 335–7
drum replacement technology 136–7

drums: controllers 47; level adjustment 180;
    sampled 211
D.S. (Dal Segno) 271
duple time signatures 268
DX-7 synthesizer 329, 335, 341–2
dynamic-based effects: attack setting 188–9;
    compressors and 186–7; expanders and gates
    192–3; knee setting 190; limiting compression
    192; makeup gain 190; ratio 188; release control
    189; side chaining 190–1; stereo linking 191–2;
    threshold level 187

early reflections 206
editing: additional 154; examples of 145–53;
    musical performance and 168–78; notation
editors and 160–5; quantization and 154–9; tools
    for 140–1, 165–8; types of 142; workflow 142–5
Effector plug-in 227
effect variations 177–8
Electric Drum Machine/Sampler app 92
electronic instruments 325–6
electronic music: Controllerism and 246–8;
    expressive control and 248–50; live
    performance and 217–20; MainStage for 223
E-mu-Virtuoso 2000 330, 343–4
enharmonic equivalent 260, 261
envelopes: built-in 175; ways to adjust 174
equalizers: description of 193–4; graphic 197–9;
    parametric 194–7, 199
Ethernet 44
expanders and gates 192–3
expressive control 248–50

FaderPort 66, 69
faders: automation and 208–10; bus 183; control
    surfaces and 61, 62; level adjustment and 179, 181
Fairlight CMI 344–6
famous people interviews *see* interviews
fifth intervals 274, 276, 279
FireWire 43, 349
first ending 270

5-pin DIN MIDI cable 38–41
flag placement 262, 265
flange 202, 208
flat key signatures 274, 275
flat key trick 275, 276
flat notes 259, 260, 261
FL Studio 170, 226–9, 238–9
FL Studio Playlist Clips 166
FM synthesis 410, 411
forward repeat 269–70
fourth intervals 274, 276, 278
frame rates 22–3
Francis, Nick 319
Freed, Adrian 240
freezing tracks 126
frequency: bands 200; equalizers and 193, 197–9;
    notch filter and 196–7; pass filter and 194–5;
    shelving filter and 195–6
Fruity Loops *see* FL Studio

GarageBand 6, 7, *14*, 101
General MIDI (GM1) 403–4, 408
General MIDI (GM) standard 32–5, 333–4, 368
General MIDI 2 (GM2) 404–7
General MIDI Lite (GM LIte) 407–9
General Standard (GS) 35
Gigasampler 337–8
global settings 59–60
GM2 Developer Information 407
G major scale 272, 273
GM Developer Guidelines 404
GM standard 33, 36
Grand Piano Pro app *88*, 89
grand staff 258–9
graphic equalizers 197–9
groove quantization 159, 170–2
GS standard 35
guitarists, MIDI control and 216–17

half step 259, 260, 271
hard and soft knees 190, *191*

hardware: 5-pin DIN MIDI cable 38–41; adjusting
    settings for 59–63; configurations 63–70;
    controllers 46–52; control surfaces 61–3; Ethernet
    44; FireWire 43; PCI cards 45; sound generators
    52–9; summary about 70–1; USB 42–3; WiFi 45–6
harmonic system 284–5
harmony, defined 253–4
HD-MIDI protocol 353–5
Heap, Imogen 248, 249
Highly Liquid's products 322–4
Hillman, Jonathan 302–5
Holland, Kevin 323, 324
homophonic texture 254
horns 211

Implementation Chart 334–5, 361–70
importing of files 32, 145–6
intervals 277–80
interviews: C. J. Drummeller 298–302; Dr. Noize
    295–7; George Strezov 293–5; Jay Smith 316–22;
    John Staskevich 322–4; John Swihart 289–93;
    Jonathan Hillman 302–5; Kenny Bergle 308–16;
    Matt Moldover 305–8
iPad: apps for 72–3, 74–5, 243; hardware
    configuration and 70, 71; MIDI connectivity
    with 76–82; setting up MIDI studio with 75–6;
    USB and 50; WiFi option and 46
iPad instruments 73–5

J4T Multitrack Recorder app 94
Jam Boxes 246, 248
Jupiter-6 synth 340–1

Kawai SX-240 64
keyboard: controllers 47; instruments 49, 211
keyboardists, live performance and 213–15, 217
key signatures 109–11, 273–6
key switches 55–6
King, B. B. 311
knee setting 190
Korg iMS-20 75

latency, recording and 120–6
layer tracks 118, *119*
ledger lines 257–8
Lemur app 96–7, 243
level adjustment: buses 180–3; master output 184;
    track levels 179–80
lighting control 8, 10–11
limiting compression 192
live performance: Ableton Live for 229–33;
    alternative techniques for 133–4; Controllerism
    and 245–8; DAWs and 106–7; electronic music
    and 217–20; expressive control and 248–50; FL
    Studio for 226–9; MainStage for 220–4; Max/
    MSP software for 233–6; MIDI control and 216–
    17, 297, 299–300, 303–4; MIDI mapping and
    236–40; recording 106–7; sequencers and 220;
    Sonar for 224–6; traditional setups and 213–16;
    *see also* OSC protocol
Livid Instruments  317
local control messages 20, 61
Logic Pro: Chord Memorizing 165–6; click in *115*;
    control surface setup *80*; editing tools in *140*;
    Environment Window in 166, *167*; hardware
    configuration and 64–70; key signature 111;
    latency mode *125*; level adjustment in *181*;
    mapping in *54*; MIDI notes in 6; note length
    in *148*; note velocity in 143, *144*; orchestral
    template in *127*; pitch bend information in *150*;
    sample rate in *124*
loops 55, 115–16, 133
loop/sequencer/sampler apps 91–3

MaGIC protocol 350–1
Magic Seven trick 277
MainStage software 220–4, 237–8
major scales 271–3, 285
major triad 281, 282, 283, 285
makeup gain 190
Manufacturer System Exclusive messages 365
master faders 182–3, 184
Matrix view 225, 226, 238

Max/MSP software 233–6, 244, 249, 321–2
McMillian, Keith 320
Media-accelerated Global Information Carrier
    (MaGIC) protocol 350–1
melody 253, 254
MIDI channels: function description 362–3; GM1
    features and 404; hardware configuration and
    67; Proteus devices and 40; System Common
    messages and 22–3
MIDI click 115, *116*
MIDI clips 155, 158, 159, 227, 233
MIDI clock 352, 365
MIDI controllers: Ableton Live and 232–3; data
    transmission and 12–13; electronic music
    and 219; live performance and 215–6; MIDI
    mapping and 236–40; subprotocols and 24–5;
    *see also* controllers
MIDI data: composition of 15–16; controllers and
    128; DAWs and 6–7; making of sound and 3–5;
    notation editors and 162, 164; recording 105;
    sequencer apps and 101–2; transmission of 11, 39
MIDIDroide app 86, *87*, 88
MIDI drums 135–7, 215–6
MIDI events 155, 157, 158, 159, 418
MIDI files: controllers and 31–2; downloading
    131–3, 333; importing *146*, 223; standard 368–9;
    storage of 29–32
MIDI guitars 48, 61, 314
MIDI inputs 107–9, 120, 122
MIDI instruments 328–30
MIDI interface 41, 64–70, 292, 317, 332
MIDI keyboard 74, 90, 95, 162
*MIDI: Let's Share the 'Secret '* (White) 412–15
MIDI Machine Control (MMC) 62–3, 367
MIDI Manufactures Association (MMA) 19, 310
MIDI mapping: Ableton Live and 239–40;
    description of 236–7; FL Studio and 238–9;
    MainStage software and 237–8; Sonar and 238
MIDI messages: binary numbers and 27–9;
    Running Status process and 36–7; summary of
    374; types of 17–25

MIDI Mixer app 94
MIDI Mode 60, 67
MIDI Monitor 102, *103*
MIDI Network Setup 77, *79*
MIDI notes 7, 52, 115, 160, 352
MIDI on Android 82–4
MIDI/OSC control apps 84–9
MIDI Outs 39, 41, 65, 331
MIDI path 120–2
MIDI ports 41, 44, 121, 331
MIDI sequence 109, 152–3, 174, 338
MIDI specifications 327, 328, 332, 335, 403–9
MIDI Studio utility 77
MIDI Thru 38, 39, 40, 67, 121
MIDI time code 9–10, 22–3, 23, 64–5, 365, 367
MIDI-to-CV convertor 57–8, 68
MIDI tracks 59, 113, 152, 171
MIDI utilities 102–3
minor triad 281, 283
mix control 207
mixing: automation in 208–12; dynamic-based
    effects in 186–93; level adjustment in 179–84;
    placement in the stereo field in 184–6; spectral
    based effects in 193–201; time-based effects in
    202–8
mLAN protocol 348–9
mobile devices: iPad apps and 72–3; iPad
    instruments and 73–5; MIDI connectivity and
    75–82, 338–9; MIDI on Android and 82–4; *see
    also* musical instrument apps
mockups 13, 295
modulation wheel 127, 128
Moldover, Matt 246, 305–8, 319
Mono Mode On messages 21–2, 60, 61
Monophonic Mode 60
monophonic texture 254
MOTU MIDI Express XT 65–70
MPC60 workstation 346–7
multiband compression 200
multimedia applications 233, 234, 236
Multitimbral Mode 61

multi-track recording apps 93–4
music: chord progressions and 285–8; circle of
    fifths and 276; elements of 251–4; harmonic
    system and 284–5; intervals and 277–80; key
    signatures and 273–6; Magic Seven trick and
    277; major scales and 271–3; MIDI for making
    413–15; notation 254–63; road maps and
    269–71; texture 254; time signatures and 263–9;
    triads and 280–4
musical alphabet 258
musical instrument apps: AC-7 Core 77–80; on
    Android platform 84–94, 243; considerations
    for choosing 95–6; for controllers 99–100; for
    drum machines 91, 92; for iPad 73–5, 243;
    Reactable 248; third part software 81–2
Musical Instrument Digital Interface (MIDI):
    anecdotes 293; articles 409–18; benefits of 290,
    295, 297, 300–1, 304, 306; different roles of
    8–11; drum machines 335–7; early computers
    and 330–2; early days of 326–8; future of
    348–55; Implementation Chart 334–5, 361–70;
    instruments 328–30, 339–47; interface 332; key
    to using 12–13; limitations of 290, 295, 297, 300,
    304, 351–3; making music with 413–19; making
    of sound and 3–5; mobile revolution 338–9; vs.
    OSC 244–5, 250, 352–3, 416–19; presence of 2–3;
    software for 337–8; successful use of 6–7; things
    to know about 1; as a time saver/waster 13–14;
    use by famous people 8; web and 332–4
musical performance, ways to achieve goal of
    168–75
musical road maps 269–71

naming scheme 241
NAMM show 310, 319, 327, 353, 412
natural notes 259–60
Ney-Fi app 81
Non-Commercial System Exclusive messages 365
notation editors: DAWs and 7, 109; editing in
    162–5; note entry and 161–2; working with
    160–1

notch filter 196–7

Note-On and Note-Off Velocity 363–4

Note On and Off messages 17, 37, 244, 352

notes: adding 161–2; adjusting start time and length of 142–3, 147–8, 164; adjusting velocity of 149, *153*; clefs 256; dotted 266–7; double triggered 20; GM standard and 32, 33; key signature setting and 109; looping of 55; Mono Mode On and 21–2; natural 259–60; sending of 6; sixteen 267–8; Song Position Pointer and 23

note values 155–6, 262–3

Omni Mode 60

Omni Mode On and Off messages 21

one-man-bands 220, 222–3

OSC protocol: development of 240; devices for 242–4; features of 240–2; vs. HD-MIDI 354–5; vs. MIDI 244–5, 250, 352–3, 416–19

panning 184–5

parameters: AC-7 Core app and 99; Caustic 2 app and 91; CC messages and 19; local control 20–1; Omni Mode Off 21; strength and sensitivity 157; swing 157–8; SysEx messages 24

parametric equalizers 194–7, 199

parts per quarter note (PPQN) 26–7

pass filter 194–5

PCI cards 45

percussion tracks 135–7, 151

piano keyboard 259–60

pitch bend information *145*, 150

pitch bend range 32, 33, 35, 364

plate reverb 204–5

player pianos 3–4, 325

Poly Mode On messages 22

Polyphonic Aftertouch messages 17–18

Polyphonic Mode 60–1

polyphonic texture 254

power chords 288

precautionary accidentals 262

pre-delay 205

Program Change messages 18

Pro Tools: buffer size in *123*; click in *115*; conductor track in *112*; editing in *5*; event list *16*; hardware configuration and 65–6; MIDI Merge in *129*; MMC dialog *63*; note length in *143*; pitch bend information in *145*; quantize notation in *163*; session grid in *141*; tempo information in *172*, *173*; tempo operations in *112*

pumped synth 191

Pure Data program 247, 248

Push controller 232–3

Q amount 197, 199

quadruple time signatures 269

quantization: controlling strength of 157; groove 159, 170–2; note value 155–6; parameter 157–8; purpose of 139, 154–5; randomization and 158

Reactable synthesizer 246–8

real-time analyzer 170

real-time transformation 168

recording: additional controllers for 127–30; click track and 114–17; common ways of 105; conductor track and 111–14; examples of 129–30; latency and 120–6; live performance 106–7; MIDI files and 131–3; MIDI inputs and 107–9; musical training for 104; percussion tracks and 135–7; project settings for 109–11; sound and 118–20; summary about 137–8; templates and 126–7; triggering and 134–5

Redding, Travis 317

release control 189

Reset All Controllers messages 20

reverb effect: decay time 206; description of 202–3; digital reverbs 205; early reflections 206; mix control 207; plate reverb 204–5; pre-delay 205; reverb type 205; spring reverb 205

rhythm: defined 251–2; elements of 252–3

Roland GS standard 35

Roland Jupiter-6 340–1

Roland SPD-SX 51–2, 68
round robin triggers 55
Running Status process 36–7

S900 sampler 343
sample rate 123, 124, 208, 343, 345
samplers 52–6, 170
sampling/sequencing app 92
Scalable Polyphony MIDI (SP-MIDI) data 369, 408
second ending 270
second intervals 278
sequencers: Ableton Live 229–33; accessing velocity data in 149; alternative performance techniques and 133–4; choosing apps for 101–2; DAWs and 100–1, 220; editing and 144–5, 164; groove quantization by 159, 170–1; MIDI storage and 165–6
sequencer technology 6–7
sequencing methods 345
Sequential Circuits Prophet 600 329, 339–40
Sequential Circuit Studio 440 336, 347
seventh chords 282–4
seventh intervals 279, 282, 283
sharp key signatures 273, 274
sharp key trick 276
sharp notes 259, 260, 261
shelving filter 195–6
"shift-click" method 183
side chaining 190–1
signal attenuation 188
simple meters 268
sixteen notes 267–8
sixth intervals 279, 284
Smith, Dave 322, 329
Smith, Jay 316–22
SMPTE time code 9–10, 23
software synths 123, 234
Sonar (Live Matrix) 224–6, 238
Sonar X2 Matrix 166
Song Position Pointer 23, 366

Song Select 23, 366
sound: MIDI and 3–5; mixing and 210–12; recording and 118–20
sound generators: samplers 52–6; synthesizers 56–9
spectral-based effects: boutique effects 201; equalizers 193–9; multiband compression 200; sonic enhancers 201
spring reverb 205
staff: defined 255; grand 258–9; ledger lines and 257–8
Standard MIDI files (SMF) 31
Staskevich, John 322–4
status messages 16, 17, 22, 29, 36, 37
stereo field, placement in 184–5
stereo linking 191–2
Strezov, George 293–5
Studio 440 drum machine 336, 347
subdividing system 267, 268
Swihart, John 289–93
Symphony Pro 2, 165
synthesizers 56–9
System Common messages 22–3
System Exclusive messages 24
System Real-Time messages 23

Tangible objects 246, 247, 248
television shows, MIDI-based soundtrack for 2–3
templates: groove 158, 159, 170, 172; quantization 171; recording and 126–7; triggering and 134
tempo: defined 252–3; maps 31, 113–14, 130; before recording 111, 112
tempo changes 172–4
third intervals 278
threshold level 187
time-based effects: chorus 208; delay 207–8; flange 208; pitch shifting 208; reverb 202–7
time signatures: bottom numbers for 264; counting beats process and 265–6; description of 263–4; dotted notes and 266–7; duple, triple and quadruple 268–9; notation protocol and

265; simple meters and 268; sixteen notes and 267–8; ties and 266
timing inaccuracies 120, 121
tonality 272, 273
TouchDAW app 88–9
TouchOSC app 81–2, 84, 86, 243–4
track automation 175–7
track levels 179–80
tracks setup 152
transformation tools 166–8
transposition 59, 60, 150, 151, 167
treble clef 255, 256
triads: chord symbol protocol for 282–4; components of 281; construction 281–2; description of 280
triggering: how it works 134–5; MIDI Mode and 60; MIDI notes and 352; Omni Mode and 50
triple time signatures 268, 269

Universal Serial Bus (USB) *see* USB
Universal System Exclusive messages 364–5
USB: Akai MPK88 and 50; Android devices and 83; FaderPort and 69; MIDI devices 42–3; MIDI inputs and 108; MIDI transmission over 352; Roland SPD-SX and 51–2

van der Rest, Nathan 348
VCA group 183, 340
V chord progression 285, 286, 287
V-Control app 81
velocity, adjusting 149
velocity layers 53–4, 118
voice leading process 286, 287

wavetable synthesis 410–11
White, Tom 409, 411
WiFi option 45–6, 76, 83
Wright, Matt 240
written scores 291, 295, 297, 302, 304–5

XG standard 35
XMF File Types 369

Yamaha DX7 synth 341–2
Yamaha XG standard 35

Zeta Instrument Processor Interface (ZIPI) 349–50
ZGE Visualizer 227, 229
ZIPI protocol 349–50
zone rangers 54–5